Parts and Wholes in Semantics

Parts and Wholes
in Semantics

■■■

FRIEDERIKE MOLTMANN

OXFORD

UNIVERSITY PRESS

OXFORD
UNIVERSITY PRESS

Oxford   New York
Auckland   Bangkok   Buenos Aires   Cape Town   Chennai
Dar es Salaam   Delhi   Hong Kong   Istanbul   Karachi   Kolkata
Kuala Lumpur   Madrid   Melbourne   Mexico City   Mumbai   Nairobi
São Paulo   Shanghai   Taipei   Tokyo   Toronto

Copyright © 1997 by Friederike Moltmann

First published by Oxford University Press, Inc.
198 Madison Avenue, New York, New York 10016

www.oup.com

First issued as an Oxford University Press paperback, 2003

Oxford is a registered trademark of Oxford University Press

Library of Congress Cataloging-in-Publication Data
Moltmann, Friederike.
Parts and wholes in semantics / Friederike Moltmann
p. cm.
Includes bibliographical references and indexes.
ISBN 0-19-509574-X; 0-19-515493-2 (pbk.)
1. Semantics. 2. Whole and parts (Philosophy) I. Title.
P325.M59   1997
401'.43—dc20   96-9891

1 3 5 7 9 8 6 4 2

Printed in the United States of America
on acid-free paper

Preface

The relation between parts and wholes plays an important role in the way we conceive of things. Different kinds of entities have different kinds of part structure: artifacts and organisms have parts which have a particular function within the whole; quantities of water have subquantities as parts; groups of entities (like groups of tables, people, events, or facts) have group members or subgroups as parts; and events, states, and actions may have other events, states, or actions as parts. When using natural language, we often refer to things and say something about their parts or the integrity of the whole.

The goal of this book is to show that very general notions of part and whole play a pervasive role in the semantics of natural languages and are crucial in the understanding of a broad range of phenomena. The notions of part and whole are involved in the mass-count distinction, in various quantificational constructions, in distributive interpretations of predicates, and in the lexical meaning of many expressions in various natural languages. In this book, I argue that a particular notion of part structure is relevant in natural language semantics. This notion is novel in two general respects. First, it is not generally transitive, closed under sum formation, and extensional (identifying entities that have the same parts). The reason for this, basically, is that this notion involves the concept of *integrated whole* in certain ways. Second, part structures, under the new notion, are context-dependent or variable. On the one hand, this means that an entity may have different part structures in different *situations*. On the other hand, it means that an entity may have different part structures in different (temporal, spatial, qualitative, or object-induced) *dimensions*. The variability of part structures, as I will argue, is the source of systematic apparent ambiguities in a broad range of natural language constructions involving the parts of an entity. Moreover, it plays a role in particular semantic selectional restrictions of predicates and semantic operations.

The notion of part structure as it is conceived in this book deviates in fundamental ways from traditional notions of part structure, those common both in philosophy and in linguistic semantics. According to the traditional view, part structures are not variable; rather, an entity has exactly one part structure in all contexts. Moreover, the part relation in, at least, most recent traditions in philosophy and linguistics generally is an extensional notion — that is, a set-theoretic or extensional mereological notion.

Besides providing a theory of part structures for natural language and a general framework for formally analyzing part-structure-related phenomena, this book establishes a number of results that are of independent interest. One of them concerns the status of *situations*. A part structure of the sort relevant in natural language semantics is relative to a situation, where such a situation may be either a particular situation the speaker refers to or a situation that is described by the sentence. Hence the semantically relevant part structures are *situated part structures*. Since such situated part structures determine the availability of distributive interpretations of predicates and the satisfaction of semantic selectional requirements, this leads to the view that predicates do not take entities as arguments, but rather pairs consisting of an entity and a situation. Correspondingly, every noun phrase will denote not a single entity, but rather a pair consisting of an entity and what I call a 'reference situation' (or, given the generalized-quantifier treatment of noun phrase denotations, it will denote a set of sets of pairs consisting of entities and situations).

Two other claims made in this book concern the mass-count distinction. First, the mass-count distinction as a syntactic distinction between nominal categories is independent of the semantic mass-count distinction in the following way: there are expressions that apply to both mass nouns and count nouns but have a lexical meaning that specifies the part structure of an entity as that of a group, rather than a quantity. Second, the mass category is—both syntactically and semantically—the unmarked category among the categories singular count, plural, and mass. Two examples from English indicate that if a category does not have a mass-count distinction, it will count as a mass, rather than a count, category: verbs (with respect to the Davidsonian event-argument place) and clauses.

This book is organized as follows. Chapter 1 gives a general outline of the theory of situated part structures with its most important empirical motivations; it is supplemented by an appendix discussing in greater detail some related proposals in the previous literature. Chapter 2 presents the formal semantic framework that is used in the subsequent chapters; it also gives a treatment of distributivity, a central phenomenon among part-whole phenomena in natural language. The following chapters treat the various empirical subject matters. Chapter 3 is about what I call 'part-structure-sensitive semantic selection'—that is, semantic restrictions imposed by predicates, readings of a predicate, or semantic operations on the part structure of an argument. It also gives a semantic analysis of what I call 'perspective shifters', expressions such as *as a teacher* and *as a whole* in adnominal position. This is because part-structure-sensitive perspective shifters such as *as a whole, together, individual,* and *whole* interact in certain ways with part-structure-sensitive semantic selection. Chapter 4 treats various phenomena displaying an interaction between quantification and part structures. It gives new analyses of plural and mass quantifiers such as *all, many,* and *much,* and discusses quantifiers ranging over the parts of an argument (e.g., *all* and *whole*). Chapter 5 analyzes certain classes of expressions that specify part structures independently of the categories mass and count, namely frequency expressions (e.g., *frequent(ly)* and *rare(ly)*) and certain metrical and vague determiners in German. Chapter 6 is about expressions involving part structures that are relativized to a particular dimension: first, part-structure modifiers such as *together, alone, as a whole, individually* in adverbial position; second, expressions of completion such as *completely* and *partially* in various languages; and third, quantifiers ranging over the parts of a concrete event, such as *simultaneously* and *same/different* in the internal reading. Finally, Chapter 7 discusses the mass-count distinction when applied to verbs and clauses.

Only the first chapter and, to some extent, the second chapter are presupposed by the subsequent chapters. Any among Chapters 3-7 may be read more or less independently of the others.

Acknowledgments

Many people have been of help at various stages of this book. In particular, it has profited from comments from the audiences of presentations at the Massachusetts Institute of Technology, the University of Amsterdam, Stanford University, the University of Southern California in Los Angeles, the Conference on Language and Logic in Tucson, 1989, and the Workshop 'Formal Mereology and Conceptual Part-Whole Theories' at the European Artificial Intelligence Conference (EAIC) in Amsterdam, 1994, and the participants of my course 'Complex Part Structures and Natural Language' at the Seventh European Summer School in Logic, Language and Information in Barcelona, 1995. For discussions or comments on parts of earlier versions of the manuscript, I would like to thank in particular Renate Bartsch, Kit Fine, Irene Heim, Jim Higginbotham, Ed Keenan, Stanley Peters, Barry Schein, Barry Smith, Martin Stokhof, and the referee for Oxford University Press. For technical help with the preparation of the manuscript, I would like to thank Mark Brand. Finally, I wish to thank my father for his support over many years.

New York City   F.M.
March 1997

Contents

Parts and Wholes in Semantics

1

Introduction

1.1. Part structures in the semantics of natural language

There are many devices in natural language that, directly or indirectly, make reference to the part structure of an entity. This book investigates a broad range of such linguistic phenomena involving part-whole relations. Its goal is to provide a unified account of part-whole phenomena on the basis of a notion of part structure that is novel in several respects.

The novelty of this notion consists in the way it contrasts with the notion of part structure that has been most prominent in more recent discussions in philosophy and in linguistics, namely that of *extensional mereology*.[1] The part relation of extensional mereology is transitive, closed under sum formation, and extensional (that is, entities are identical just in case they have the same parts). Moreover, it is generally (in extensional mereology and elsewhere) assumed that entities have exactly one part structure.

The view of part structures presented in this book is a very different one. On this view, the part relation lacks formal properties such as transitivity, extensionality, and closure under sum formation inherently. What plays a more important role than such properties is whether an entity or its parts are *integrated wholes* (which they are, for example, in virtue of having a certain shape or by being connected in space and time). Moreover, an entity need not have a single part

---

[1] An extensional mereological part relation is used mainly for the semantics of definite plural and mass NPs in the lattice-theoretical approach of Link (1983, 1987), Sharvy (1980), and Simons (1983, 1987). This approach has subsequently been carried over to the semantics of events by Hinrichs (1985), Bach (1986), and Krifka (1989, 1990). Other applications of extensional mereological part relations concern generics and mass quantification. For example, Burge (1972) analyzes the referent of *gold* in *gold is widespread* as the mereological sum of all gold quantities (see also Ojeda 1991, 1993). Roeper (1983), Bunt (1985), and Lønning (1987) treat quantified mass NPs such as *all water* as involving quantification over the subquantities of the (maximal) quantity of water.

structure; rather, the part structure of an entity is *variable*. There are two ways in which the part structure of an entity is variable.

First, an entity may have different part structures in different situations, either by being divided differently into parts in these situations or by consisting of parts that are related to each other in different ways in these situations. The possibility of having different part structures in different situations is due to two properties of situations. First, a situation may include information about accidental properties of entities, and an entity may be an accidental integrated whole in one situation, but not in another. Having integrity of a particular sort (e.g., being connected in space) need not be essential for an entity. Second, a situation may contain only partial information about an entity. Hence in a given situation, an entity may fail to be an integrated whole simply because the situation fails to provide the relevant information about integrity.

An entity may also have different part structures in different *dimensions*. This holds especially for events: an event may have both a spatial and a temporal part structure, and, moreover, it may have different part structures correlating with different sorts of event participants. Finally, entities may have part structures in particular qualitative dimensions such as color.

Thus, the new notion of part structure has two general characteristics:

1. *The Importance of Integrity in Part Structures*
   The notion of integrated whole plays a crucial role in part structures.
2. *The Variablity of Part Structures*
   The part structure of an entity is variable in two ways:
   a. one and the same entity may have different part structures in different situations or under different perspectives;
   b. one and the same entity may have different part structures in different dimensions, where such dimensions are space, time, or more general aspects of an entity, such as the way the entity relates to other objects (e.g., event participants) or some qualitative dimension.

What are integrated wholes and what role does the notion of integrated whole play in part structures? I will give a precise answer to these questions later in this chapter. For the moment, the following intuitive characterization of integrated whole should suffice. Integrated wholes are entities that have integrity to a sufficient degree — for example, by having a certain shape, or by consisting of parts that are connected in space or time and are separated from other entities in those dimensions. We will see that the notion of integrated whole plays an important role in many phenomena in natural language. Let me mention the following main areas in which the notion is central.

First, the notion of integrated whole is at the heart of the *mass-count distinction*. Count nouns such as *ball*, *chair*, or *horse* always express properties that define an entity as an integrated whole. By contrast, mass nouns such as *water* and *wood* fail to express such properties.

Second, the notion of integrated whole plays a crucial role in certain *semantic selectional requirements*. Many predicates and semantic operations impose semantic selectional restrictions that involve the part structure of an argument. For example, certain predicates such as *compare* require arguments that lack integrity themselves but consist of parts that are integrated wholes (i.e., have a group-like part structure). This means that those predicates generally allow only for plural NPs as in (1a), but not singular count NPs as in (1b), where '#' marks semantic unacceptability:

    (1) a. John compared the fish and the meat / the beans.
          b. # John compared the basket of fruit / the meal / the wine.

    Third, the notion of integrated whole is involved in the *lexical meaning* of expressions like *together, alone, whole,* and *individual. Together* characterizes an entity as an integrated whole, whereas *alone* characterizes an entity as not being part of an integrated whole. *Whole* (as in *the whole family*) puts an entity under a perspective in which it is not an integrated whole, and *individual* (as in *the individual children*) puts an entity under a perspective in which it is not an integrated whole but consists of parts that are (essential) integrated wholes.

    Also, the notion of integrated whole is, at least in part, responsible for why extensional mereological properties do not hold of the semantically relevant part structures: integrity may block transitivity, restrict sum formation, and be the source of the failure of extensionality.

    It is striking that, even though natural language abounds in phenomena involving the notion of integrated whole, this notion itself has not systematically been used in semantic analyses of natural language constructions. Semantic theories have usually employed an extensional mereological notion of part structure, a notion that involves only the ordering relation 'is part of' among parts, but not other relations among parts which could establish integrity.

Let us turn to the second characteristic of the new notion of part structure, the variability of part structures. One phenomenon involving entities with different part structures in different situations consists in the various *distributive readings* that predicates with plural arguments display. For example, (2) may describe a situation in which the men lifted the table individually or a situation in which certain subgroups of the men lifted the table together:

    (2) The men lifted the table.

In the first case, the part structure of the group of men in the relevant situation consists of individual men; in the second case, it consists of the relevant subgroups of men.

    The possibility of an entity's having different part structures in different situations shows up also with the various readings that *quantifiers* may exhibit ranging over the parts of an entity — for example, *all* in (3):

    (3) All the students found a solution.

In (3), *all* expresses universal quantification over the parts the group of students has in the relevant situation. Example (3) may be true either if every single student found a (possibly different) solution (in which case the parts of the group of students are the individual students), or if certain relevant subgroups of students each found a (possibly different) solution (in which case the parts of the group are those subgroups). (The second reading is harder to get, yet not impossible, cf. Section 1.5.4.)

In examples like (2) and (3), the part structure of the relevant entity is largely contextually determined, subject only to general principles of part structure individuation. But there are also expressions that lexically characterize an entity with a particular kind of part structure. An example is the event quantifier *frequently*, as in (4):

(4)   Yesterday, John exercised frequently.

Frequently in (4) specifies that the (complex) event of John's exercising yesterday consists of many subevents separated in time.

The second respect in which the part structures of an entity are variable was that an entity can have different part structures in different *dimensions*, in an appropriately extended sense of 'dimension' (including not only space and time, but also more general aspects with respect to which an entity may be qualified). An entity has a part structure in a given dimension just in case the parts in that part structure are distinguished from each other by properties belonging to that dimension. The dimension dependency of part structures plays an important role in natural language semantics. It manifests itself most prominently in apparent ambiguities that systematically arise with expressions involving parts and wholes. We can distinguish wo sorts of such phenomena which correlate with two ways in which an entity may have different part structures in different dimensions: [1] an entity may be an *integrated whole* in one dimension, but not in some other dimension, and [2] an entity may have *different sets of parts* in different dimensions.

The first case can best be exemplified by expressions like *together*, whose semantic function is precisely to specify that an entity is an integrated whole in a particular situation. *Together* has several readings — for example, a spatiotemporal proximity reading, as in (5a), and a group-action reading, as in (5b) (cf. Lasersohn 1990):

(5)   a. John and Mary sat together.
      b. John and Mary work together.

These two readings can be traced to the fact that the group consisting of John and Mary can be specified as an integrated whole in two different dimensions: in the dimension of space-time, which is the dimension relevant in (5a), and in the dimension of John and Mary's activities, which is relevant in (5b).

The second case of an entity's having different part structures in different dimensions consists in the entity's having different sets of parts in different dimensions. This case can best be illustrated with expressions making reference to the parts of an *event*. Event part quantifiers display systematic apparent ambiguities whenever an event is specified as having parts in more than one way (provided it does not specifically make reference to temporal parts like frequency adverbials). One such event part quantifier is expressed by *simultaneously*, as in (6), where it ranges over the parts of a complex event of John praising and criticizing Ann and Sue:

(6) John praised and criticized Ann and Sue simultaneously.

In (6), *simultaneously* may compare either the subevents of praising and criticizing or the subevents involving Ann and Sue. In the first case, *simultaneously* applies to the part structure of the complex described event in the dimension of the event type; in the second case, it appliesto the part structure in the dimension of the object participants.

Completely as in (7) allows for an apparent ambiguity also with simple event predicates:

(7) The clouds completely disappeared.

On one reading of (7), every individual cloud has disappeared (to some standard degree); on the other reading, the state of the clouds (as a whole) is one of total invisibility. On the first reading, 'completeness' is measured with respect to the participant-related part structure of the event of the clouds' disappearance; on the second reading, it is measured with respect to the event-type-related part structure (consisting of the degrees of visibility).

Events differ from most kind of entities that are not events — that is, from objects — in that they quite naturally have multidimensional part structures. Such part structures may include a part structure that corresponds to an event type, a part structure where the parts correlate with the parts of a participant, and a part structure that corresponds to the location of the event. Linguistically, this means that, whenever an expression makes reference to the parts of an event (without qualifications) and applies to an event with n different part structures in different dimensions, the sentence will exhibit n different readings.

We have seen from a few central examples how the notion of part structure as characterized earlier manifests itself in natural language. What is crucial is that such part structures have to be taken as relative to *situations*. For example, the two readings of (3) involve two different situations, one in which the group of students is divided into particular subgroups and one in which it is divided into individual students. A situation carries a certain amount of information about an entity, such as whether the entity itself or its parts are integrated wholes, and the semantically relevant part structure of an entity depends on such information. What information is contained in the relevant situation depends on the meaning of relevant parts of the sentence and on the nonlinguistic context. Because of the dependency on a situation, part structures in the semantically relevant sense can be called *situated part structures*, and the part relation they involve can be called the *situated part relation*.

The relation between situated part structures and the information in the relevant situation can then be characterized as follows:

The dependence of part structures on situations
1. The situated part relation is a weak relation from a formal point of view. Whether certain formal conditions (transitivity, closure under sum formation) hold of situated part structures depends on the information in the situation, in particular whether or not entities are characterized as integrated wholes in the relevant situation.
2. Part-structure-related information in a given situation is provided in a variety of ways:
   a. by the specific concepts expressed by count and mass nouns
   b. by part-structure-related lexical meanings of expressions such as *frequent(ly)*
   c. by implicit information provided by the nonlinguistic context.

This is the basic picture of the account of part-structure-related linguistic phenomena in terms of situated part structures. In what follows, I want to lay out in a formally more explicit way the basic assumptions and principles of this account, and, in particular, introduce the notion of situated part structure against the background of the extensional mereological notion. First of all, however, certain basic assumptions concerning the semantics of singular count, plural, and mass NPs should be made explicit.

1.2. The analogy of the semantics of singular count, plural, and mass noun phrases

The notion of part plays a prominent role in the semantics of plurals and mass nouns in two ways. First, the extensions of plural and mass nouns are naturally ordered by a part-of relation. Second, there are many constructions with singular count, plural, and mass NPs that involve a part-of relation.[2] An assumption that is often made and that I will share is that the semantics of plural, mass, and singular count NPs is analogous. More specifically, the semantic difference between plural, mass, and singular count NPs results from plural, mass, and singular count nouns expressing different kinds of concepts, with plural nouns expressing concepts of

---

[2] A treatment of definite and indefinite plural and mass NPs within mereology is given in Sharvy (1980), Link (1983), and Ojeda (1993), and of quantified mass NPs in Bunt (1985), Lønning (1987), and Roeper (1983). Their proposals are essentially compatible with the general view of plural and mass nouns taken here. However, it is incompatible with a view according to which plurals are associated with different logical types than singular NPs (cf. Bennett 1972, 1974) or any view according to which plurals play a fundamentally different role in sentence meaning than singular NPs.

A very different treatment of definite NPs, not using mereology, has been given by Schein (1986, 1994) (see also Higginbotham/Schein (1989)). Here definite singular and plural NPs are treated as a sort of second-order quantifier.

groups, mass nouns concepts of *quantities*, and singular count nouns concepts of *individuals*.

There are a number of semantic parallelisms among definite singular count, plural, and mass NPs which support the view that definite plural and mass NPs (such as *the children* and *the water*) are, like definite singular NPs, referential NPs, referring to a single entity: a group in the case of plurals, and a quantity in the case of mass NPs.

First, like singular count NPs, definite plural and mass NPs allow for collective predicates which hold of the group or quantity, without necessarily holding of its parts, as in (8a) (with verbs) and (9a) (with nouns):

(8) a. The men gathered.
    b. The wood is heavy.
(9) a. The sum of these numbers is greater than 2.
    b. The weight of the wood is 10 pounds.

Second, definite plural and mass NPs do not enter scope relations with quantified NPs or binding relations with NPs containing *same* or *different*. Thus, the examples in (10) contrast with those in (11), and the ones in (12) with those in (13):

(10) a. The students found a mistake.
     b. The students found a different mistake.
(11) a. Every student found a mistake.
     b. Every student found a different mistake.
(12) a. The wood is of a very good or very bad quality.
     b. The wood is of the same quality.
(13) a. All the wood is of a very good or very bad quality.
     b. All the wood is of the same quality.

Examples (10a) and (10b) are most naturally understood as involving only one mistake, whereas (11a) and (11b) may involve as many mistakes as there are students.[3] Similarly, for (12a) to be true, the entire wood quantity must be of either good quality or bad quality. But for (13a) to be true, good and bad quality may be

---

[3] Speakers differ with respect to indefinite NPs in object position, as in (10a) (an issue I will come to in Chapter 2); but the data are clear with indefinite NPs in subject position, as in (1a), as opposed to (1b):.

(1) a. A mistake was found by every student.
    b. Every student found a mistake.

Indefinite NPs in subject position can never have a reading in which they distribute over the group members of a plural object NP: (1a) can only be understood as involving one mistake. By contrast, (1b) easily allows for a reading in which *a mistake* takes narrow scope with respect to *every student*.

found in different subquantities of the wood. Furthermore, (12b) and (13b) show that definite mass NPs cannot bind *same* (and hence enforce a discourse-related interpretation), in contrast to quantified mass NPs, as in (13b).[4]

These parallelisms support the view that definite plural and mass NPs are, like definite singular count NPs, referring NPs, referring to groups and quantities, respectively. The question then is, How can they refer to groups and quantities? Most plausibly because of the content of the nouns in question, whose extension consists of sets of groups and quantities. In its most general form, this view takes the form of the following Uniformity Condition:[5]

(14) *Uniformity Condition*
      Plural (mass) nouns express group (quantity) concepts in all syntactic
      contexts in which they occur.

---

[4] A potential third parallelism between definite mass and plural NPs and singular count NPs has been pointed out by Löbner (1987). It concerns the unacceptability of a sentence in which a homogeneous predicate holds only of a part, not the whole, of the referent of a definite NPs. This is attributed to the presupposition of homogeneous predicates that they must either hold of every part of an argument or fail to hold of every part. Löbner claims that this holds for singular count NPs, as in (1) (being about a chair with red and blue stripes), plurals as in (2a), as well as mass NPs, as in (3a):

(1) # The chair is blue.
(2) a. # The chairs are blue.
     b. Every chair is blue.
(3) a. # The wood is dry.
     b. All the wood is dry.

If the chair in (1) is half red, half blue, then (1) seems to lack a truth value. Similarly, if some of the chairs are red and some blue, (2a) appears to lack a truth value. By contrast, in such a situation, (2b) with a quantified singular count NP is certainly false.

The reason for this that Löbner gives is that if the entities that plurals refer to are considered groups and if members or subgroups are taken as the parts of those groups, then (2a) violates the presupposition of homogeneous predicates: *blue* either holds of only a part of the group of chairs or fails to hold of only a part of the group of chairs.

Similarly, in a situation in which the wood is half dry and half wet, (3a) is neither true nor false, but (3b) is certainly false. Some speakers, though, judge (2a) and (3a) then false, rather than truthvalueless. Thus, the data on which this third parallelism is based may not be so safe.

[5] This assumption has often been maintained for definite and indefinite plurals such as *the men* and *men*. For example, Link (1983) treats as the same the meaning that *the man* and *the men* and *a man* and *men* have in a sentence, but he assigns different meanings to the nouns *man* and *men*. However, the assumption has not systematically been made for all kinds of plural NPs, for instance not for *all the men*, *all men*, or *few men*. As we will see in Chapter 4, not only definite and indefinite NPs but also quantified NPs can be treated in a uniform manner on the basis of the situated part relation.

The Uniformity Condition is not without problems, though, especially concerning the case of plurals, an issue I will come back to in Chapter 5.[6] However, in general, the Uniformity Condition can be maintained in problematic cases by invoking independent principles of the individuation of the part structure of groups and quantities (and sometimes conditions of syntactic agreement for the distribution of plurals).

How are the concepts expressed by singular count, plural, and mass nouns distinguished — that is, what does the mass-count distinction consist in? There are two views of the mass-count distinction: the extensional mereological view and the present one, both of which I will discuss in subsequent sections. On both views, the concepts expressed by plurals are obtained in a systematic way from the concepts expressed by the corresponding singular nouns. Thus, if *sum* is some appropriate operation of sum formation, the extension of a noun f in the plural, f_{pl}, will be as in (15):[7]

---

[6] Certain constructions with plurals seem to go against the Uniformity Condition, for example those in (1) (cf. Roberts 1987):

    (1) a. The men believed that they / * he were / was alone.
          b. They found their / * his key.

But here syntactic agreement seems to be involved, since this phenomenon is not specific to plurals, but applies to other categories as well — for instance, tense (sequence of tense), as in (2a), and person (pronouns *de se*), as in (2b):

    (2) a. John thought that he was happy.
          b. John thought that he was female.

So (1) simply shows that 'plural' is a syntactic category that must satisfy conditions of agreement in certain 'subordinate contexts'. In these contexts, plural pronouns may be interpreted as singular.

Another construction consists of plural quantifiers that do not seem to range over groups, but only over individuals (as in *all men have a passport*). However, as I will argue in Chapter 4, there are independent conditions by which plural quantifiers are allowed to range over individuals only and which explain their tendency not to quantify over groups.

[7] In nonmereological accounts of plural reference, plurals generally have been taken to denote sets of individuals (cf. Bennett 1974, Scha 1981, Hoeksema 1983, Bunt 1985, and Landman 1989). The reason is that mereological part relations appear at first sight inappropriate for plurals; plurals rather seem to involve set membership (as in Bennett 1974, Scha 1981, and Hoeksema 1983). Bunt (1985) therefore constructs a system (called 'ensemble theory') which comprises mereology for mass nouns and set theory for plurals. However, an extensional mereological part relation can be used for plurals as well if the part relation for plurals is distinguished from the part relation for mass nouns. The main difference between the two part relations is that the mereology for plurals is atomic (the individual members of groups being atoms), whereas the mereology for mass nouns is not atomic.

Set theory has gained new interest in the semantics of plurals and collective NPs in Landman (1989), who argues that it has two properties that make it superior to a simple lattice structure for the semantics of plurals and collective NPs. Set-theoretical structures

(15) $[f_{pl}] = \{x \mid (\exists X)(x = sum(X) \ \& \ X \neq \emptyset \ \& \ X \subseteq [f_{sing}])\}$

Following the account of definite NPs of Sharvy (1980), a definite plural NP such as *the men* then refers to the maximal group of men and a definite mass NP such as *the water* to the maximal quantity of water:[8]

(16) a. $[the\ water] = sum(\{x \mid x \in [water]\})$
      b. $[the\ men] = sum(\{x \mid x \in [men]\})$

Plural and mass nouns are parallel semantically also as regards conjunction. Conjunction of both plural and mass NPs may be interpreted by sum formation, as in the examples in (17) (with (17a) having the reading in which the men resemble the women):

(17) a. The men and the women resemble each other.
      b. The wine and the water resemble each other.

For the interpretation of *and* in such cases, an operation of sum formation *sum* always applies to a set of entities, regardless of whether those entities are individuals, groups, or quantities:

(18) For entities $x_1, \ldots, x_n$, $[and](\{x_1, \ldots, x_n\}) = sum(\{x_1, \ldots, x_n\})$

The analogy between the semantics of plural, mass, and singular count NPs holds not only for definite and conjoined NPs; it also extends to quantification. English exhibits quantification over the parts of whatever entities singular, mass, or plural NPs refer to; and often the same quantifiers are used to quantify over the parts

---

are a specific kind of lattice, namely free lattices. In free lattices, a situation such as the following may not arise: *a* is the sum of *c* and *d*, and *a* is the sum of *e* and *f*, with *c, d, e,* and *f* being distinct. That is, the sum of a set *X* of individuals must be different from the sum of any set of individuals different from *X*. However, this condition fails to apply to a group whose identity does not depend on its members. For instance, groups denoted by *committee* or *directors* may have members that completely change in the course of events. This even holds for groups such as the one denoted by *the students at MIT*.

[8] The analysis of definite plural and mass NPs in terms of reference to sums of entities satisfying the relevant predicate is not the only possible account. An alternative analysis, which preserves the Russellian account of definite descriptions is to take *the men in the room* to refer to the unique group satisfying the predicate *men in the room,* and *the water in the tub* to refer to the unique quantity of water satisfying the predicate *water in the tub.* The uniqueness condition would be satisfied by general conditions on the universe of discourse (which is as usual contextually determined) and Gricean maxims as follows. If a speaker utters an expression that must refer to a unique entity and if there are in principle several entities satisfying the conditions, then the addressee should conclude that the universe of discourse intended by the speaker contains only one of these potential referents. A speaker may intend the universes of discourse for definite plural or mass NPs to contain only the maximal group or quantity satisfying the relevant predicate (which is the most prominent one, having the highest degree of integrity).

of individuals, quantities, or groups. This is so, for instance, in the partitive constructions in (19):

> (19) a. all of / some of / part of the book
>   b. all of / some of / part of the wine
>   c. all of / some of / part of the books

In these examples, *all*, *some*, and *part* range over the parts of either individuals, groups, or quantities, and so require that a part relation applies to individuals, groups, and quantities.

In general, there are two possible ways to account for the analogy between plural, mass, and singular count NPs:

1. By assuming distinct, but analogous, extensional mereological part relations for the extensions of singular count, mass, and plural NPs
2. By assuming one and the same part relation for all three domains of entities, and imposing weaker conditions on the part relation than the extensional mereological ones.

My account is based on the second, not the first, strategy. I will start, though, by discussing the first alternative, laying out in more detail the extensional mereological view of part-whole relations.

1.3. The traditional view of part structures

Let me make explicit the assumptions and consequences of the extensional mereological view of part structures. There are various extensional mereological theories of the part relation. These theories differ in their intended applications, as well as in how they characterize the notion of part.[9] But they all have certain features in common. Extensional mereological theories of the part relation generally share the assumption that the part relation is transitive, extensional, and closed under sum formation. A typical extensional mereological theory postulates the four axioms (20a–d) with extensionality in (20e) as a theorem.[10] Here < is an extensional mereological part relation:

---

[9] See Simons (1987) for an overview of extensional mereological theories.

[10] Extensionality can be derived from antisymmetry and reflexivity as follows. Suppose for all z, $z < x$ iff $z < y$ and $x < x$ and $y < y$. Then $x < y$ and $y < x$. Hence, by antisymmetry, $x = y$. If extensionality is not desired as a property of part structures, as will be discussed below, then either reflexivity or antisymmetry have to be given up. For the notion of part structure that I will define later, I will not assume reflexivity.

(20) a. $x < y$ & $y < z \rightarrow x < z$ (transitivity)
      b. $x < x$ (reflexivity)
      c. $x < y$ & $y < x \rightarrow x = y$ (antisymmetry)
      d. For any nonempty set X, $(\exists x)\, x = sum_<(X)$ (closure under sum
          formation)
      e. $((\forall z)(z < x \leftrightarrow z < y)) \rightarrow x = y$ (extensionality)

The notion $sum_<$ in (20) is best defined as in (21b) on the basis of the overlap
relation $O_<$ given in (21a):[11]

(21) a. *Definition*
          $x \, O_< y$ iff $(\exists z)(z < x$ & $z < y)$
      b. *Definition*
          For a nonempty set X,
          $sum_<(X) = \iota x[(\forall y)(y \, O_< x \leftrightarrow (\exists z)(z \in X$ & $y \, O_< z))]$

According to (21b), the sum of a set X is the entity that overlaps another entity y
just in case y overlaps with some other entity in X.

In most extensional mereological theories, more axioms than those in (20) are
posited, though a part structure just satisfying (20a–e) is assumed in Link (1983) for
the extension of plural and mass nouns. For present concerns, only the basic
properties given in (20) are important.

A way of capturing the analogy of the semantics of plural, mass, and singular
count nouns discussed at the beginning of this section is to apply the same sort of
part relation to the domains of groups, quantities, and individuals. In fact, for the
first two domains, this has been done, for example, by Simons (1983, 1987) and
Link (1983).[12] Then, the extension of a mass noun is a substructure of a part

---

[11] This definition has been proposed by Simons (1987), who argues that it is more
adequate than the definition of *sum* as the least upper bound (supremum) of a set. The
latter definition allows for the model given in (1), where w is the supremum of both the
set $\{x, y\}$ and the set $\{y, z\}$:

(1) w
        $/ \ | \ \backslash$
        $x \ \ y \ \ z$

Landman (1989) criticizes the definition of *sum* as least upper bound for the same
reason. He proposes a different solution to the problem, however — namely, the use of
sets for the semantics of plurals (cf. fn. 7).

[12] The view that distinct part relations should apply to different domains of entities — in
particular, the plural and the mass domain — was first expressed by Sharvy (1980).
Sharvy proposed that definite plural NPs such as *the children* refer to the sum of all the
children with respect to the plural-specific part relation, and definite mass NPs such as
the water refer to the mereological sum of all the water quantities with respect to the
mass-specific part relation.

structure $(X, <_m)$, and the extension of a plural noun is a substructure of another part structure $(Y, <_i)$, where $<_m$ is the part relation for quantities and $<_i$ is the part relation for groups.[13]

The application of extensional mereological part relations to all three kinds of entities requires a separation of the domain of individuals, the domain of groups, and the domain of quantities, each with its own part relation (the distinct relations $<_m$ and $<_i$ above). Such a separation in fact has been made by Sharvy (1980), Link (1983), and Simons (1983) (at least for groups and quantities). The distinction between the three different domains of entities each having its own part relation is conceptually required by two formal properties of extensional mereological part relations: *transitivity* and *extensionality*.

It is quite obvious that the distinction between the domain of groups and the domain of individuals is required by transitivity: the parts of a group usually are considered the individual members, but generally not the proper parts of individual members. But a single part relation applicable to both domains would yield parts of individuals as parts of a group.

The distinction between the domain of quantities and the domain of individuals is necessary because of both transitivity and extensionality. Suppose no distinction is made. Then, for example, if any material part of a ring counts as a part of the ring, by extensionality, the ring and the gold in the ring must be identical. But clearly this is wrong. The gold in the ring and the ring have different life histories — for example, they usually start and cease to exist at different times. Or in more linguistic terms, the gold in the ring and the ring differ in whether particular predicates of existence are true of them. Certainly, the time of existence is essential for the identity of an entity. Thus, at least for semantic purposes, the gold in the ring and the ring should be treated as distinct entities.[14]

Other cases of the wrong result coming from the application of the same part relation to quantities and individuals are due to transitivity in conjunction with extensionality. For example, a chair made of wood has certain distinguished parts:

The view that different part relations should be distinguished for individuals and quantities was in a more elaborate way adopted by Link (1983) and Simons (1983). In general, it is either implicit or explicit in extensional mereological approaches to the part relation that yet another part relation has to be distinguished for individuals. However, constructions involving the parts of an individual have generally not been discussed.

[13] The logic for plurals and mass nouns developed by Link (1983) uses two algebras $(E, v, <_i)$ and $(D, v, <_m)$, for the plural and mass domain, respectively. E, the domain of entities, is an atomic Boolean algebra with the join operation v for the formation of groups and an ordering $<_i$ (the part relation that relates group members or subgroups to goups). D, a subset of E, is a semilattice with join v (sum formation for quantities) and ordering $<_m$ (the part relation holding among quantities). The extension of a plural noun such as *children* is a subset of E, and the extension of a mass noun such as *water* is a subset of D.

[14] This criterion of identity, the 'life-histories principle', has been defended by Wiggins (1981). But see Lewis (1986) for a different view.

the legs, the back, and the seat. These are the parts that a referential NP such as *the parts of the chair* usually refers to and a quantified NP such as *all of the chair* usually ranges over (therefore permitting the appositive extension in *the parts of the chair / all of the chair — the legs, the back, the seat*). Suppose the same (transitive) part relation that applies to the mass referent of *the wood of the chair* applies to the individual referred to by *the chair*. Then, contrary to intuition and semantic facts, any material part of the functional parts of the chair — any piece of a leg or the back etc. — would necessarily count as a part of the chair; and, again, by extensionality, the chair would be identical to the wood of the chair. But, generally, the chair and the wood the chair consists of have different life histories. Hence, again, they should be treated as different entities.

The strategy that is generally taken on an extensional mereological approach for blocking undesirable consequences of transitivity and extensionality is to differentiate among part structures for different domains of entities, a strategy chosen by Sharvy, Link, and Simons. On such an account, the domain of groups will be ordered by a different part relation than the domain of quantities; and again, the domain of individuals may have its own part relation.

This is not the only way of solving the problem, however. The same result can be obtained by an alternative strategy, which is the one I will take. Instead of assuming different domains of entities each with its own part relation, transitivity and extensionality can be treated as properties holding of the part relation not absolutely but only under certain conditions. Then the problems mentioned above do not arise, and the part relation can be considered a single relation applying to individuals, quantities, and groups.

The choice between these two alternatives is not arbitrary. Rather, there are conceptual and empirical criteria that decide between them. The extensional mereological approach with distinctions among different part relations for different domains of entities predicts that no failure of extensionality should arise within one and the same domain. But this is not the case. Certainly, among individuals, extensionality may fail in both directions. First, two objects may have been made of the same material and even consist of the same parts but still be different. For example, two committees may consist of the same members (and maybe even the same subcommittees) but yet be different in function. Second, an individual may persist in flux, the gain and loss of parts. This is the most common objection against the extensional mereological notion of part when applied to individuals (see Simons 1987 for a recent discussion). As a way out of this problem, one might restrict extensional mereology to quantities and pluralities (as Simons 1987 suggests). However, extensionality may fail even in the domain of groups, as we will see.

Also, transitivity may fail in the domain of individuals (cf. Rescher 1955, Cruse 1979). To take an example from Rescher (1955), the nucleus is a part of the cell, and the cell is a part of the organism; but the nucleus does not count as a part of the organism. Similarly, a page is naturally a part of a book, and the book is naturally a part of a library; but the page does not intuitively count as a part of the library. Thus, the following two inferences are invalid:

(22) a. # The nucleus is a part of the cell.
<u>The cell is a part of the organism.</u>
The nucleus is a part of the organism.
b. # This page is a part of this book.
<u>This book is a part of the library.</u>
This page is a part of the library.

One might therefore choose the strategy that could be taken in order to avoid the extensionality problem — that is, to adopt a special, nontransitive part relation for individuals and restrict extensional mereological part relations to groups and quantities.

However, restricting extensional mereological part relations to groups and quantities does not solve the general problem. At least in the context of natural language semantics, transitivity failure occurs even within the plural and the mass domain. Transitivity may fail because a group may have a part structure in which only certain subgroups, and no individuals, are parts. Also, quantities may have a discrete part structure, in which certain subquantities, but not all smaller units, count as parts. For example, on one reading of (23a), only the maximal group of men and the maximal group of women count as parts of the group denoted by *the men and the women*. Similarly, on one reading of (23b), only the maximal subquantity of water and only the maximal subquantity of wine count as parts of the quantity denoted by *the wine and the water*:

(23) a. John compared the men and the women.
b. John compared the wine and the water.

Even extensionality may fail with groups. Suppose the judges are the same persons as the teachers. Then transitivity failure occurs in (24) on the reading on which the judges collectively earn more money than the teachers taken together:

(24) The judges earn (collectively) more money than the teachers.

So extensionality and transitivity as properties of extensional mereological part relations require that different part relations be distinguished for different domains of entities. Without transitivity and extensionality, a uniform part relation could apply to all three kinds of entities. But not only 'across domains', even within one and the same domain, failure of transitivity and extensionality may occur. Thus, it appears that there are no strong reasons to take the part relation to be extensional and transitive. But if extensionality and transitivity are given up, there is no need for a distinction among domains of entities; rather, a single part relation suffices for individuals, groups, and quantities.

I will argue for a uniform, weak notion of part that, at the same time, incorporates conditions under which the part relation is transitive and extensional in a particular context. With this notion, strict formal properties as captured by the extensional mereological axioms are less important than the information about

entities or their parts in a given context — in particular, properties that characterize
an entity or its parts as integrated wholes.

1.4.   The mass-count distinction: the extensional mereological account

The mass-count distinction obviously is a syntactic distinction among nouns (or
perhaps occurrences of nouns).[15] Mass and count nouns differ in whether they
allow for the plural and which determiners they take. But the mass-count distinction
as a purely formal distinction is also associated with a distinction in content. When
a noun is a count noun, we know that it refers to entities of some kind; and when it
is a mass noun, we know that it refers to entities of another kind. In the following, I
will contrast two approaches to the mass-count distinction as a distinction in
content: the *extensional mereological approach*, which I will argue against, and the
information-based approach, which I will propose instead and which is based on
the notion of integrated whole.

On the extensional mereological approach to the semantic mass-count
distinction, singular count nouns, mass nouns, and plurals are characterized by
formal properties of their extensions that are defined in terms of extensional
mereological part relations. The properties characterizing plural and singular count
noun extensions are defined in terms of the plural-specific part relation, and the
property characterizing mass noun extensions is defined in terms of the mass-
specific part relation.

On the extensional mereological approach to the mass-count distinction,
generally two formal properties are postulated for the extensions of mass nouns as
opposed to singular count nouns: *cumulativity* (i.e., if a set contains two entities, it
also contains their sum) and *divisivity* (i.e., if a set contains an entity, it also
contains any of its parts).[16]

Cumulativity is defined in (25), where <, as usual, is an extensional
mereological part relation:

(25) *Definition*
        A nonempty set X is *cumulative* iff
        $(\forall x)(\forall y)\,(x \in X \,\&\, y \in X \rightarrow sum_<(\{x, y\}) \in X).$

Divisivity is defined in (26):

---

[15] For an extensive discussion of what exactly the mass-count distinction applies to, see
Schubert/Pelletier (1989).

[16] Cumulativity as a characteristic property of mass noun extensions was first proposed by
Quine (1960). Divisivity was proposed by Cheng (1973). Both conditions have been adopted
by ter Meulen (1981), Roeper (1983), and Lønning (1987).

(26) *Definition*
A nonempty set X is *divisive* iff $(\forall x)(\forall y)(x \in X \ \& \ y < x \rightarrow y \in X)$.

If a set is both cumulative and divisive, it is homogeneous:

(27) *Definition*
A nonempty set X is *homogeneous* iff X is cumulative and divisive.

For the extensional mereological characterization of *plurals*, another property is generally used — namely, atomicity, the property a set has if it consists only of sums of sets of atoms. It is defined in (28b) by means of the notion of atom given in (28a):

(28) a. *Definition*
a is an *atom* in a set X iff $(\neg \exists x)(x \in X \ \& \ x < a \ \& \ x \neq a)$.
b. *Definition*
A set X is *atomic* iff for every $x \in X$, $x = sum(Y)$ for a set Y of atoms in X.

There is a strong and a weak version of the extensional mereological account of the mass-count distinction. On the strong version, homogeneity is taken as the characteristic of mass nouns, as in (29), where [ ] is the denotation function:

(29) *Extensional mereological characterization of mass nouns (strong version)*
If a noun f is a *mass noun*, then $[f]$ is homogeneous (in every model).

Singular count nouns are characterized in terms of the notion of atom, as in (30):

(30) *Extensional mereological characterization of singular count nouns*
If a noun f is a *singular count noun*, then all the elements in $[f]$ are atoms (in every model).

Since an atom is the sum of its singleton, the extension of a singular count noun will also be atomic.

Singular count noun extensions often do not include all the parts of an object that is in their extension. Hence singular count noun extensions are not generally divisive with respect to the part relation among individuals. But the extension of a mass noun, being divisive, still may consist only of atoms. A stronger condition therefore may be imposed on mass noun extensions — namely, that they not include any atoms and thus consist of entities that are indefinitely divisible (cf. Ojeda 1993). Consisting only of atoms and consisting of no atoms then would make up the difference between singular count and mass nouns.

Plural nouns have an extension that is the closure (under sum formation) of the extension of the corresponding singular count noun. Hence plural noun extensions will be atomic and cumulative:

(31) *Extensional mereological characterization of plural nouns*
      If a noun *f* is a *plural* noun, then [*f*] is atomic and cumulative (in every
      model).

The extensional mereological characterization of plural and mass nouns hinges
crucially upon part relations that are specific to the domain of singular count nouns,
plurals, and mass nouns, and such part relations lead to a number of conceptual and
empirical problems. There are both problems with the strong version of the
extensional mereological account and with weaker versions that one might propose
instead.

One of them arises with divisivity for mass noun extensions, namely as the so-
called *minimal-parts problem*, which was pointed out by Quine (1960). It consists
in that a sufficiently small part of a quantity of a mass noun referent often is not a
referent of the mass noun again. For example, a part of a single piece of a quantity
referred to as 'furniture' may itself not be furniture again. A weaker version of the
extensional mereological account, therefore, gives up divisivity as a characteristic of
mass noun extensions and takes only cumulativity as the defining property
(following Quine 1960). The mass-count distinction then is drawn as in (32):

(32) *Extensional mereological characterization of mass and count nouns*
      (weak version)
      a. If a noun *f* is a *mass noun*, then [*f*] is cumulative (in every model).
      b. If a noun *f* is a *singular count noun*, then [*f*] consists only of atoms
          (in every model).
      c. If a noun *f* is *plural*, then [*f*] is atomic and cumulative (in every
          model).

The minimal-parts problem clearly puts into question also the characterization of
mass noun extensions as not containing any atoms. But if divisivity and lack of
atoms for mass nouns is given up, then there is no extensional mereological
criterion distinguishing particular mass and count nouns anymore. A particular mass
noun could very well have an atomic extension.

A way of avoiding the minimal-parts problem while maintaining divisivity and
lack of atoms for mass nouns might be to reevaluate the status of those properties.
Divisivity and lack of atoms may be considered only perceived, not actual,
properties of mass noun extensions.[17] However, such a view is not very satisfactory
since it does not yield a decidable criterion for the mass-count distinction.

Another problem with the extensional mereological account concerns the
distinction between mass nouns and singular count nouns in terms of the notion of
atom. It appears that there are singular count nouns that may include nonatoms in

---

[17] This view has been taken by Bunt (1985), according to whom "the use of mass nouns
is a way of talking about things as if they were a homogeneous mass, i.e. as having a
part-whole structure, but without singling out any particular parts and without any
committment concerning the existence of minimal parts" (Bunt 1985, p. 46).

their extension (with respect to the plural-specific part relation) — for example, the nouns *entity, object,* or *sum*.[18] The nouns also pose a problem for the characterization of mass and plural nouns in terms of cumulativity. One strategy in this case is to emphasize the distinction between the plural-specific and mass-specific part relations by which the notions of atom and sum are defined and distinguish them from an ontological part relation, a strategy I will come to below. Alternatively, one might adopt a conceptual view of the notion of atom on which the extension of a singular count noun would consist not of atoms in any ontological sense but only of entities perceived as atoms (and similarly for sums). But here such a view is even less plausible than in the case of divisivity.

A general conceptual problem with the extensional mereological account, having to do with the first strategy just mentioned, is that it ultimately does not provide any language-independent criteriom for the mass-count distinction. It relies crucially on part relations that are not independently identifiable in the world, but rather are identifiable only by recourse to the relevant category of the nouns in question. For whether the plural-specific or whether the mass-specific part relation obtains between two objects can be decided only by looking at what nouns have been used to refer to those objects.

The most important empirical inadequacy of the extensional mereological account of the mass-count distinction is this. The extensional mereological account predicts that mass nouns should have a homogeneous or cumulative extension in all contexts, and plurals should have an atomic and cumulative extension in all contexts. That is, the extensional mereological account attributes absolute formal properties to mass and plural nouns as their defining semantic characteristics. But as a matter of fact, extensional mereological conditions may be suspended under certain circumstances — namely, when there is information about the integrity of particular entities or their parts from sources other than the nouns being used. On the account that I will propose, cumulativity and homogeneity have only a derived status; what is more crucial for the distinction between mass and count nouns than such properties is whether nouns characterize entities as integrated wholes.

1.5. A new notion of part structure for natural language

We can now turn to the notion of situated part structure and the information-based account of the mass-count distinction that goes along with it. What is crucial about situated part structures is that they depend in certain ways on information given by the linguistic or nonlinguistic context. This information crucially involves properties that characterize an entity or its parts as integrated wholes, and it is responsible for the failure of transitivity and closure under sum formation. Such part-structure-specific information is related to, but in principle independent of, the

---

[18] For similar examples, see Griffin (1977), who discusses and criticizes extensional mereological criteria for the related distinction between sortals and nonsortals (see the appendix to this chapter).

mass-count distinction. Singular count nouns characteristically specify an entity as an integrated whole, whereas mass nouns do not. But there are other ways of providing information about integrity than by count nouns. Integrity may also be conveyed by particular lexical items, by certain construction types, or by the nonlinguistic context.

Also, the new notion of part structure uses a single, sufficiently general part relation, which then allows for simple and uniform semantic analyses of a broad range of constructions. In these analyses, semantic differences between constructions are often not located at the level of sentence meaning, but rather arise from the way the part structures of the entities involved are characterized and from the way they are individuated in the relevant context.

In the following, I will first show the relevance of the notion of integrated whole for the mass-count distinction, where the notion of integrity will be left at an intuitive level. Then I will give a formal definition of one notion of integrated whole, which is the most important one for the phenomena under investigation. Finally, I will specify the role this notion plays in part structures.

1.5.1. The information-based account of the mass-count distinction

The notion of integrated whole plays a central role in the mass-count distinction. This can best be seen from the ways in which singular count nouns are converted into mass nouns and mass nouns into singular count nouns. If the singular count noun *apple* is used as a mass noun, it loses the components of its meaning that define an apple as an integrated whole — in particular, the properties of shape. *A lot of apple* and *a little apple* refer to 'apples' either implying the loss of the apples' integrity or disregarding their integrity. This is intuitively seen in the contrast between (33a) and (33b):

(33) a. The salad contains an apple.
     b. The salad contains apple.

Example (33a) strongly suggests that the salad contains a whole apple, whereas (33b) preferably is understood in the sense that the salad contains only pieces of apple, that is, 'apple' without its usual shape.

More generally, singular count nouns differ from mass nouns in that they characterize an entity as an integrated whole. Let me call properties that characterize an entity as an integrated whole *whole-properties*. Then, singular count nouns, but not mass nouns, must express whole-properties as part of their lexical meaning. Nouns in whose lexical meaning properties of form or gestalt play a central role typically do not allow a conversion into mass nouns. For example, the count nouns *picture, ball*, or *statue* are impossible as mass nouns (* *a lot of picture / ball / statue*).

The converse process of converting mass nouns into count nouns shows the same thing. There are a variety of ways in which whole-properties can be introduced so as to allow a mass noun to be converted into a count noun. For instance, quantities in particular contexts often are associated with natural measures. This is what makes the count noun use of *beer* possible in *three beers*. Another way of converting mass nouns into count nouns is by letting the noun refer to kinds, as in *three wines*.

There is an issue, however, as to what it means for a count or mass noun to express or fail to express whole-properties. Generally, it matters not so much how the described entity actually happens to be, but rather whether it is regarded as an integrated whole or not. One reason for that is that the same entity can be referred to both by a mass NP and a count NP. For example, a piece of wood can be referred to both by *the wood* and by *the piece of wood*. Moreover, there are mass nouns, for example *furniture* or *clothing*, which seem to apply to entities that consist of integrated wholes. When such mass nouns are used to refer to an entity *x*, however, it is implied that the integrity of the parts of *x* is not relevant or not perceived as integrity. For the picture one has in mind when applying *furniture* or *clothing* to an entity seems to be a more or less homogeneous mass.

A way to account for this behavior of mass and singular count nouns is to take noun extensions as being relative to *situations* — that is, partial specifications of entities with properties. A situation need not represent an entity with all the properties it has, but may contain only partial information. Hence, an entity may be an integrated whole in the actual world, but need not be one in the relevant situation. And the same entity may be an integrated whole in one situation but not in another. Moreover, the notion of situation may be extended so that it can also represent the way a speker views entities — that is, represent information about merely conceived properties and relations that hold of entities. I will come back to the notion of situation, both in its formal aspects and in its further empirical applications, later in this chapter.

If the extension of a noun is conceived of as a function from situations to functions from entities (or *n*-tuples of entities) to truth values (see Section 1.5.4.), the distinction between singular count, plural, and mass nouns in terms of the conceptual information associated with nouns can be given in the following way:

(34) *The information-based account of the mass-count distinction*
   a. If *f* is a *mass noun*, then for any minimal situation *s* and entity *x*
       such that $[f]^s(x) = 1$, *x* is not an integrated whole in *s*.
   b. If *f* is a *singular count noun*, then for any situation *s* and entity *x*,
       if $[f]^s(x) = 1$, then *x* is an integrated whole in *s*.

The characterization of mass noun extensions in (34a) uses minimal situations. The reason for this is this. Suppose a mass noun *f* holds of an entity *x* in a situation *s*, and *s* is not minimal in carrying the information given by *f* about *x*, then *x* may still be an integrated whole in *s* — namely, if the information about the integrity of *x* in *s* comes from a source other than *f* itself.

The most important and empirically relevant feature of the information-based account of the mass-count distinction (as opposed to the extensional mereological one) is the following. If the semantic differences between singular count nouns, plurals, and mass nouns reduce to a distinction in conceptual information (that is, the presence or absence of integrity conditions), then these distinctions may, in a concrete case, be suspended — namely, if the relevant context, in some other way, influences the integrity of an entity independently of the conceptual meanings of the nouns being used. There are various ways in which integrity conditions can be provided independently of the use of count nouns. Essentially three such ways can be distinguished:

1. Nonlinguistic background information about the part structure of entities
2. The meaning of more complex constructions in which the nouns occur — for instance, conjunction or modification by conjoined NPs, PPs, or relative clauses
3. Part-structure-related lexical meanings

If the referents of an NP or its parts are specified as integrated wholes in one of these ways, then the extensional mereological properties that are associated with the category of the noun in question may be suspended. But this means that whether extensional mereological properties hold of entities and the actual subextensions of nouns depends on integrity conditions wherever they may come from.

There is a class of potential counterexamples to (34). Certain singular count nouns — for instance, *entity*, *unit*, *thing*, *piece*, and *part* — do not explicitly characterize an entity as an integrated whole; nonetheless, they syntactically classify as count nouns in that they take the plural and allow for cardinality quantifiers (such as *three* as in *three things*).[19] However, it turns out that these nouns also semantically act as count nouns. For example, they do not allow for mass predicates, as seen in (35a), and they cannot act as predicates of mass or plural NPs, as seen in (35b, c):

(35) a. This thing / This entity is an apple / # is apple.
     b. The leg / # The wood are a part of the table.
     c. The two legs are parts of the table / # a part of the table.

This thing in (35a) refers to an entity that is viewed as an integrated whole, but *apple* as a mass noun may hold of an entity only when it is not viewed as an integrated whole. In other words, *this thing* refers to an entity that is an integrated whole in the relevant situation, whereas *apple* may hold of an entity in a situation only if the entity is not an integrated whole in that situation.

Example (35b) illustrates the converse case. The predicate *a part of the table* in (35b) expresses a property that can hold only of an entity viewed as an integrated whole — that is, an entity in a situation in which it is an integrated wholes. Thus,

---

[19] In the philosophical literature — for example, Griffin (1977) — such nouns are discussed as 'dummy sortals' and distinguished from true sortals such as *chair* (cf. Appendix, Section 1A.2.).

a part of the table can be true of an entity and a situation referred to by *the leg*, but not the entity and the situation referred to by *the wood*.[20]

The semantic 'count status' of the nouns in question is obvious also from the way a question such as How many things are there? is answered. Generally, only entities that are integrated wholes are counted, not sums or parts of such entities which themselves lack integrity. However, what kinds of integrated wholes are counted is left unspecified; it depends entirely on the type of entity itself.

Thus, nouns like *entity, unit, thing, piece*, and *part* do not fail to impose integrity, but rather impose *implicit integrity conditions*, which have to be provided by the nonlinguistic context.

There is one additional condition imposed by these nouns. They generally do not require just that the entities be integrated wholes in the relevant situation, but rather that they be *essential* integrated wholes. For one cannot refer to a quantity of wood that forms an accidental integrated whole (by being connected in space and time) as *the entity, the thing, the piece*, or *a part*. Given this, the noun *thing*, for example, will carry the following lexical condition:

(36) *Semantic condition on* thing
  For an entity x and a situation s, if $[thing]^s(x) = 1$, then x is an essential integrated whole in s.

Thus, even count nouns that do not describe an entity as an integrated whole in a particular way carry implicit integrity conditions as part of their meaning.

So far I have restricted myself to mass nouns and singular count nouns and have left out plurals. Plurals by definition cannot ascribe whole-properties to an entity. This follows from the meaning of plurals as group concepts. A plural noun describes an entity x only on the basis of whole-properties of the parts (i.e., the members) of x, namely the whole-properties expressed by the corresponding singular noun. Thus, plurals generally characterize an entity only by nonrelational properties of the members it is composed of and therefore generally do not characterize it as an integrated whole. (Only the maximal group denoted by a plural constitutes a (weak) integrated whole, an issue I will come back to later.)

Given (34), being an integrated whole or failing to be one in the relevant situation is only a necessary, not a sufficient, condition for an entity to be described by a count noun or a mass noun respectively. This is adequate, since there are various ways in which even the referent of a mass noun (in a given situation) may count as an integrated whole or as consisting of integrated wholes, as we will see.

---

[20] The noun *part* acts both as a count noun and a mass noun. As expected, as a mass noun, it does not require an entity to be an integrated whole and thus can apply to quantities and groups:

(1) a. The wood is part of the chair.
   b. The legs are part of the table.

Thus, from the properties an entity x has in some situation, it is not predictable whether x will belong to the extension of a noun that is syntactically mass or count.

1.5.2. Characterizations of integrated wholes

Let me now turn to the notion of integrated whole. The notion of integrated whole is not new, but rather has played a role in philosophy for a long time. The most recent and detailed discussion of this notion and its history is given in Simons (1987). The notion of integrated whole is a difficult one, and it is hard to give a unified definition of it — should that be possible at all. Hence it may not be possible to state what is common among all count nouns.

But fortunately, for most of the analyses of natural language constructions given in this book, a rather simple notion of an integrated whole of a particular kind suffices. This is the notion of *R-integrated whole*. This notion comes from Simons (1987) and is defined in (37), where a division of an object is taken to be a set of (general) parts completely exhausting the object:

> (37) An entity x is an *R-integrated whole* if there is a division of x such that every member of that division stands in the relation R to every other member and no member bears R to anything other than members of the division.

Formally, an R-integrated whole will be defined on the basis of a number of auxiliary notions. One of them is the notion of mereological division of an entity in (38), where $O_<$ is the relation of mereological overlap:

> (38) *Definition*
> For a nonempty set X and an entity x,
> X is a *mereological division* of x (DIV(X, x)) iff
> $(\forall y)(y \in X \rightarrow y < x)$ & $(\forall y)(y < x \rightarrow (\exists z)(z \in X$ & $z\,O_<\,y))$.

For an entity to be an integrated whole, the division must be closed and connected under some relation. The notions of closure and connectedness under a relation are defined as follows:

> (39) *Definition*
> For a nonempty set X and a two-place relation R,
> X is *closed* under R (CL(R, X)) iff
> $(\forall x)(\forall y)(x \in X$ & $(xRy \lor yRx) \rightarrow y \in X)$.
> (40) *Definition*
> For a nonempty set X and a two-place relation R,
> X is *connected* under R (CON(R, X)) iff
> $(\forall x)(\forall y)(x \in X$ & $y \in X \rightarrow xRy \lor yRx)$.

Now an integrated whole under a relation R, an R-integrated whole, can be defined as in (41), where R_{trans} is the transitive closure of R (i.e., $xR_{trans}y$ iff there are entities $x_1, \ldots, x_n$ such that xRx_1 & $\ldots$ & x_nRy):

(41)   *Definition*
      For a nontrivial two-place relation R and an entity x,
      x is an *R-integrated whole* (R-INT-WH(x)) iff there is a nonempty set
      X such that DIV(X, x), CL(R_{trans}, X), and CON(R_{trans}, X).

The specification 'nontrivial' in (41) is required in order to exclude integrated wholes being defined on the basis of relations such as difference or identity.

Given (41), the parents of John are an integrated whole on the basis of the relation 'having John as a child with', and a pile of books is an integrated whole because the books form a mereological division which is closed and connected under the transitive closure of the relation 'lies immediately below'.

A special kind of R-integrated whole can be defined on the basis of a one-place property. Any one-place property F defines a relation FF, which holds of a pair just in case F holds of each of its members:

(42)   *Definition*
      Let F be a nontrivial one-place property,
      FF(x, y) iff F(x) and F(y).

An FF-integrated whole is simply a maximal entity that can be divided into parts that all have the property F.

The notion of FF-integrated whole is quite important in the context of natural language semantics. In particular, it has an important application to definite plurals. Given the view that definite plurals such as *the books on the shelf* refer to the maximal group of entities satisfying the corresponding singular N' as given in Section 1.2., the referent of *the books on the shelf* is an FF-integrated whole, where F is the property expressed by *book on the shelf*.

The notion of R-integrated whole is a very simple notion of integrated whole; and of course, R-integrated wholes are not the only kind of integrated whole. As is discussed in Simons (1987), there are a number of other notions of integrated whole. For example, R-integrated wholes require that the members of the division stand in a single relation to each other. But there are integrated wholes of more complex types, which involve more than one relation. For example, there are various kinds of forms that define objects as integrated wholes but involve more than one relation. Another notion of integrated whole is based not (or not only) on relations holding among the parts of an object but on the function the entire object has. In this case, the entity is an integrated whole because it has a certain function with respect to other objects. Furthermore, entities may be integrated wholes on the basis of functional dependencies among their parts.

It is not easy to give formal definitions of types of integrated wholes other than R-integrated wholes. In fact, it is not clear whether there is at all a unified definition of different sorts of integrated wholes. However, the other notions of integrated whole, though they certainly may be important for the lexical semantics of count nouns, do not play a direct role in the kind of part-structure-related phenomena discussed in this book. They therefore can be neglected. For the present purposes, the notion of R-integrated whole usually suffices. For the more general notion of integrated whole, I will henceforth use the abbreviation 'INT-WH' (that is, INT-WH(x) iff x is an integrated whole).

The notion of integrated whole has two important general properties. First, being an integrated whole is a matter of *degree*, rather than an absolute property. An entity may have a greater degree of integrity than some other entity, and a whole-property may represent a greater degree of integrity than some other whole-property. The relative nature of integrity plays a role in natural language semantics — for example, by the fact that an entity that is an R-integrated whole on the basis of a property is an integrated whole to a weaker degree than an entity that is an R-integrated whole on the basis of an (irreducible) relation. Thus, the referent of *the people* has a weaker degree of integrity than the referent of *the line of people*. We will see empirical manifestations of this difference in Chapter 3.

The second important property of integrity is that it may manifest itself in a particular *dimension*. An object may have integrity in one dimension, but fail to be an integrated whole in some other dimension. To give a simple example, Kurdistan is an integrated whole culturally to a high degree; but it is not an integrated whole to the same degree politically. Of course, an entity may also have integrity in more than one dimension or in all relevant dimensions. The fact that integrity may obtain only relative to a particular dimension is empirically relevant in that it is responsible for certain systematic apparent ambiguities of expressions of integrity such as *together* and *alone*, as will be discussed in Chapter 6.

The restriction of integrity (of a certain degree) to a particular dimension corresponds to the more general fact that a part structure may be relative to a particular dimension. An entity may also have different sets of parts in different dimensions.

The notion of integrated whole not only plays a role in the general distinction between mass and count nouns; it may also be expressed directly by particular expressions of the object language. There are a number of expressions in English whose semantic function is ascribing integrity or the lack of it to an entity or its parts. Among those that ascribe integrity to an entity are *as a whole*, *as a group*, and *together*; among those that ascribe the lack of integrity are *whole* (as an adjectival modifier), *entire*, and *alone*; and among those that ascribe integrity to the parts of an entity are *individual* and *separate*. For the semantics of these expressions (which will be discussed in detail in Chapters 3 and 6), only the notion of R-integrated whole is needed.

1.5.3. Formal properties of part structures

Earlier, it was mentioned that the notion of integrated whole is responsible for the failure of transitivity and, to some extent, extensionality. Let me now show why.

Let us first consider failure of extensionality with individuals. Two objects that consist of the same parts may be different — for instance, when they differ in arrangement or form. A simple example is a chair and a table made of the same parts. The difference between the chair and the table is due to the fact that the parts enter different spatial relations to each other in the two cases (and these relations are essential for the two objects). Essential relations among parts such as those underlying the form of an object may also underlie the difference between referents of collective NPs and referents of plurals constituted of the same individuals. For instance, the distinction between the referent of *the line of dots* and the referent of *the dots* consists in that the former, but not the latter, requires that certain spatial relations hold among the parts (the individual dots).

So particular integrity conditions may be crucial for the identity of entities that have the same parts, and two entities that have the same parts are identical only if they share the same (essential) whole-properties. We can then formulate the following Extensionality Principle:

(43) *Extensionality Principle*
$(\forall x)(\forall y)((\forall z)(z < x \leftrightarrow z < y) \ \& \ \neg \ \text{INT-WH}(x) \ \& \ \neg \ \text{INT-WH}(y)$
$\rightarrow x = y)$

A tempting assumption then is that individuals are, in some way, composed of their parts and, possibly, some essential whole-properties.[21] However, such a conception of individuals is usually inadequate. An individual x and a group or quantity y composed of the same parts generally differ not only in that x is essentially an integrated whole but also in that x, unlike y, generally allows for the loss, addition, or replacement of parts. For example, the referent of *the orchestra members* does not stay the same when members of the orchestra are taken away, added, or replaced, whereas the referent of *the orchestra* may stay the same under such circumstances.

Issues about individuation like these, however, are rather unimportant for the phenomena dealt with in this book, since they do not so much involve the individuation of entities *per se* as the part structures entities have in particular situations. For those phenomena, it generally only matters whether or not an entity is an integrated whole in a situation, not whether it is an integrated whole essentially or not.

Let us turn to transitivity. Like extensionality, the question whether the inference from $x < y$ and $y < z$ to $x < z$ is allowed for given x, y, and z can be traced to the presence or absence of integrity, namely the integrity of y. Consider the part

---

[21] This would correspond to Fine's (1982) notion of *qua*-object, which is an aggregate of a quantity and a property.

relation applied to groups, where y is a person, z a group with y as a member, and x a leg of y. Then the inference to $x < z$ is intuitively invalid. The reason appears to be that individuals are integrated wholes, and their integrity may block transitivity. One might then propose the following condition on part structures: if x is a part of y, y a part of z, and y an integrated whole, then x is not a part of z.

However, this condition would be too strong. It would exclude many cases of acceptable part structures, for example that of a human body. My hand is a part of my arm, which is an integrated whole, and my arm is a part of my body; but my hand also is a part of my body. A weaker transitivity principle is required which simply does not require transitivity if the intermediate entity y is an integrated whole:

(44) *Transitivity Principle*
$(\forall x)(\forall y)(\forall z)(x < y \ \& \ y < z \ \& \ \neg \ \text{INT-WH}(y) \to x < z)$

The Transitivity Principle allows transitivity failure also for the parts of an individual. Let us consider the case given in (22a) of an organism, a cell of the organism, and its nucleus. The nucleus fails to be a part of the organism because the cell is an integrated whole. Similarly for the example in (22b) of the library, the book, and the page: the page fails to be a part of the library because the book is an entity with integrity of its own. These two examples contrast with a case in which the inference is valid: a piece of paper may be a part of a loose collection of papers on my desk, and this collection may be a part of the stuff of papers on my desk. In this case, the paper may be considered a part of the stuff on my desk. The reason is that the collection of papers does not have the integrity that may prevent transitivity.[22]

---

[22] Example (44) leaves open whether if y is an integrated whole, x will be part of z. For answering this question, it is illuminating to consider some further examples such as (1a) and (1b), in which the intermediate items, the book and the lobster, are integrated wholes, but transitivity goes through:

(1)   a.   This page is part of the book.
           The book is part of my written work.
           This page is part of my written work.
      b.   This claw is part of the lobster.
           The lobster is part of the dinner.
           The claw is part of the dinner.

The reason why transitivity goes through in (1a) and (1b) has to do with the nature of the whole: *my written work* in (1a) and *the dinner* in (1b) do not necessarily have parts that are integrated wholes. The difference between the referent of *the library* and *my written work* is that the former must be constituted of certain *kinds* of parts — namely, books, which in a way are *functional parts* of the library (though not essential parts; it matters not so much whch books are in the library, but only that they are books). By contrast, the referent of *my written work* need not consist of integrated wholes: any entity as long as it is something written by me may count as a part of my written work; no part of my written work need be an integrated whole for my written work to be what it is. So it

We have seen that the presence of integrity may block extensionality and transitivity for the ontological part structure of entities. The Transitivity Principle also applies to situated part structures, which I will discuss in the next section.

1.5.4. Situated part structures

Let us recall the two phenomena mentioned earlier that involve situated part structures: distributive interpretations of predicates, as is possible in (2), repeated here as (45a), and universal quantification over parts, as in (3), repeated here as (45b):

(45) a. The men lifted the table.
      b. All of the students found a solution.

As was mentioned earlier, (45a) and (45b) display different readings, depending on whether the predicate applies to group members or subgroups of the group of men or students. The possibility of such readings can be traced simply to the fact that the group in question has different part structures in different situations.

There are two possible alternative views, though, of the multiple readings of sentences with distributivity and part quantification. The multiple readings might instead be considered either a matter of *vagueness* or a matter of *ambiguity*.[23] There are good arguments, however, against both views.

That they are not a matter of vagueness can be seen from the fact that, with one and the same group, a sentence involving part quantification or distributivity and its negation can be true, depending on which context the speaker has in mind. For instance, (46a) and (46b) can both be true if the plural NPs are evaluated with respect to different situations in which the students are divided differently into subgroups. Similarly for (47a) and (47b), examples of the sort discussed by Gillon (1987):

(46) a. All of the students collaborated.
      b. All of the students did not collaborate.
(47) a. The students collaborate.
      b. The students did not collaborate.

An argument that the readings in question are not a matter of ambiguity is that not any possible division of the relevant entity into parts yields an available reading.

---

appears that transitivity is conditioned as in (2), where 'FP(y, z)' means that y is a functional part of z — i.e., y falls under the part sortal associated with z:

(2) $(\forall x)(\forall y)(\forall z)(x <_s y \ \& \ \neg FP(y, z) \ \& \ y <_s z \rightarrow x <_s z)$

[23] See Gillon (1987) for the view that the readings are cases of multiple ambiguity.

Thus, (46a) cannot be true with respect to a division of the students into subgroups that is not relevant at all in the context.

The multiple readings are hence best treated as a matter of context-dependent part structures. Further support for this view comes from the fact that such readings arise systematically with all constructions in natural language that involve the parts of an entity (without making reference to specific kinds of parts). All these constructions pattern exactly the same way with respect to which parts of the entity may or have to be relevant, as we will see.

Distributivity and part quantification occur not only with plural NPs but also with mass NPs, as in (48a) and (48b) (in a situation in which the furniture as a whole is not light, but only the individual pieces); and the partitive construction is possible also with singular count NPs, as in (48c):

(48) a. The furniture was light.
     b. All of the furniture was light.
     c. All of the wall is green.

Both distributivity and part quantification need not involve all physical parts of the entity in question, but only parts that are relevant in the context. This is the case even with individuals: the predicate *is green* in (48c) need not hold of all physical parts of the wall; some small parts of the wall may not be considered relevant.

Situated part structures are part structures that entities may have only *accidentally* in a given situation. A typical case of an accidental part structure is a division of a group or a quantity into particular subgroups or subquantities. What is essential for the identity of groups and quantities is only that they are ultimately constituted of certain individuals or certain stuff, not that they are divided into particular subgroups or subquantities. They have such part structures only in particular situations.

The semantically relevant part structures should be restricted to a situation also because of *partiality*. In a situation of full information, there may be a lot of properties that could define an entity or its parts as integrated wholes. However, usually, only some of these properties will be relevant in a given context of communication, and these will be the properties for which the entity or its parts are specified in the intended situation.

What is the formal status of the situation involved in distributivity and part quantification? I assume that every referential NP is evaluated with respect to a particular situation the speaker has in mind, namely what I call a *reference situation*. A reference situation may specify an entity only partially — that is, only with respect to what the speaker considers relevant. In different reference situations, then, entities may have different part structures. Thus, (45a) and (45b) on their different readings are evaluated with respect to different reference situations in which the men or the students are divided into whatever counts as the relevant parts. But the sentence meanings of (45a) and (45b) will always be the same. (45b) will always have the logical form in (49b), where s' is the reference situation and the definite NP *the students* is treated as referring to the maximal group of students or the sum of the set of all groups of students, as in (49a) (more about this later):

(49) a. $[the\ students]^{s'} = sum_{<_S}\,'([students]^{s'})$

   b. $(\forall x)(x <_S\,'[the\ students]^{s'} \rightarrow x \in [found\ a\ solution])$

Let me say some more about the treatment of situations and partiality. Formally, I will treat situations (which may act as reference situations) as primitives, as in Humberstone (1981) and Kratzer (1989a), but unlike in Situation Semantics (Barwise/Perry 1983). Every situation is associated with a set of entities, the set of entities occurring in the situation. This is the *domain* of the situation, formally *D(s)*, for a situation *s*. Partiality is accounted for by making use of a third truth value # ('Undefined') besides 1 (True) and 0 (False). A predicate has to be specified whether it is true, false, or neither true nor false, but undefined, of an *n*-tuple. Formally, *n*-place predicate denotations can then be construed as functions from situations to functions mapping *n*-tuples of entities to one of the truth values 1, 0, or #. Thus, '$[student]^{s}(x) = 1$' means '*x* is specified as a student in *s*', '$[student]^{s}(x) = 0$' means '*x* is specified as not being a student in *s*', and '$[student]^{s}(x) = \#$' means '*x*'s being a student in *s* is left open'.

We can now turn to the formal properties of situated part structures. The two readings of (44a) (one quantifying only over individuals and one quantifying only over certain groups) impose certain conditions on situated part structures. Given that only certain subgroups may count as the (situated) parts of a group, the situated part relation may not be transitive. Furthermore, the situated part relation may not be closed under sum formation. Otherwise, any group of subgroups of an entity *x* would count as a part of *x* in the relevant situation, which should not be the case. But, lacking transitivity and closure under sum formation, the situated part may not be an extensional mereological relation.

Without transitivity and closure, however, the part structure of an entity in a situation is not uniquely determined. So the question arises, What divisions of a group or quantity into parts are possible? Part structures depend on the context; but at the same time, they are restricted in certain general ways. In fact, there is a preference scale among the potential part structures of an entity described in the sentence: certain part structures are strongly preferred; others are possible, but harder to get; some are entirely impossible. In the case of plural quantification with a predicate that can hold both of individuals and groups as in (45a), the most natural reading is the one in which the group members and only they constitute the relevant parts. If proper subgroups are to be the relevant parts, additional background knowledge about such subgroups is required. This also holds for the case of distributivity with plurals with a predicate that can be true both of groups and individual members, as in (45b). So, whenever a construction involves the relevant parts of a group, the individual members are the 'preferred' parts. Certain potential part structures of a group *x* are excluded, namely those in which parts of group members count as parts of x. For example, (50) can never mean that the parts of the individual chairs — the legs, the seats, and the backs — are triangular:

(50) # The chairs are triangular.

With quantification and distributivity with mass NPs, the most prominent reading of an (appropriately neutral) predicate is the one in which there are no distinguished parts of the quantity, but the predicate holds of all actual parts. Thus, (51a) hardly allows for a reading in which the subquantities of a contextually divided quantity of wood weigh two pounds. Such a reading, however, is for some speakers available in (51b) in a situation in which several bars of gold each contain two grams of copper:

(51) a. The wood weighs two pounds.
      b. The gold contains two grams of copper.

Thus, the situated part relation has to satisfy two conditions: first, it should be sufficiently weak to allow for all part structures that underlie the available readings; second, it should capture the restrictions that are imposed on part structures in a given situation.

Like the ontological part relation, the situated part relation is subject to the Transitivity Principle, though now relativized to a situation. Thus, if in the relevant situation, certain subgroups are specified as integrated wholes as in (45a) and (45b) and certain subquantities as in (48b) and (48c), then transitivity need not hold. Thus, we get the following condition on situated part structures, where the notion of integrated whole INT-WH is now conceived as a two-place relation between entities and situations:

(52) *Transitivity Principle (for situated part structures)*
      $(\forall x)(\forall y)(\forall z)(x <_s y \ \& \ y <_s z \ \& \ \neg \ \text{INT-WH}(y, s) \rightarrow x <_s z)$

Let us turn to closure under sum formation. The possibility that in (45b) only individuals or only certain subgroups of the group of students count as the parts of the referent of *the students* is not due to the prohibition against transitivity alone. A further principle is required which blocks the formation of sums in that case.[24] A plausible principle blocking sum formation is the following: a set X has a sum x in a situation s in the sense of $<_s$ just in case the elements in X are not integrated

---

[24] For, if sum formation were unrestricted, then any sums of parts of an entity x would count as parts of x. Suppose y is the sum of two parts x and x' of z and is different from z. Then if y is not a part of z, either z is a part of y, or the sum of y and z is different from both y and z. But then, in the first case, y is not the sum of x and x', since it has to be minimal. In the second case, both y and z are the sum of x and x', contradicting the definition of 'sum' in (21b).

wholes in *s* or else *x* is an integrated whole itself in *s*. Thus, we have the following condition on what can be called *situated sum formation*:[25]

(53) *Restriction on situated sum formation*
　　　If for a nonempty set X of entities and a situation s, for every x', $x' \in X$, INT-WH(x', s), then $sum_<(X) \in D(s)$ only if INT-WH$(sum_<(X), s)$.

Here another part relation $<$ has been used, which, unlike the situated part relation $<_s$, is closed under sum formation. This should not be an extensional mereological part relation, though, because of the familiar problems arising with extensionality, such as the persistence of an entity in flux — the loss and addition of parts. The relation $<$ may be considered transitive, though. Then $<$ is simply a more general part relation than the situated part relation $<_s$. In fact, $<_s$ should be a restriction of $<$. I will call $<$ simply the *general part relation*, and the parts of an entity in the sense of $<$ its *general parts*.

The restriction on sum formation (53), at first sight, appears to raise one problem, though. Unrestricted sum formation seems necessary in order to account for why definite plural NPs always have a referent (as long as there is at least one entity of the relevant sort). But actually, (53) does not delimit the existence of the referents of definite plurals such as *the children on earth*, even though the referents are sums of integrated wholes (e.g., the individual children). As referents of definite plurals, sums form integrated wholes, namely by being maximal entities of a certain sort (*FF*-integrated wholes).

I can now introduce the formal notion of situated part structure, making use of the general part relation relation $<$ as an auxiliary notion:

(54) *Definition*
　　　A *(situated) part structure* is a triple $(s, (D(s), <_s), (E, <))$ satisfying:
　　　a. $D(s) \subseteq E$
　　　b. $<_s \subseteq <$
　　　c. $(\forall x) \neg x < x$
　　　d. $(\forall x)(\forall y)(\forall z)(x < y \& y < z \to x < z)$
　　　e. $(\forall B')(B' \subseteq E \& B \neq \varnothing \to \exists x\, x = sum_<(B'))$
　　　f. $(\forall x)(\forall y)(\forall z)(x <_s y \& y <_s z \& \neg\, \text{INT-WH}(y, s) \to x <_s z)$
　　　g. $(\forall X)(X \subseteq D(s) \& X \neq \varnothing \& (\forall x)(x \in X \to \text{INT-WH}(x, s)))$
　　　　$\to (sum_<(X) \in D(s) \to \text{INT-WH}(sum_<(X), s)))$

---

[25] Critics of extensional mereology have emphasized that mere sums must satisfy additional conditions, conditions on integrity, in order to count as entities, and that therefore a theory of the part relation should not freely allow for sum formation (cf. Simons 1987). Condition (53) poses a weaker requirement. It does not generally require that sums be integrated wholes; they need to be integrated wholes only if they are the sum of entities that are themselves integrated wholes. This has, for instance, the effect that the part structure of a quantity referred to as *the water* (in a context that does not impose integrity on subquantities of water) is closed under sum formation, and, hence, together with transitivity, contains all subquantities of the water as parts.

The notion of integrated whole in a situation INT-WH is in principle definable in terms of the properties an entity has in the relevant situation. However, since I have not given a general definition of integrated whole, this can be done only for R-integrated wholes:

(55) For a situated relation R, an entity x, and a situation s,

R-INT-WH(x, s) iff for all y and y' $y <_s x$, $y' <_s x$, $R^s trans(y, y') = 1$, and

for every y, $y <_s x$, for no z, $\neg z <_s x$ and $R^s trans(z, y) = 1$.

We have seen that relevant properties of the part relation have to be relativized to situations, in particular to the information about integrated wholes in those situations. But this means that, relative to a given situation, a full extensional mereology may emerge; that is, restricted to the domain of that situation, the part relation may be extensional, transitive, and closed under sum formation:

(56) *Extensional mereology in a local context*
If for a situation s, for no x, $x \in D(s)$, INT-WH(x, s), then $(D(s), <_s)$
is extensional, closed under sum formation, and possibly transitive.

Let me turn to the definition of the extension of plurals. In an extensional mereological approach, the extension of a noun f in the plural is defined as in (57):

(57) $[f\text{pl}] = \{x \mid (\exists X)(X \subseteq [f\text{sg}]\ \&\ X \neq \varnothing\ \&\ x = sum_<(X))\}$

A parallel definition can be given on the basis of the situated part relation. For this purpose, it is useful to introduce the partial operation of *situated sum formation* $sum_{<s}$ for a situation s. The operation $sum_{<s}$ is a partial function mapping a set X of entities to the sum (in the sense of $sum_<$) of X as just in case the latter is in the domain of s:

(58) *Definition*
For a nonempty set X and a situation s,

$$sum_{<s}(X) = \begin{cases} sum_<(X), \text{ if } sum_<(X) \in D(s) \\ \\ \text{undefined otherwise.} \end{cases}$$

When is the sum of a set in the domain of a situation? Given (53), clearly, the sum x of a set X is in a situation s just in case either x is an integrated whole in s or X does not have integrated wholes as elements.

The extension of the noun f in the plural in a situation s can now be defined as follows:

(59) $[f\text{pl}]^s = \{x \mid (\exists X)(X \subseteq [f\text{sg}]^s\ \&\ X \neq \varnothing\ \&\ x = sum_{<s}(X))\}$

According to (59), an entity x is in the extension of the plural of f with respect to a situation s iff x is the sum of a nonempty subset of the extension of the singular of f. If an entity x is in the extension of a plural noun in a situation s, then (59) allows the part structure of x in s to take various forms: the part structure may consist only of individuals, only of subgroups, or both; and if a subgroup x' is a part of x in s, then the parts of x' need not be individuals, but may still be subgroups.

1.6. Summary

In this introductory chapter, I have given an overview of the various empirical domains in which part structures play a role, and I have presented an outline of the theory of situated part structures as the part structures relevant for natural language semantics. This theory was contrasted with the traditional extensional mereological approach most often taken in linguistic and philosophical semantic analyses.

We have seen that three different part relations had to be distinguished: [1] the ontological part relation, [2] the semantically relevant, situated part relation, and [3] the general part relation. The general part relation only served to help define certain properties of the other part relations, in particular the restriction on sum formation. (It will later be used also for other purposes — for example, for the meaning of *whole* and *wholly* discussed in Chapters 3 and 6.)

The emphasis so far has been on the importance of situated part structures for particular linguistic phenomena. It still has to be seen what exactly the role of situated part structures is in sentence meanings. This is an issue I will address in the next chapter. There I will also present a general semantic framework that, together with the notion of situated part structure presented in this chapter, will serve as the basis for the analyses of the phenomena discussed in detail in the subsequent chapters.

Appendix:
Comparison with Other Approaches

We have seen the most important features of the account of part-whole phenomena in natural language in terms of situated part structures. In this appendix, I want to discuss some related notions and approaches — namely, other notions that have been used in linguistic semantics and philosophy that are related to the notion of integrated whole, and other approaches to the mass-count distinction that are similar in spirit to the information-based account.

1A.1. Notions related to the notion of integrated whole in other semantic approaches

There are a number of analyses of particular constructions in the semantic literature which employ notions that are related to the notion of integrated whole in the present account. In this section, I will briefly discuss some of those notions and compare their function and nature with the present notion of integrated whole.

One of the notions that plays a similar role to the notion of integrated whole is the notion of an *atom* in Link's (1983) lattice-theoretical account of mass nouns and plurals. As was already mentioned, Link's account is an extensional mereological one in which a mereology for groups is distinguished from a mereology for quantities. The mereology for groups is atomic, whereby the atoms are the individuals in the extension of the corresponding singular count noun. The atoms are the smallest parts a group may have (with respect to the plural-specific part relation). Hence atoms play the role of integrated wholes, preventing parts of individuals from being parts (in the relevant sense) of groups.

However, the notion of atom is conceptually not satisfactory for a number of reasons. First, this notion is a purely formal one; it leaves totally open under what conditions an entity counts as an atom. Second, there is no natural way of specifying when groups themselves may be integrated wholes and hence count as atoms. Link (1987) introduces yet another part relation for mereologies that include groups as atoms. But again, it is left open under what conditions a group may count as an atom. Furthermore, the notion of atom, when applied to groups, is purely extensional. No means are provided for distinguishing groups that are different entities but yet composed of the same members.

Thus, a theory that employs the notion of atom in the algebraic sense to give entities the status of integrated wholes still requires an account of the conditions under which an entity may count as an atom.

Another notion similar in function to the notion of integrated whole when applied to groups is the notion of *group* in Landman (1989). Landman employs singleton-set formation in order to represent the difference between referents of collective NPs such as *committee* ('groups' in his terminology) and referents of plurals such as *the children* (which do not act as 'groups' in a strict sense, but only as 'sums' in Landman's terminology). A group in Landman's sense is formally construed as a set. Referents of definite plurals that act as mere sums, but not as 'groups', are construed as lattice-theoretical sums, whereas referents of collective NPs and definite plurals with a collective interpretation as singleton sets containing lattice-theoretical sums.

As Landman himself observes, one problem with this account is that set theory is not rich enough to account adequately for all distinctions among collective NPs, in particular, distinctions among 'groups' that are different yet composed of the same members — for instance, committees that consist of the same members but differ in function.

Besides that, there are other objections to this application of set theory. Despite the potential technical usefulness of set theory for some cases of nontransitivity, it seems hard to give any content to the operation of singleton-set formation in the context of natural language semantics. There are three general objections against the use of singleton sets. First, the relation between individuals and their singletons is not correlated with a systematic semantic operation (since it depends merely on the collective or distributive reading of the predicate). Moreover, the operation cannot be given a reasonable interpretation as a cognitive principle of individuation. Finally, Landman's notion of group suffers from the same problem as Link's notion of atom: no conditions are stated under what circumstances entities count as groups, and there is no way of distinguishing among groups consisting of the same members.

Another notion related to the notion of integrated whole is Krifka's (1989, 1990) notion of *natural measure*. Natural measures include concepts like 'piece', 'liter', 'loaf', and 'bunch'. Krifka assumes that natural measures constitute a separate component in count nouns. Then, for example, the noun *animal* would be semantically composed of some mass concept corresponding to *animal* and a natural measure, such as 'organism'. Support for this view of the meaning of count nouns comes from so-called classifier languages. In such languages, the natural measure is expressed separately from the noun by 'classifiers'. Krifka does not provide a definition or characterization of natural measures, but states only certain general formal properties that natural measures should have.

The notion of natural measure covers part of what the notion of integrated whole covers. In fact, a natural measure is a specific kind of integrated whole. But there are integrated wholes that are not natural measures — for instance, subgroups of a group that are integrated wholes in a particular situation (e.g., by spatial closeness or interaction among group members). Since such integrated wholes play an important role in natural language semantics, the notion of natural measure is insufficiently general for the present purposes.

To sum up, notions that play a role similar to the notion of integrated whole have already been employed in semantic analyses. But either these notions are not given any specific content and are purely extensional (as in the case of Link and Landman), or they play only part of the role the notion of integrated whole should play (as in the case of Krifka's notion of natural measure).

1A.2. The notion of integrated whole and the notion of sortal concept

The notion of whole-property is closely related also to an important notion in the philosophical literature on identity, the notion of *sortal* or *sortal concept*. This notion plays a prominent role in the debate about relative identity, the question of whether identity statements necessarily involve a sortal concept such as *man* as in (A1) (cf. Geach 1962, Griffin 1977, Wiggins 1981):

(A1)   This is the same man as that one.

Sortals, as the notion is used in the philosophical literature, are count nouns like *man* or *tree*, but not mass nouns or count nouns like *thing*.[26]

The crucial difference between the notion of sortal concept and the notion of integrated whole is that sortal concepts always provide a principle of individuation, which allows for counting entities and reidentifying an entity across different times and possible worlds. Thus, sortal concepts involve essential properties that an entity falling under the concept cannot lose without losing its identity or falsifying certain identity statements (depending on the philosophical view of identity). The notion of integrated whole, by contrast, is independent of the issue of individuation. It subsumes both essential and accidental integrity. Sometimes, integrity conditions that are expressed by a particular noun certainly individuate different entities — for example, the conditions of form that constitute a statue. But in other cases, integrity conditions expressed by singular count nouns are only accidental properties which an entity may lose without losing its identity. For example, *the pile of rice* and *the rice*, intuitively, refer to the same entity, even though only *the pile of rice*, but not *the rice*, characterizes the entity as an (accidental) integrated whole.

Mere intuition, though, is not the only criterion for deciding whether entities are identical or not in the context of 'natural language ontology', for there are semantic criteria for deciding whether entities are considered identical or not. One such criterion comes from verbs of existence. The fact that what is expressed by *pile of rice* does not individuate a new entity besides the rice can be seen from the fact that predicates of existence are inappropriate, as in (A2a). Other examples are given in (A2b–c). The examples contrast with (A3), where the sortal *band* provides a principle of individuation and hence allows for predicates of existence.

(A2)   a.   # The pile of rice does not exist anymore, because the rice is spread all over the floor.
         b.   # The group of children does not exist anymore, because the children dispersed.
         c.   # That patch of snow does not exist anymore because it was used to build the snowman.
(A3)   The band does not exist anymore because its members became soloists.

The issues discussed in this book are neutral with respect to ontological problems of identity and individuation. The only assumptions I make are assumptions about the *semantically relevant level of reference*. Here, part structures are situated part structures which underlie quantification over parts, distributivity, and other part-

---

[26] In the philosophical literature, there are various proposals for defining the notion of sortal. These definitions are basically of the same nature as the semantic characterizations of count nouns that have been proposed: they use either extensional mereological properties (see Griffin 1977 for a discussion) or the property of being countable (cf. Strawson 1960, Griffin 1977). Gupta (1980), by the way, uses the notion of sortal in a very different way, as a modal term covering both mass and count nouns.

structure-related phenomena; and situated part structures are independent of the identity of entities.[27]

1A.3. Related approaches to the mass-count distinction

The information-based account of the mass-count distinction which uses the notion of integrity is not entirely new. Similar views of the mass-count distinction have sometimes been expressed in the literature, though generally in a rather intuitive and informal manner. An example is the cognitive-semantic approach of Langacker (1987a, 1987b). The crucial notion in Langacker's characterization of the mass-count distinction is that of a *boundary* (see also Jackendoff 1990). Count nouns specify entities as having a boundary (in some dimension), whereas mass nouns specify entities as not having a boundary. The mass-count distinction then is a conceived distinction between different kinds of entities, rather than an objective distinction. On Langacker's view, the heterogeneity and homogeneity of count noun and mass noun extensions is supposed to follow from the notional distinction between mass and count nouns, which consists not in objective properties but in conceived properties of individuals and masses. Langacker, however, does not give a definition or explicit characterization other than the intuitive one of the notion of boundary.[28]

---

[27] Not only the notion of an integrated whole has been discussed in the philosophical literature in relation to individuation; the notion of part has, too. This is the issue of the so-called mereological essentialism (cf. Chisholm 1973; see also the discussion in Simons 1987). Clearly, from the point of view of situated part structures, the question of whether parts should be considered as essential or not receives the same answer as the question about the status of integrity.

[28] Gillon (1992) also presents a view on the mass-count distinction that deviates from the traditional mereological view based on cumulativity and divisivity as properties of mass noun extensions. Yet his view is a mereological one in a different way and not based on the notion of integrated whole.

2

The Formal Semantic Framework and the Treatment of Distributivity

2.1. General issues concerning sentence meaning

In this chapter, I will outline a formal framework of compositional semantics within which the present approach to part-structure-specific constructions can be cast. This framework provides the basis for a first explicit application of the theory of parts and wholes to distributivity phenomena, which I will give at the end of this chapter. However, first some general remarks about the treatment of sentence meanings are in order.

Let me recall that one crucial aspect of the semantically relevant part relation is that it is relativized to situations. This relativization serves two purposes:

1. Situations carry part-structure-related information that is not essential for the identity of an entity, and such information may be linguistically provided — for instance, by singular count nouns.
2. Situations may carry only partial information about an entity, in particular about its part structure. Most importantly, not all properties that define an entity or its parts as an integrated whole need to be present in a situation.

The required notion of situation carries partial information about the world which, usually, involves a temporally and spatially limited part of it. However, situations need not, like events or states, be temporally or spatially connected. In these two respects, the required notion of situation corresponds to the notion of Situation Semantics (Barwise/Perry 1983).

What is the status of situations in sentence meanings? One crucial function of situations is that they may act as reference situations with respect to which an NP may be evaluated.[1] Moreover, predicates (in a particular reading) may hold of an

---

[1] The notion of reference situation as a situation associated with referential NPs comes close to the notion of resource situation that Barwise/Perry (1983) use in the context of Situation Semantics. The resource situation for an NP, as conceived by Barwise and Perry, is a situation the speaker envisages when uttering the NP. The NP is to be evaluated

argument only relative to a reference situation. For example, in (1), *lifted the table*, in a distributive reading, holds of the referent of *the men* only relative to a reference situation in which the group of men is divided into the relevant parts (individuals or subgroups):

(1) The men lifted the table.

The reference situation of an NP basically carries the descriptive information provided by the NP itself and possibly contexually given information.[2]

A sentence involves not only the reference situations associated with an NP but also a set of possibly different situations, the set of *described situations*. The described situations correspond to what is asserted by the sentence; they constitute the proposition the sentence expresses. In particular, they carry the information provided by the predicate. In (1), generally, only the described situation, not the reference situation, carries the information expressed by the predicate *lifted the table*. But the way the predicate applies to the argument (the group of men) depends on the reference situation, which determines the relevant parts over which the predicate distributes.

Besides reference situations, a sentence meaning may of course involve other contextually given components such as the time of utterance, the speaker, and the addressee. In order to capture such context-dependencies, the meaning of a sentence should be conceived as a function from n sequences of reference situations and other relevant indices to sets of described situations, where n is the number of referential NPs in the sentence. However, in this book, I will simplify sentence meanings,

---

relative to that NP. The particular application of resource situations that Barwise and Perry had in mind were specific definite NPs with incomplete descriptive content, as in (1):

(1) The man came.

In the resource situation for *the man* in (1), *the man* refers to the unique entity satisfying the property expressed by the noun *man*.

There are major differences, though, between the notion of resource situation and the notion of reference situation. Unlike reference situations, resource situations are supposed to be completely independent of the described situations. A general question, then, is, Given a situation-semantic approach to sentence meaning, are both resource situations and reference situations required, or can one be reduced to the other? Rather than answering this question, I will, for the present purpose, restrict myself to the notion of reference situation, and simplify sentence meanings so that no other indices besides reference situations will be used. Reference situations then also (perhaps inadequately so) serve as the basis for evaluating definite NPs.

[2] Gillon (1992) presents a view of the various distributive readings of definite plural NPs according to which the predicate is evaluated with respect to a set of subgroups formed from the relevant individuals, whereby the choice of this set is determined pragmatically (though it is not elaborated exactly how). Thus, Gillon's (1992) view comes close to the present one.

reducing them to those aspects that are immediately relevant for the analysis of part-whole phenomena investigated in this book. In particular, I will disregard all indices except the reference situations. So sentence meanings will simply be construed as functions from reference situations to sets of described situations. Reference situations only carry presuppositional, not assertive, information of a sentence. Thus, the truth and falsehood of a sentence now has to be relativized to reference situations: a sentence S will be true or false relative to reference situations $s_1, \ldots,$ s_n for some number n.

For the purpose of compositionally building up sentence meanings as functions from reference situations to described situations, the denotation of every expression will be conceived of as a function from situations to extensions. It then depends on the composition of the sentence meaning whether the situations will turn out to be reference situations or described situations. The noun *man*, for example, will always denote a function from situations to functions from entities to truth values. But when *man* occurs in an NP as in *the man*, the situations will become reference situations; and when it occurs in a predicate as in *John is a man*, the situations will become described situations. Also the denotations of verbs are construed as functions from situations to extensions. Thus, *distinguish* will denote a function from situations to functions mapping triples consisting of an event, an agent, and a pair $<x, s>$ (with x being an object and s a reference situation) to truth values. With verbs, the situations in general will become described situations.

The notion of reference situation is related to (though different from) the notion of *resource situation* in Situation Semantics (Barwise/Perry 1983). A resource situation is also a situation associated with the evaluation of a referential NP, but its sole function is to uniquely identify the referent of an incomplete definite description. As Barwise and Perry point out, resource situations ultimately depend on the speaker's intention, and the same holds for reference situations.

In Situation Semantics, sentence meanings are basically relations between discourse situations and described situations, and resource situations are construed as functions of the discourse situation. A function then assigns a resource situation to the discourse situation and every occurrence of a referential NP in the sentence. Similarly, one may consider reference situations as dependent on the discourse situation, although, as we will see in Chapter 3, the ways in which a reference situation may depend on the speaker's intentions are much more restricted than in other cases of context-dependency. Again, I will simplify sentence meanings and disregard the possible dependence of reference situations on the speaker's intentions.

There are constraints on reference situations that, when properly stated, would have to involve other parameters neglected in this simplification. Most importantly, there is a minimality condition on reference situations. According to this condition, reference situations should be the smallest situations containing the information that is given by the description provided by the referential NPs and perhaps some other contextually given information:

(2) *Minimality Condition on reference situations*
The reference situation of a referential NP is the smallest situation containing the information expressed by the referential NP and perhaps other contextually given information.

The general effect of this condition can be seen in almost all natural language phenomena that involve parts and wholes. The condition basically guarantees that part structures are made available on the basis of information only, that is, only on the basis of integrity conditions as expressed by the description the speaker uses, not integrity conditions that entities or their parts may satisfy independently of that.

The Minimality Condition may be considered a pragmatic requirement, a consequence of Gricean maxims of rational communication. It basically says that the reference situation with respect to which a speaker intends his utterance to be understood should match the information provided by the referential NPs as much as possible. Hence it can be considered a condition enforced by the necessity for the speaker to 'communicate' to the addressee which reference situation he has in mind.

Given the notion of situated part structure, the Minimality Condition has an important general implication. It implies that there is a close relation between part structures of entities and the information that is given: part structures must themselves be communicated. This means that the addressee has to construe part structures according to the information he receives or that is presupposed, and the speaker has to know this when using a description for the intended part structure. Part structures that are individuated in this way consist of the relevant aspects of the ontological part structures of entities in the situation of communication. Thus, reference situations will represent relevant aspects of (ontological) part structures, not necessarily part structures as they actually are. More generally, then, information about the part structure of entities has to some degree the same status as propositional information. It is information that must either be conveyed explicitly or belong to the common ground that the addressee shares with the speaker.

2.2. Compositional situation semantics for simple constructions

I can now outline the general semantic framework that I will assume in this book. It is important to keep in mind that this framework is designed only to capture the most relevant aspects of the constructions to be discussed; it neglects many other aspects of meaning — tense, for example — and it certainly does not claim to be a complete theory of natural language semantics. But it certainly is possible to extend this fragmentary framework to more complex cases and to other kinds of constructions.

Sentence meanings will be built compositionally as functions from reference situations to described situations. For this purpose, the meaning of all (nonsyncategorematic) expressions is construed as a function from situations to extensions. Semantic composition then basically consists in operations on such functions. All expressions with lexical content, regardless of their syntactic category, express such a function.

If an expression is a noun, verb, or preposition, it will denote a function from situations to sets or relations, or, more accurately, to functions mapping an entity or an *n*-tuple of entities to one of the truth values 1 (True), 0 (False), or # (Undefined). I will call such functions *situated sets* or *situated relations*.

I will assume a generalized-quantifier treatment for all non-predicative NPs. This is not merely a technical decision, but rather is motivated by the semantics of *as*-phrases and other perspective shifters discussed in Chapter 3. As will be discussed in greater detail below, an NP will then denote a function mapping a situation (a reference situation) to a function from situations (described situations) to a set of situated sets. I call generalized quantifiers of this sort *situated generalized quantifiers*.

I assume the Davidsonian (1967) view of verb meanings according to which every verb has an additional argument place for *events*. By convention, I take this to be the first argument position of the verb. Then, a verb taking *n* syntactic arguments will denote a situated $(n+1)$-place relation. Verbs sensitive to the part structure of an argument take as arguments not objects but rather pairs consisting of an object and a situation (a reference situation). *Distinguish*, for example, is sensitive to the part structure of its object argument, because for evaluating *John cannot distinguish the students*, one has to know whether the sentence is about individual students or groups of students (cf. Chapter 4). Hence *distinguish* denotes a situated relation between an event of distinguishing, an agent, and a pair $<x, s'>$ consisting of an object *x* that is being distinguished and a reference situation s'. *Distinguish* assigns a triple $<e, x, <y, s'>>$ relative to a situation *s* the truth value 1 iff in *s*, *e* is an action or state of distinguishing *y* relative to s' by *x*. In this case, we have $[distinguish]^s(e, x, <y, s'>) = 1$. Nouns formally have the same type of meaning. For example, the noun *man* denotes a function from situations to sets so that '$[man]^s(x) = 1$' is to be read '*x* is a man in *s*'.

I will use λ-notation to designate both functions and relations. For example, '$\lambda s \lambda e x y [R^s(e, x, y) = 1]$' will denote a function from situations *s* to a three-place relation between events *e*, and entities *x* and *y*. For the sake of familiarity or simplicity, I will often characterize extensions of expressions that are functions from *n*-tuples to truth values 1, 0, or # simply by specifying the positive part by a λ-expression. Thus, the extension of *French word* in a situation *s* may be given simply by the expression '$\lambda x[[French]^s(x) = 1 \ \& \ [word]^s(x) = 1]$'.

Let me now turn to the treatment of situated generalized quantifiers. On an extensional generalized-quantifier account, generalized quantifiers as the denotations of NPs are either relations between sets or sets of sets (cf. Barwise/Perry 1983). Given the role of reference situations and described situations, the denotations of NPs as generalized quantifiers now have to be construed in the following way: NPs now denote partial functions mapping a (reference) situations s' to a function from (described) situations *s* to sets of situated sets *P* (which are functions from situations *s* to mapping pairs $<x, s'>$ to truth values, where *x* is an entity and s' the reference situation). The extensions of some basic NPs can then be given as follows, where s' is a reference situation:

(3)
$$[\![the\ man]\!]^{s'} \begin{cases} = & \lambda s \lambda P[P^s(<\iota x[[\![man]\!]^{s'}(x)=1], s'>)=1] \\ & \text{if } \iota x[[\![man]\!]^{s'}(x)=1] \text{ is defined} \\ = & \text{undefined otherwise.} \end{cases}$$

(4) a.
$$[\![the\ men]\!]^{s} \begin{cases} = & \lambda s \lambda P[P^s(<sum_{<s'}(\{x\mid [\![men]\!]^{s'}(x)=1\}), s'>)=1] \\ & \text{if } sum_{<s'}(\{x\mid [\![men]\!]^{s'}(x)=1\}) \text{ is defined} \\ = & \text{undefined otherwise} \end{cases}$$

b.
$$[\![the\ water]\!]^{s'} \begin{cases} = & \lambda s \lambda P[P^s(<sum_{<s'}(\{x\mid [\![water]\!]^{s'}(x)=1\}), s'>)=1] \\ & \text{if } sum_{<s'}(\{x\mid [\![water]\!]^{s'}(x)=1\}) \text{ exists} \\ = & \text{undefined otherwise.} \end{cases}$$

(5) a. $[\![every\ man]\!]^{s'} = \lambda s \lambda P[\{<x, s'>\mid [\![man]\!]^{s'}(x)=1\} \subseteq \{<x, s'>\mid P^s(<x, s'>)=1\}]$

b. $[\![some\ man]\!]^{s'} = \lambda s \lambda P[\{<x, s'>\mid [\![man]\!]^{s'}(x)=1\} \leftrightarrow \{<x, s'>\mid P^s(<x, s'>)=1\} \neq \varnothing]$

Implicit in this construal of situated generalized quantifiers is yet another technical step: according to (3)–(5), *every* argument position of a predicate is now occupied by pairs consisting of entities and situations. This is necessary also for nontechnical reasons since distributivity (which is sensitive to the part structure of an entity in a situation) involves *all* argument positions of verbs and also some other categories, as will be discussed later in this chapter. For the sake of simplicity, though, I will often disregard the situation component of the argument of a predicate when representing the meaning of a sentence.

I will adopt a particular conception of meaning composition, which is not so much motivated by the phenomena dealt with in this book but by general considerations of simplicity, flexibility, and linguistic adequacy. As already mentioned, I assume the same type of meaning for all categories of lexical expressions. On the view of compositionality that I adopt, the composition of sentence meanings is based on systematic correlations between syntactic relations or functions and semantic operations.[3] Formally, it is based on a relation between syntactic relations of functions R and semantic operations O, which may differ from language to language. For English, I will call this relation *corr*. Thus, we may have $<R, O> \in corr$ for a syntactic relation or function R and its associated semantic operation O.

Meaning composition then works as follows. If constituents $f_1, \ldots, f_n$ in a syntactic structure S stand in the syntactic relation R in S, i.e., if $<f_1, \ldots, f_n> \in R(S)$, then the application of O to the meanings of $f_1, \ldots, f_n$ gives the meaning of the syntactic string consisting of $f_1, \ldots, f_n$, i.e., the meaning of $f_1^\wedge \ldots ^\wedge f_n$. Let [ ] be the semantic interpretation function. Then we have:

(6) Let $<R, O> \in corr$ for a syntactic relation R and semantic operation O. Then, for constituents $f_1, \ldots, f_n$ in a syntactic structure S,

---

[3] See Lieb (1983) and Moltmann (1992a, 1992b) for this conception of compos-itionality.

if $<f_1, \ldots, f_n> \in R(S)$, then $[f_1{}^\wedge \ldots {}^\wedge f_n] = O([f_1], \ldots, [f_n])$.

I will later use various syntactic relations and correlated semantic operations. For the present, however, I will introduce only very simple and elementary syntactic relations and semantic operations.

In general, when specifying a syntactic relation R, I will simply appeal to standard syntactic functions that are wellestablished in the syntactic literature.

First, I will introduce the syntactic relations correlated with definite plural and mass determiners. I will adopt a syncategorematic treatment of the determiner and hence will assign it the empty set as its denotation. For definite plural and mass NPs in subject position (with an intransitive verb), we then have:

(7) a. *The syntactic relation for definite determiners*
        For constituents f and g in a syntactic structure S,
        $<f, g> \in \mathrm{DEF}_{pl/m}(S)$ iff $f = the$, g an N', and $f{}^\wedge g$ is a plural or mass
        NP in the subject position in S.
     b. *The semantic operation for definite determiners*
        Let A be a situated set.
        For a situation s',
        $def_{pl/m}(\emptyset, A) = \lambda s \lambda P[P^S(sum_{<s}{}'(\{x \mid A^{s'}(x) = 1\}), s') = 1]$
     c. $<\mathrm{DEF}_{pl/m}, def_{pl/m}> \in$ corr

I will refrain from spelling out analogous definitions for singular count NPs, which involve the ι-operator.

I will also assume a syncategorematic treatment for *every* and *some*, though I will spell this out only for *every*:

(8) a. *The syntactic relation for* every
        For constituents f and g in a syntactic structure S,
        $<f, g> \in \mathrm{SING\text{-}QUANT}_{every}(S)$ iff $f = every$, g an N', and $f{}^\wedge g$ is a
        singular NP in subject position in S.
     b. *The semantic operation for* every
        Let A be a situated set.
        For a situation s',
        $sing\text{-}quant_{every}(\emptyset, A>) = \lambda s \lambda P[\{<x, s'> \mid A^{s'}(x) = 1\} \subseteq$
        $\{<x, s'> \mid P^S(<x, s'>) = 1\}]$
     c. $<\mathrm{SING\text{-}QUANT}_{every}, sing\text{-}quant_{every}> \in$ corr

Later (Chapter 5), we will see that the same operation applies to plural and mass NPs that are existentially or universally quantified (the difference residing only in whether the NPs range over individuals, groups, or quantities).

The correlations in (7) and (8) account for NPs in subject position only. It is merely a technical matter, though, to generalize this treatment of situated generalized quantifiers to NPs in object position. Of course, scope relations then have to be taken into account, though this is an irrelevant issue for the present concerns.

Next, I will define the syntactic relation of argumenthood and the semantic operation of argument satisfaction for subjects of intransitive verbs. Existential quantification over the event arguments is conceived as part of the semantic operation of argument satisfaction:

(9) a. *The syntactic relation of argumenthood for subjects*
   Let f be an intransitive verb and g an NP in a syntactic structure S.
   $<f, g> \in ARG(S)$ iff f is the subject in S with respect to g.
   b. *The semantic operation of argument satisfaction*
   Let Q be a situated quantifier and R a two-place situated relation.
   For a situation s',
   $arg(Q^{s'}, R) = \lambda s[Q^{s'}(s)(\lambda x[(\exists e) R^s(e, x) = 1]) = 1]$
   c. $<ARG, arg> \in corr$

Let me illustrate with an example how the meaning of a simple sentence will be composed. Based on the relevant definitions, the denotation of (10a) (in the relevant respects) is built as in (10b–d), and, similarly, the denotation of (11a) will be built as in (11b):

(10) a. The children are distinguishable.
   b. $[the\ children]^{s'} = \lambda s \lambda P[P^s(<sum_{<s}'(\{x' | [children]^s'(x') = 1\}), s'>) = 1]$
   c. $[are\ distinguishable]^s = \lambda exs'[[distinguishable]^s(e, <x, s'>) = 1]$
   d. $[The\ children\ are\ distinguishable]^{s'} = \lambda s[[the\ children]^{s'}(\lambda xs'[(\exists e)[are\ distinguishable]^s(e, <x, s'>) = 1]) = 1] = \lambda s[(\exists e)[are\ distinguishable]^s(e, <sum_{<s}'(\{x' | [children]^s'(x') = 1\}), s'>) = 1]$
(11) a. *Every child left.*
   b. $[Every\ child\ left]^{s'} = \lambda s[[every\ child]^{s'}(\lambda x[(\exists e)[left]^s(e, <x, s'>) = 1]) = 1]$

Another important syntactic relation is *modification*. Modification is associated with the semantic operation of intersection of argument places of relations. As a syntactic relation, it subsumes modification by adverbials (expressing event predicates) and (absolute) adjectives. For a modifier denoting a situated set and the constituent modified denoting an n-place situated relation, we have:

(12) a. *The syntactic relation of modification*
   For constituents f and g (with an n-place extension) in a syntactic structure S, $<f, g> \in MOD1,n(S)$ iff f is a modifier (of an appropriate kind) of g in S.
   b. *The semantic operation of modification*
   Let P be a situated set and R an n-place situated relation.
   For a situation s,
   $mod1,n(P^s, R^s) = \lambda x_1 \ldots x_n[P^s(x_1) = 1\ \&\ R^s(x_1, \ldots, x_n) = 1]$
   c. $<MOD1,n, mod1,n> \in corr$

Note that the semantic operation of modification, unlike the operations for determiners, will not differentiate between reference and described situation. It yields a relation with only one argument position for situations.

Let us apply the definitions to the following examples:

(13) a. walk slowly
      b. French woman

We get the syntactic relations in (14a) and (14c), which are evaluated as in (14b) and (14d):

(14) a. <*slowly, walk*> ∈ MOD^{1,2}(S)
      b. For a situation s,
          [*walk slowly*]^s = λex[[*walk*]$^s(e, x) = 1$ & [*slowly*]$^s(e) = 1$]
      c. <*French, woman*> ∈ MOD^{1,1}(S)
      d. For a situation s,
          [*French woman*]^s = λx[[*French*]$^s(x) = 1$ & [*woman*]$^s(x) = 1$]

In this section, I have introduced only very basic syntactic relations and semantic operations for elementary sentences. However, it should be clear that this fragmentary framework can be extended to other, more complex cases. I have refrained from further technical elaborations, since this might distract from the more basic concern of this book, that is, the role of part structures in natural language.

The general framework that I have introduced is novel in regard to the role situations play in the evaluation of expressions, namely in that the evaluation of every expression depends on a reference situation. Sentence meanings, though, have been radically simplified and reduced to only those aspects that are immediately relevant for the part-whole phenomena that are the subject matter of this book. In the next section, we will see a first application of this account of sentence meaning to distributivity. This, though, requires first a general discussion of the phenomenon of distributivity itself.

2.3. The treatment of distributivity

The treatment of distributivity that I will give first requires some general clarifications concerning the relevant set of data and also a brief exposition of previous accounts of distributivity. I will first present relevant empirical data that have been discussed in the literature and, introducing a distinction between two types of distributivity phenomena, set those data in a new light. I will then discuss previous accounts of distributivity, though only in a very general way, by isolating a few very general parameters with respect to which theories of distributivity may differ from each other. Given these parameters, I will present a new account of distributivity and show how it applies to both types of distributivity phenomena.

2.3.1. The problem of distributivity and types of distributivity phenomena

There are two different types of distributivity phenomena that should be distinguished. The first type of distibutivity, *type 1 distributivity* for short, is exemplified in the examples in (15) in situations in which each man individually lifted the piano in (15a), and each man showed a different woman the picture in (15b):

(15) a. The men lifted the piano.
      b. The men showed the women the picture.

This type of distributivity is not limited to definite plural NPs. It is also found, for example, with indefinite plurals as in (16), on a reading on which, for a group of four men and a group of two pianos, each one among the men lifted one of the pianos, and each one of the pianos was lifted by one of the men:

(16) Four men lifted two pianos.

Type 1 distributivity is possible with a plural NP in any argument position of a verb. Furthermore, argument positions are independent of each other with regard to distributivity. For subjects and objects, this was seen in (15b), which also allows for readings in which only the subject or only the object exhibits a distributive reading.

Type 1 distributivity is found not only with verbs but also with prepositions, adjectives, and nouns, as in (17):

(17) a. The women sat on the chairs.
      b. The women are proud of their sons.
      c. the first chapters of the books

In the relevant readings, each woman sat on a different chair in (17a), each woman is proud of only her own son in (17b), and (here the only plausible reading) each book has only one first chapter in (17c).

There are locality constraints on type 1 distributivity. Consider (18):

(18) a. John heard the rumor that Mary and Bill won.
      b. The detectives found out that the two students were guilty.

Example (18a) does not allow for a reading in which John heard the rumor that Mary won and John heard the rumor that Bill won; (18b) does not allow for a reading in which each of the detectives found out that a different student was guilty. Basically, type 1 distributivity is clause-bound. For the present purpose, the mere fact that type 1 distributivity is constrained suffices; the precise nature of the constraints need not concern us.

The second type of distributivity, *type 2 distributivity*, is exemplified in (19) with readings in which each student works with a different computer in (19a) and each neighbor gave his dog a different fur coat in (19b):

(19) a. These students work with a computer.
     b. All my neighbors gave their dog a fur coat. (Roberts 1987)

The second type of distributivity characteristically involves an indefinite object NP which seems to take narrow scope with respect to the quantifier ranging over the parts of the referent of the subject NP responsible for distributivity.

This type of distributivity is also found in (16) on a reading on which everyone of four men lifted two pianos.[4]

There are constraints on the availability of type 2 distributivity that are of a different nature from those on type 1 distributivity. Type 2 distributivity is impossible when the indefinite NP is in subject position and the NP 'to be distributed over' in object position. For example, (20) may only be about one computer:

(20) A computer revealed the mistakes.

A parallel asymmetry can be observed for prepositions, adjectives, and nouns:

(21) a. the books about an artist
     b. a book about the artists
(22) a. the mothers proud of a boy
     b. a mother proud of the boys
(23) a. the mothers of a boy
     b. a son of the women

(21a) can refer to a group of books each one of which is about a different artist. By contrast, (21b) cannot refer to as many books as there are artists (*a book* taking narrow scope with respect to the distributor associated with *the artists*). Similarly, (22a) can refer to a group of mothers proud of their own boys. By contrast, (22b)

---

[4] Other plural determiners such as *most* and *few* in fact seem to enforce a distributive interpretation of the predicate (cf. Scha 1981, Roberts 1987):

(1) Most / Few men lifted the piano.

But, as has often been noted, *most* and *few* also allow for collective predicates — in contrast to singular count quantifiers such as *every* and *each* (see also Chapter 4):

(2) a. Most / Few philosophers agree.
    b. # Every / Each philosopher agrees.

Thus, the possibility of collective predication seems to be systematically tied to the plural category of the NP. See Chapter 4 for a detailed discussion of plural quantifiers.

cannot refer to as many different women as there are boys (*a mother* taking narrow scope with respect to the distributor associated with *the boys*). Finally, (23a) can refer to a group of more than one woman (each having a different son). By contrast, (23b) cannot possibly refer to as many sons as there are women.

A comparable asymmetry is not found with type 1 distributivity. Thus, (15b) allows for distributivity applying to the subject, to the direct object, or to both.

Keeping these characteristics of distributivity phenomena in mind, we can now turn to the ways in which distributivity can be, and in fact has been, analyzed.

2.3.2. Ways of treating distributivity

In the following, I will not discuss any particular proposal about distributivity in any detail. Rather, I want to isolate three very general parameters with respect to which theories of distributivity may differ from each other. The possibilities of treating distributivity will be considered mainly from the point of view of empirical adequacy, without regard of the technical details of particular formal proposals.

Granted that type 1 and type 2 distributivity constitute distinct phenomena, the following discussion can be restricted to type 1 distributivity. I will later return to the treatment of type 2 distributivity.

The treatment of type 1 distributivity involves basically three parameters:

1. *The status of the distributivity phenomenon*:
   Are the various distributive and collective readings a matter of *vagueness* or *ambiguity*, or something else? And, if they are a matter of ambiguity, how many different meanings are involved?
2. *The location of distributivity*:
   Is distributivity a property of *NPs*, *determiners*, *nouns*, or the *predicate*?
3. *The nature of distributivity*:
   Is distributivity a lexical property of expressions, or does it function as a separate element in the syntactic structure of a sentence (i.e., as an implicit distributivity operator)?

The literature on distributivity is vast, but the various proposals can be classified according to the three parameters and so allow for a rather simple overview. Gillon (1987) is an advocate of the ambiguity account in its strongest form. Intermediate positions have been taken by Scha (1981), Link (1983), and van der Does (1991, 1994). Verkuyl/van der Does (1991) represent the other extreme point on the scale, treating all readings as a matter of vagueness. Scha (1984), Verkuyl/van der Does (1991), and van der Does (1992, 1994) locate distributivity in determiners. Gillon (1987) locates it in the noun. A number of scholars assume an implicit distributivity operator that is represented in sentence meaning like any other quantifier. They include Link (1983), Lønning (1987), Roberts (1987), Lasersohn (1989), and Heim/Lasnik/May (1991).

The account that I will propose is located with respect to the parameters 1–3 as follows. Concerning parameter 1, it assumes neither vagueness nor ambiguity to account for multiple readings of plural sentences; rather, it traces the multiple readings to different contexts — more precisely, different reference situations, in which the group in question has different part structures. Thus, it assumes a uniform meaning both of NPs and of predicates for the different distributive and collective readings. Concerning parameter 2, it assumes that distributivity is located in the predicate — more precisely, the verb (or perhaps prepositions or nouns). Concerning parameter 3, it assumes that distributivity is a lexical property of verbs.

In the following subsections, I will discuss approaches to distributivity in very general terms with respect to these three parameters, and I will give general criticisms mainly from an empirical point of view.

2.3.2.1. Distributivity as ambiguity, vagueness, and context dependency

What criteria are there for deciding the status of distributivity? Gillon (1987) argues for multiple ambiguities on the basis of negation. He observes that both (24a) and (24b) may be true if (24a) involves a different division of students into subgroups than (24b) does:

(24) a. The students collaborate.
      b. The students do not collaborate.

This should be impossible if the multiple readings were a matter of vagueness. But, as we will see in the next section, ambiguity is not the only alternative to vagueness.

A treatment that assumes multiple ambiguities makes predictions that are not confirmed by the facts. First, it predicts that all readings are equally available. But this is not the case. A simple example is (25):

(25) The children weigh 200 pounds.

Example (25) basically has only two readings: one in which each child weighs 200 pounds and one in which the entire group of children weighs 200 pounds. Readings in which certain subgroups of children weigh 200 pounds are unavailable.

Second, a treatment in terms of ambiguity predicts that a predicate should be incompatible with a conjunction of two modifiers, one specifying a distributive, the other a collective, reading. But this is not the case, as can be seen with the conjunction of the distributive and collective modifiers *individually* and *together* in (26):

(26) The men lifted the piano individually and together.

The fact that (26) is perfectly acceptable clearly shows that *lift* should have a general meaning comprising both a collective and a distributive reading. *Individually* and adverbial *together* will be analyzed in Chapter 6.

As was already mentioned above, there are intermediate positions between the one represented by Gillon (1987) (who assumes a maximal number of ambiguities) and the one represented by Verkuyl/van der Does (1991) (who assume one and the same sentence meaning for the various readings). Clearly, wherever those accounts draw the demarcation line, the same criteria decide whether more than one meaning is involved.

2.3.2.2. Locating distributivity

What criteria are there for deciding whether distributivity should be located in the NP or in the predicate? An argument against Gillon (1987), who locates distributivity in the NP, was pointed out by Lasersohn (1989). The problem for Gillon's account is the observation made by Dowty (1986) and Lønning (1987) that a plural NP allows for a conjunction of two predicates: one of which has a collective reading, the other one a distributive reading. Such a case is (27) on a reading on which the men collectively lifted the piano and individually lifted the chair:

(27) The men lifted the piano and lifted the chair.

Lasersohn proposes that a VP denotes both individuals and groups (or sets) of individuals, and an implicit adverbial operator in the VP has the effect that if the VP applies to a group or set, it also applies to the elements of the group or set. Thus, (27) would have the representation in (28), where D is the distributivity operator:

(28) The men lifted the piano and D [lifted the chair].

Thus, distributivity on Lasersohn's account is located in the predicate.

If this account should capture the various distributive readings (involving subgroups) that are available, it requires a corresponding number of distributivity operators (associated with the various divisions of groups into subgroups). But then it makes a more problematic prediction in that conjoined predicates should be able to distribute 'differently' — that is, they should be able to distribute over the members of different divisions of the group into subgroups. Thus, (29a) should not have a reading on which the men lifted the table in subgroups and lifted the chair individually. On this reading, (29a) would be represented as in (29b), where D' is a distributivity operator ranging over certain subgroups, and D the operator ranging over individuals:

(29) a. The men lifted the table and lifted the chair.
    b. The men D' [lifted the table] and D [lifted the chair].

Such a reading does not seem to be available for (29a), however. Thus, it appears that distributivity, when it applies to several predicates, must apply 'in the same way' (i.e., with respect to the same division of the groups into subgroups).

2.3.2.3. The status of distributivity

Often it is proposed that distributivity should be accounted for on the basis of an implicit distributivity operator (cf. Lasersohn 1989, Link 1983, Roberts 1987, and Heim/Lasnik/May 1991). A general issue that arises with implicit distributivity operators, however, is how to get the distributive readings on which the predicate holds only of some subgroups and not the individuals. As mentioned in the previous section, the various distributive readings would require multiplying the number of distributivity operators (to match the number of possible divisions of the group referred to by the plural NP). But an implicit-distributivity-operator approach does not necessarily require multiple operators.

Roberts (1991), who also assumes the presence of an implicit distributive operator for distributive readings, proposes a solution to the problem based on a single operator. She suggests that, like other quantifiers, a distributivity operator may have a contextually restricted quantification domain so that only contextually relevant parts will be in the domain.

The problem with Roberts's account is that, unlike other cases of contextually restricted quantification domains, there are much stricter conditions on what is to be contained in the restriction of a part quantifier. For instance, the elements in the restriction must somehow cover the entity, which would not have to be the case if the quantifier domain could be arbitrarily restricted. In this respect, implicit part quantification as in (30a) differs from overt part·quantification as in (30b). For in (30a), everyone among the men must be involved (individually or with others) in a lifting of the table, whereas (30b) can be true if only a contextually relevant subset of the committee members was involved in a lifting of the table:

(30) a. The men lifted the table.
     b. All the members of the committee lifted the table.

An account of distributivity based on an implicit distributivity operator predicts that the distributivity operator can take wide scope over other quantifiers. Sometimes, this seems to be the case, and in fact, those cases were one of the motivations of the approach (cf. Roberts 1987). For instance, (31) has a natural reading in which each student individually wrote an essay:

(31) The students wrote an essay.

It does not generally hold, however. In particular, the distributivity operator cannot take scope over an NP in subject position as in (20), repeated here as (32):

(32) A computer revealed the mistakes.

We will see further restrictions on apparent quantifier scope interactions with type 2 distributivity later.

2.3.3. An account of distributivity based on situated parts structures and disjunctive lexical meanings

2.3.3.1. The proposal

I propose an account on which the distinction between the strict collective reading and the various distributive readings is traced neither to an ambiguity of the NP nor to the presence or absence of an implicit distributive operator, but rather to a general lexical property of verbs (and other lexical categories) — that of having a disjunctive lexical meaning of a certain sort. Furthermore, I treat the choice between the various distributive readings not as a matter of ambiguity but rather as a matter of an argument having different part structures in different situations. Thus, distributivity is, to some extent, reduced to different situations the sentence is about.

This treatment of distributivity crucially involves situated part structures, so that entities — in particular groups — may have different part structures in different situations. Not only groups but also quantities may have situated part structures. And as was already mentioned in Chapter 1, distributivity also occurs with mass NPs. An example from Gillon (1992) is given in (33a) describing a situation in which the pieces of jewelry in a display contain one ounce of gold each. An example involving an accidental division of a quantity of wood into parts — let's say different piles of wood — may be (33b), on a reading on which each pile suffices to heat a room (though, as was mentioned in Chapter 1, such readings are rather marginal):

(33) a. The jewelry contains just one ounce of gold.
　　　b. The wood suffices to heat a room.

With situated part structures, the range of potential distributive readings is accounted for in the following way. If a predicate f applies distributively to a group or quantity x in a situation s, this means that f holds of all parts of x in s, i.e., all y such that $y <_s x$. The ability of verbs in English to have a distributive interpretation can be formulated as a postulate on lexical meanings of verbs as in (34) (which, for the sake of simplification, is formulated only for two-place verbal relations):

(34) For any intransitive verb meaning R and situations s' and s,
　　　if $R^s(e_i, <x_j, s'>) = 1$ (for all $i \in I, j \in J$, for sets of natural numbers I
　　　and J), then $R^s(sum_{<s}'(\{e_i \mid i \in I\}), <sum_{<s}'(\{x_j \mid j \in J\}), s'>) = 1$.

I will assume that verbs always have disjunctive lexical meanings with one disjunct representing the verb meaning in its nondistributive version and the other disjunct in its distributive version. This yields the following general schema for verb meanings, where 'f_{lit}' represents only the 'literal' non-distributive reading of the verb f:

(35) *The general disjunctive meaning of (transitive) verbs (in English)*
　　　For an (intransitive) verb f and situations s and s',

$[f]^S = \lambda ex[[f_{lit}]^S(e, <x, s'>) = 1 \lor (\forall x')(x' <_{s'} x \to (\exists e')(e' <_s e$
$\& [f_{lit}]^S(e', <x', s'>) = 1)]$

The notion of a distributive interpretation can now be construed as in (36a), and the notion of a strict collective interpretation as in (36b):

(36) a. *Distributive interpretation*
   For entities e and x, a verb f, and situations s and s',
   f is interpreted distributively in s with respect to e, x, s and s' iff
   $[f]^S(e, <x, s'>) = 1$, and for every x', $x' <_s x$, there is an event e',
   $e' <_s e$ and $[f]^S(e', <x', s'>) = 1$.
   b. *(Strict) collective interpretation*
   For entities e and x, a verb f, and situations s and s',
   f is interpreted (strictly) collectively in s with respect to e, x, s and
   s' iff $[f]^S(e, <x, s'>) = 1$, and there is no e', $e' <_s e$, such that for
   some x', $x' <_s x$, $[f]^S(e', <x', s'>) = 1$.

This also accounts for the case of conjoined collective and distributive predicates in (27). Here, *lifted the piano* holds of an event that does not have proper parts falling under the predicate *lifted the piano*, whereas *lifted the chair* does hold of an event consisting of subevents falling under the predicate (so that every part of the group of men is the agent of one such subevent).

To apply this account of distributivity to a concrete example, let us consider (37a) with the denotation in (37b):

(37) a. The men lifted the piano.
   b. $\lambda s[(\exists e)[lift]^S(e, <sum_{<s'}(\{ x \mid [men]^{s'}(x) = 1 \}), s'>,$
   $<\iota x [[piano]^{s''}(x) = 1], s''>) = 1)]$

Example (37b) is compatible both with distributive and collective interpretations. For *lift* can hold of a triple $<e, x, y>$ under three circumstances. First, *lift* holds of $<e, x, y>$ 'literally' (with the nondistributive disjunct). Second, it may be that for any part e' of e, *lift* holds of $<e', x, y>$ (given e has proper parts) (a repetitive reading). Third, it may be that for any part e' of e, there is a part x' of x and a part y' of y such that *lift* holds of $<e', x', y'>$ (again, given e has proper parts) (a distributive reading). A distributive reading can manifest itself in a multitude of distinct ways — depending on what the parts of the group are in the reference situation.

The account of distributivity that I have given presupposes that the Davidsonian event argument may in principle always be a group event, rather than a single event. This is required anyway, namely for repetitive readings. In the case of a repetitive reading, the event argument is a group of events; but, unlike in the distributive case, it consists of single events that all have the same participant (see also Hinrichs 1985, Langacker 1987a, Jackendoff 1990, and Moltmann 1992a for repetitive readings). If the members of an event group stand in the relation denoted by the verb to parts of a participant group, the result is not a repetitive, but rather a distributive, reading of the verb.

There is cross-linguistic evidence for the assimilation of repetitive and distributive readings of verbs. In certain languages, as discussed in Blevins/Levin (1987), a verb whose event argument is a group event is marked with a special distributive morphology, regardless of whether this group event constitutes a repetitive or a distributive interpretation. This morphology distinguishes two subextensions of a verb, one in which the event arguments are single events and one in which they are group events. Still other languages make a further distinction between repetitive and distributive interpretations. This then leads to the conclusion that it is a specific fact about English that it systematically allows any verb to take group events as arguments.

Let us briefly look at the following more complex case:

(38) The four men lifted the six pianos.

Here the same semantic representation and the same readings are allowed. In the reading in which *lift* distributes over all three argument places, we might, depending on the reference situations, get 16x36 readings, though not all of them are equally available for general reasons.[5]

2.3.3.2. Consequences of the proposed account of distributivity

The account of distributivity that I have proposed makes the correct predictions regarding the characteristics of distributivity discussed above.

First, it predicts that distributivity, since it is treated as a lexical feature, should be restricted to arguments of the same lexical predicate. We have seen that this corresponds to the facts.

Second, it accounts for the fact, shown earlier by example (25), that not all distributive readings are equally available, because the potential part structures of an entity may differ in status: they may be either merely allowed, preferred, or disallowed. Consider also (39), which has only two salient readings:

(39) The boxes are expensive.

---

[5] Plural sentences with indefinite NPs such as (1) have additional readings, involving possibly more than six pianos — for instance, for each man a different group of six pianos:

(1) Four men lifted six pianos.

However, these readings arguably come about because determiners such as *four* have a second function as quantifiers (cf. Milsark 1977) (cf. Chapter 4).

Example (39) says either that each box is expensive or that the entire collection of boxes is expensive. Readings on which certain subcollections of boxes are expensive are perhaps not totally excluded, but readings in which the parts of the individual boxes are expensive are unavailable. This scale of acceptable readings follows from the fact that the individual boxes, as well as the entire, maximal group of boxes, are integrated wholes. Subgroups of boxes may count as integrated wholes, but this requires additional contextual information. Parts of individual boxes cannot count as parts of the group of boxes because of the integrity of the individual boxes.

Another correct prediction of the account is the possibility of conjunctive adverbial modifiers such as *individually and together*. For verbs themselves have disjunctive lexical meanings.

Finally, the account predicts that distributivity, being a lexical property of verbs, should not be able to interact in scope with other quantifiers in a sentence.

The account so far has been limited to type 1 distributivity. However, it also provides a way to account for type 2 distributivity. First, some general remarks about type 2 distributivity.

As was mentioned above, type 2 distributivity has often motivated an implicit distributivity operator, which can interact in scope with indefinite NPs. However, it appears that type 2 distributivity is much more restricted than the implicit-operator account would predict. Type 2 distributivity is possible, it seems, only when the VP denotes a 'sufficiently well-established' property. Compare (40a) with (40b) and (41a) with (41b):

(40) a. The students work with a computer.
     b. The students discovered a computer in a classroom.
(41) a. The students wrote an essay.
     b. The students interpreted an essay by a German poet.

In (40a), *work with a computer* describes a relatively well-established property (as it is common to classify people according to whether they work with a computer or not). Hence, the property of working with a computer can be attributed to each individual student. But in (40b), *discovered a computer in a classroom* is a predicate that in general does not express a well-established property (for instance, it does not express a property that could form a natural basis for classifying students). A similar contrast holds for (41), between *wrote an essay* and *interpreted an essay by a German poet*.

This indicates that type 2 distributivity occurs only with complex predicates that are *lexicalized*. Thus, given that type 1 distributivity only involves the verb, it appears that the relevant semantic operation associated with distributivity (type 1 as well as type 2) applies only in the lexicon. This gives the following generalization about the categories that distributivity can apply to:

(42) *The location of distributivity in the lexicon*
'Distributivity' applies only to lexical categories (V, N, P) and projections of lexical categories as far as they are lexicalized.

The distributivity operation in its most general form, then, is as follows:

(43) *The distributivity operation (definition schema)*
Let f be an n-place predicate (a lexical category or a projection thereof) and $s_1, \ldots, s_n$ reference situations. Then the disjunctive distributive meaning of f with respect to the mth argument place of f is the function $D^m([f])$ such that for any situation s,

$Dm([f])(s) = \lambda x_1 s_1 \ldots x_m s_m \ldots x_n s_n [[f]^S(<x_1, s_1>, \ldots, <x_n, s_n>) = 1 \vee (\forall x_m')(x_m' <_{sm} x_m \to (\exists x_1') \ldots (\exists x_{m-1}')(\exists x_{m+1}') \ldots (\exists x_n')(x_1' <_{s1} x_1 \& \ldots \& x_{m-1}' <_{sn} x_{m-1} \& x_{m+1}' <_{sm+1} x_{m+1} \& \ldots \& x_n <_{sn} x_n \& [f]^S(<x_1', s_1>, \ldots, <x_m', s_m>, \ldots, <x_n', s_n>) = 1))]$

Given (42), (43) applies only in the lexicon. In English, in fact, (43) applies to all lexical entries with respect to all argument places. In the languages mentioned earlier, though, in which distributivity is marked in the verbal morphology, it would not apply to certain argument places — in particular, the event argument place. Instead, the distributivity operation would be tied to a particular morphological category for those argument positions.

In the case of the lexicalized VP *work with a computer*, distributivity applies to the relation $\lambda ex[(\exists y)([computer]^S(y) = 1 \& [work\ with]^S(e, x, y) = 1)]$ (the extension of the lexicalized VP in a situation s), affecting the second argument place.

Type 2 distributivity is special also in that it is restricted to certain types of determiners — in particular, to simple indefinite NPs. Partitive NPs generally do not yield the distributive reading. For example, a distributive interpretation is hard to get in (44a). Furthermore, objects with quantifiers like *few* as in (44b) do not easily yield a distributive reading:

(44) a. The mothers saw one of the children.
b. The students saw few movies.

The same distinction can be observed for the distributive interpretation in NPs. In fact, with NPs, the relevant contrasts seem even stronger:

(45) a. the mothers of a handicapped child
b. the mothers of one of the handicapped children
(46) a. the mothers of a few children
b. the mothers of few children

Example (45a) has a plausible interpretation, but (45b) implies that one and the same child has several mothers. Similarly for (46a) and (46b).

This restriction on the determiner indicates that only certain NPs can undergo lexicalization rules in English, forming complex predicates — namely, simple indefinite NPs. Furthermore, there are restrictions with respect to the syntactic argument position. Examples like (20) (= 32) show that subject NPs cannot undergo the lexicalization rules (a generalization for which there is independent evidence). Thus, the lexicalization rules for English, comprise the following condition:

(47) *Condition on lexicalization (in English)*
     For a verb f and an argument g, $[f^\wedge g]$ may be a complex lexical item
     only if g is a simple indefinite NP and an internal argument of f.

In this chapter, I have given an outline of the general semantic framework, and I have proposed a new account of distributivity based on disjunctive lexical meanings. This account was applied first to type 1 distributivity, but with some further assumptions about lexicalization in English, it was applicable to type 2 distributivity as well.

3

Semantic Selection, Part Structures, and Perspectives

There are two sorts of semantic phenomena besides distributivity that involve part structures: [1] part-structure-sensitive semantic selectional requirements of predicates, readings of predicates, and semantic operations and [2] quantification over parts. Both phenomena are main motivations for the notion of situated part structure given in Chapter 1. Part-structure-sensitive semantic selection and part quantification involve part structures that depend on the information about parts and wholes in the relevant situation — in particular, information about the integrity of entities or their parts. Such part structures, moreover, involve a part relation that lacks transitivity and closure under sum formation as inherent formal properties.

In this chapter, I will discuss the first type of phenomenon, semantic selectional requirements that involve the part structure of an argument. These requirements are conditions on the part structure of an argument that are imposed by certain predicates, particular readings of predicates, and certain semantic operations. Like presuppositions and sortal correctness conditions, such part-structure-sensitive selectional requirements have to be met in order for the sentence to be acceptable — that is, in order for it to be either true or false (on the relevant reading).

Three main results about part-structure-sensitive semantic selection will be established:

1. Certain semantic selectional requirements involve the part structure of an entity. Crucially, such a part structure may be specified by information about integrity that is provided independently of the specific content of singular count, plural, or mass nouns.
2. These part-structure-sensitive semantic selectional requirements involve situated part structures.
3. Which entities satisfy the part-structure-sensitive semantic selectional requirements depends on very general semantic properties of the relevant predicates, readings of predicates, and semantic operations.

There are two semantic selectional requirements that relate the applicability of predicates, semantic rules, or readings of predicates to particular types of part structures of their arguments: one requirement is what I shall call the *Accessibility Requirement* and the other is what I shall call the *Integrated Parts Requirement*.

There are two important results to be presented about the Accessibility Requirement. First, an entity may be specified as having a part structure with or without integrity independently of the use of singular count nouns (for example, by the use of a modifier with the adjective *whole*). Second, the Accessibility Requirement has to be met not by an argument *per se* but by an argument in the relevant reference situation. The crucial evidence for this comes from the observation that certain expressions, which I call 'part-structure-sensitive perspective shifters' (such as *as a whole* or *together*) influence part-structure-sensitive semantic selection. These expressions modify the reference situation but not the entity itself. The semantics of part-structure-sensitive perspective shifters leads to a general discussion and semantic analysis of *as*-phrases (such as *as a teacher* or *as a prime number*), which, as I will argue, pattern together semantically with expressions like *together* and *alone*.

The most important overall result about the Integrated Parts Requirement will be that entities may be specified as having the part structure of a group in a variety of different ways without the use of plural nouns. Moreover, the Integrated Parts Requirement will confirm the sensitivity of part-structure-sensitive semantic selection to reference situations.

3.1. The Accessibility Requirement

3.1.1. The basic data and the generalization

The core data that motivate the Accessibility Requirement comprise the fact that collective NPs such as *the group of children* and *the family* and plural NPs such as *the children* and *the family members* behave differently in systematic ways with respect to certain predicates, readings of predicates, and semantic operations. This holds regardless of whether or not *the group of children* and *the children* refer to the same entity, an issue I will address in more detail later. Plural and collective NPs differ in that one and the same predicate may be true of an entity referred to by a collective NP, but false or inapplicable with respect to possibly the same entity referred to by a plural NP and vice versa. This is illustrated in (1)–(6), where semantic unacceptability or lack of truth value is indicated by '#':

(1) a. He compared the family members.
    b. # He compared the family.
(2) a. The faculty members are distinguishable.
    b. # The faculty is distinguishable.
(3) a. Between the chairs, there was a snake.
    b. # Between the group of chairs, there was a snake.
(4) a. He classified the people.
    b. He classified the group of people.
(5) a. John counted the ten children.

      b. John counted the groups of children.
(6) a. He recognized the family members.
      b. He recognized the family.

Example (4a) clearly means something different than (4b). In (4a), John may have dealt with individual people; but in (4b), John must have dealt with the people as a group. Also, (5a) may be true, without (5b) being true, and vice versa. For example, (5b) may be true if there are two groups of children and John counts two; but in this case, (5a) is false. Moreover, if each group of children has five members, and John counts ten, (5a) is true, but (5b) is false.[1] Similarly, (6a) may be true, without (6b) being true, and vice versa.

    There are many predicates that pattern in a parallel way to the predicates in (1)–(6). They include *discriminate, enumerate, list, mix,* and *shuffle.*

    The different behavior of plural and collective NPs with respect to readings of predicates mainly concerns distributive readings: plural NPs do allow, but collective NPs generally do not allow, for a distributive interpretation of the predicate. For instance, the predicate *lifted the piano* may distribute over the members of a group of men if the group is referred to by a plural NP, but not if the group is referred to by a collective NP, as the contrast between (7a) and (7b) indicates. The same holds for the predicates *heavy* in (8) and *small* in (9):

(7) a. The men lifted the piano.
      b. The group of men lifted the piano.
(8) a. The chairs are heavy.
      b. The group of chairs is heavy.
(9) a. The apples are small.
      b. The group / set of apples is small.

The Accessibility Requirement also applies to semantic operations that make reference to the parts of an argument. One such operation is involved in the interpretation of reciprocals. Reciprocals generally take only plural antecedents and disallow collective NPs as antecedents:

(10) a. The family members / # The family saw each other.
       b. John introduced the people / # the team to each other.

Reciprocals are analyzed in Chapter 4 by means of an operation of quantification over the parts of the antecedent; hence they involve a semantic operation making reference to the parts of an argument and are thus subject to the Accessibility Requirement.

    Why are particular predicates and readings of predicates sensitive to the distinction between collective and plural NPs? To answer this question, the common

---

[1] The selectional requirement of *count,* that the object argument be a plural NP but not a singular count NP, was, to my knowledge, first observed by Blau (1981).

characteristic of the predicates or their readings in (1)–(6) and of distributive interpretations has to be determined.

The collective predicates in (1)–(5) that require plural NPs, *compare*, *distinguishable, between, classify*, and *count,* have the following common feature. Actions like comparing, distinguishing, classifying, and counting explicitly involve each single part of an object (i.e., the members of a group); similarly, the relation 'between' involves two parts of an argument. In this respect, the predicates differ from predicates like *blue* or *German*, which do not explicitly involve the parts of an argument and are not sensitive to the choice of plural or collective NPs:

> (11) a. The chairs are blue.
> b. The group of chairs is blue.
> (12) a. The family members are German.
> b. The family is German.

The way a predicate may involve the parts of an argument is spelled out with a concrete example in (13), which is an approximation of the lexical meaning of *distinguishable*:

> (13) *The lexical meaning of* distinguishable *(approximation)*
> λy[for any distinct parts y' and y'' of y, there is an epistemically accessible property P such that $P(y') = 1$ and $P(y'') = 0$]

Thus, the lexical meaning of *distinguishable* explicitly mentions the parts of the object argument, which clearly does not hold for the predicate *blue* or *German*.

The same semantic distinction among verbs and adjectives that is responsible for the different behavior of plural and collective NPs applies to prepositions. Prepositions like *on* do not make reference to the parts of an argument and hence are not sensitive to the choice of plural or collective NPs:

> (14) Mary lies on the pillows / the group of pillows.

By contrast, *between* has a lexical meaning that must explicitly refer to the part structure of one of its arguments, as approximately in (15):

> (15) *The lexical meaning of* between *(approximation)*
> λxy[for any two distinct parts y' and y'' of y, x is located on an appropriate connection between y' and y'']

Thus, the class of expressions that are sensitive to the distinction between plural and collective NPs (that is, that allow for plural NPs, but disallow collective NPs) appears to be exactly the class of expressions whose lexical meanings explicitly mention the parts of the entity they apply to.

Given this generalization, a crucial question is whether the selectional requirement in question is syntactic or semantic in nature. If it were syntactic in nature, this would mean that the syntactic subcategorization frame of predicates making reference to the parts of an argument should be incompatible with singular count NPs. However, there is strong evidence that the selectional requirement under discussion is not a syntactic requirement. First, the fact that the class of predicates imposing the restriction against singular count nouns is a semantically definable class suggests that the requirement is semantic in nature. Second, the requirement can show up even independently of the distinction between singular count NPs on the one hand and plural and mass NPs on the other hand. As we will see in the next section, with certain modifiers, even plural and mass NPs may violate the requirement.

In semantic terms, the requirement can be cast in the following way. A predicate that explicitly involves the parts of an argument requires that the argument have an 'accessible' part structure, and for an argument to have an accessible part structure it is necessary that it not be a referent of a singular count NP.

This condition can be carried over to the unavailability of distributive readings of predicates with collective NPs. Since the disjunct of a lexical meaning yielding a distributive interpretation explicitly refers to parts (cf. Chapter 2), distributive interpretation also falls under the Accessibility Requirement: the parts of a participant group can be correlated with subevents of the relevant event by distributive interpretation only if the part structure of the participant group is accessible. Furthermore, the Accessibility Requirement should subsume semantic operations, because of reciprocals. So accessibility of the part structure of an argument is a condition on the applicability of predicates, possible readings of predicates, and semantic operations:[2]

---

[2] Part-structure-sensitive semantic selectional requirements are, like sortal correctness conditions and presuppositions in the more familiar sense, conditions on the truth or falsehood of a sentence. But part-structure-sensitive semantic selectional requirements differ from sortal correctness conditions and presuppositions in certain respects.

Sortal correctness conditions typically impose conditions on the type of object (cf. Thomason 1972). Such a condition is, for example, the requirement of a predicate like *heavy* that its argument be a physical object:

(1) The stone / # The solution is heavy.

In contrast to sortal correctness conditions, part-structure-sensitive semantic selectional requirements impose conditions not on an argument itself but rather on an argument under a perspective (that is, an argument in a reference situation).

Presuppositions are conditions on the truth or falsehood of a sentence which may be satisfied in situations that are relatively independent of the situations described by the predicate. For instance, the presupposition of *repeat* as in (2) is that John did the mistake at any relevant time in the past:

(2) John repeated the mistake.

By contrast, part-structure-sensitive semantic selectional requirements must be satisfied with respect to the situation at the *beginning* of the process described by the predicate.

(16) *Accessibility Requirement (ACC) (preliminary version)*
    If a predicate (with a reading R) or a semantic operation P makes reference to the parts of an argument, then P can apply to an entity x (with the reading R) in a reference situation s only if x has an accessible part structure in s.

But what exactly does it mean for a part structure to be accessible? A semantic definition of accessibility on the basis of the characterization of the mass-count distinction given in Chapter 1 suggests itself. According to that characterization, collective nouns and plural nouns differ in the kind of information they convey: collective nouns, like all singular count nouns, characterize an entity in a situation as an integrated whole; plural nouns do not. Accessibility of a part structure, therefore, can be defined in terms of the notion of integrated whole: an entity x has an accessible part structure in a situation s iff x is not an integrated whole in s:

(17) *Definition*
    An entity x has an *accessible part structure* in a situation s (ACC-PART(x, s)) iff $\neg$ INT-WH(x, s).

When a plural NP refers to an entity x in a situation s, then x generally has an accessible part structure in s, since plurals do not express whole-properties. (There are exceptions to this generalization, which I will come to later.)

    The Accessibility Requirement consists in a correlation between the content of predicates or semantic operations and properties of an appropriate argument in the relevant situation. This raises the question, Why should this correlation hold? That is, why should an argument have an accessible part structure (in the technical sense of (17)) when a predicate or semantic operation makes reference to its parts? Clearly, this correlation should follow from an adequate theory of lexical meaning. Unfortunately, I will have to leave this question open.

    Accessibility in (17) is treated not as an absolute property of entities but rather as a property entities have in situations. A definition of part-structure accessibility as an absolute property would not be adequate, as we will see in Section 3.1.2.1.

    The Accessibility Requirement as stated in (16) is not yet completely correct. Two further qualifications have to be added. One of them concerns predicates that describe telic events. If the predicate is telic, it is not sufficient that it makes reference to the parts of an object in whatever way; reference to the parts of an object must pertain to the beginning of the event described by the predicate, not to the end. In particular, predicates that describe events of dividing an entity, such as *divide*, *dismember*, *slice*, *take apart*, *break*, or *smash*, should not fall under (16). Let us call such predicates *part resultatives*.[3] Part resultatives clearly are not subject to ACC, as seen in (18):

---

[3] Note that part resultatives often make reference to specific kinds of parts such as functional parts or parts with a certain shape. In fact, part resultatives are often derived from nouns that are 'part sortals' — for example, *member* in *dismember* or *slice* in *slice*.

(18) a. John divided the class / the bread loaf.
    b. John dismembered the pig.
    c. Mary sliced the cake.
    d. John took the car apart.
    e. John broke / smashed the window.

The restriction concerning part resultatives can be captured by the following general requirement on the reference situation of the NP: the reference situation should be a situation representing the object at the *beginning* of the event described by the predicate.

The other modification of the Accessibility Requirement concerns predicates as in (19) and (20), which, again, make reference to the parts of an argument without the argument being subject to ACC:

(19) a. John organized the collection of papers on the desk.
    b. Mary arranged the bunch of flowers.
    c. Sue ordered the heap of jewelry on the table.
    d. John completed the book.
(20) a. The sign is complex.
    b. John went through the paper.
    c. in the middle of the wood
    d. an overview of the book

Why are the predicates in (19) and (20) acceptable with singular count NPs? The reason is that these predicates make reference not only to *the parts* of the argument but also to the argument *as a whole*.

The predicates in (19) all describe events whose outcome is a state of the object in which it is an integrated whole. For instance, *organize* in (19a) implies that the collection of papers on the desk (as a result of John's activity) becomes an integrated whole in a certain way. Such predicates can be called *whole-resultatives*.

The predicates in (20) are not eventive, but they also make reference to the parts as well as the whole of the argument, by involving the number of parts and the configuration of the parts (*complex*), the location of an entity in the whole (*in the middle of*), or an exhaustion of the argument by its parts (*go through, overview*).

Minimal contrasts showing the difference between whole-resultatives and predicates involving parts, but not the whole, can be construed in German with the preposition *durch* 'through'. The frequent effect of adding *durch* to a verb *f* is that *f* obtains an additional meaning component specifying a certain property of the argument as a whole. As a result, the predicate then takes singular count NPs, not only plurals (as before):

(21) a. Hans numerierte die Bilder / ?? die Bildersammlung.
       'John numbered the pictures / the collection of pictures.'
    b. Hans numerierte die Bilder / die Bildersammlung durch.
       'John counted the pictures / the collection of pictures.'
(22) a. Hans zählte die Studenten / ?? die Klasse.

'John counted the students / the class.'
  b. Hans zählte die Studenten / die Klasse durch.
      'John counted the students / the class through.'

Durchnumerieren, in contrast to *numerieren*, means roughly 'number exhaustively and exclusively' or 'number in a certain order'. With the first reading, (21b) requires that John gave each of a sequence of consecutive numbers to a different one of the pictures, exhausting the pictures that way and not assigning a number to any other object or respecting a particular order among the pictures. By contrast, (21a) only means that John assigned distinct numbers (of a sequence of consecutive natural numbers) to distinct pictures. Thus, the meaning of *durchnumerieren*, in one way or other, makes reference to the whole and differs in that respect from *numerieren*.

Reference to the whole does not always suspend the Accessibility Requirement; it does so only when it pertains to the end, not the beginning, of the event described by the predicate. The predicates in (23), for example, are still subject to the Accessibility Requirement, even though they make reference to the whole:

  (23) a. John put the books / # the collection of books together.
        b. John combined the objects / # the collection of objects.

Thus, the Accessibility Requirement should be modified as in (24), which recasts (16) also in a formally more precise way:

  (24) *Accessibility Requirement (ACC) (modified version)*
        For the n-place denotation P of (a reading of) a predicate or
        semantic operation that makes reference to the parts, but not to the
        whole, of its m-th argument at the beginning of the process described
        by P (if applicable),
        if $P^s(x_1, \ldots, x_{m-1}, <x, s>, x_{m+1}, \ldots, x_n) = 1$ or 0, then
        ACC-PART(x, s).

Let us see how ACC is satisfied by (25a) with the meaning given in (25b):

  (25) a. The children are distinguishable
        b. $\lambda s[(\exists e)[\text{are distinguishable}]^s(e, <sum_{<s}\,'(\{x \mid [child]^{s\,'}(x) = 1\}), s\,'>)$
            $= 1]$

By the Minimality Condition on reference situations of Chapter 2, the referent x of *the children*, the maximal group of childen, has, in general, no other part-structure-related properties in the reference situation $s\,'$ and hence is not an integrated whole in $s\,'$ (to a sufficient degree — since x is an FF-integrated whole, a weak integrated whole). Thus, the Accessibility Requirement will be met.

In the next section, I will discuss a crucial issue regarding ACC as stated in (24), namely why it imposes a condition not simply on an entity but rather on an entity in a reference situation.

3.1.2. Semantic selection and perspectives

3.1.2.1. The influence of perspective shifters on semantic selection

The relativization of the Accessibility Requirement to a reference situation is necessary because situations can represent both essential and accidental properties of entities, and essential and accidental whole-properties play the same role in the satisfaction of ACC. An essential whole-property, for example, is the property of forming an orchestra. For when an entity x (an orchestra) loses the property of being an orchestra, x does not change; rather x ceases to exist. By contrast, to be a loose collection of papers on my desk is, intuitively, not constitutive of an entity, since it does not make much sense to say that such a collection ceases or starts to exist. Hence, it is an accidental property. Crucially, ACC is not concerned with whether a whole-property is essential or accidental. The examples in (26) show that the property of being a loose collection of papers blocks accessibility in the same way that properties like being an orchestra do:

(26) John enumerated / distinguished / compared the papers / # the (loose) collection of papers on my desk.

The satisfaction of semantic selectional requirements by both essential and accidental properties is possible not only in the case of part-structure-sensitive semantic selection. For instance, properties like having a specific height can hold of certain entities — such as bars — only if they are in vertical position, that is, only if they have a certain accidental property. Moreover, spatial properties like being behind the car or being in front of the car can hold of an entity x only if x stands in a certain accidental spatial relation to the speaker (relative to the car).

Further (and stronger) evidence that the relevant notion of part-structure accessibility does not always involve essential propertes of entities comes from the effect of certain modifiers that, intuitively, change the perspective of an entity with respect to its part structure. These modifiers can naturally be called *part-structure-sensitive perspective shifters*. Part-structure-sensitive perspective shifters may change an accessible part structure into an inaccessible part structure and, conversely, an inaccessible part structure into an accessible one. They may do this regardless of the syntactic category of the NP in question. Part-structure-sensitive perspective shifters include the phrases *as a group, together,* and *as a whole* as NP-modifiers, and the adjectival modifiers *whole, separate,* and *individual.* Part-structure-sensitive perspective shifters change the perspective of the NP-referent in such a way that the referent is viewed, for example, as an integrated whole (*as a group, as a whole, together*) or as not being an integrated whole (*whole, individual*). This is without regard of whether the descriptive content of the rest of the NP characterizes the entity in the one way or the other. This semantic effect of part-structure-sensitive perspective shifters is intuitively seen in the following examples:

(27) a. Mary liked the paintings as a whole, but not the individual
        paintings.
     b. The students as a whole / as a group / together made a good
        impression.
(28) Mary liked the whole exhibition.

The effect of *as a whole*, *as a group*, and *together* in (27a) and (27b) is that the
entity that is modified is evaluated with respect to the qualities it has as a whole, not
the qualities of its individual parts. *Whole* in (28), by contrast, has the effect that the
entity modified is evaluated with respect to the qualities of each of its parts, but not
as a whole.

The crucial observation in the present context is that the addition of *as a group*,
as a whole, or *together* to an NP blocks the accessibility of the argument. Thus, in
(29a, b), the addition of the modifiers results in predicates involving the parts of an
argument being inapplicable:

(29) a. # John counted / listed / enumerated the children as a group / as a
        whole / together. (in the sense of counting, listing, and enumerating
        individual children)
     b. # among the furniture as a group

Furthermore, the distributive reading of a predicate is impossible if the argument
is modified by *as a whole, together,* or *as a group.* This has often been noted in the
literature with respect to *together* (cf. Bennett 1974, Lasersohn 1990, Schwarzschild
1992a, 1994). The following examples all exclude a distributive reading:

(30) a. The paintings as a whole cost 1,000 dollars.
     b. John and Mary as a group / together make 1,000 dollars a day.
     c. John sold the paintings as a whole / as a group / together for
        1,000 dollars.
     d. The men as a group / together lifted the piano.
     e. The stories as a whole do not convey a clear moral (though the
        individual stories do).

Also reciprocals are incompatible with *as a whole, as a group,* and *together*:

(31) a. # The stamps as a whole resemble each other.
     b. # The children together / as a group hate each other.

Whole as an adjectival modifier has the opposite effect to *as a whole, as a
group,* and *together. Whole* shifts the perspective of an object with respect to its part
structure in such a way that it puts the totality of the parts of an entity into focus, as
in (28). Crucial for the present concerns is that the addition of *whole* to an NP can
turn an otherwise inaccessible part structure into an accessible one. Thus, a singular
count NP modified by *whole* allows for predicates subject to Accessibility

(32a, b) and for distributive readings (32c, d), and it is compatible with reciprocals (32e, f):

(32) a. John counted / enumerated / listed the whole class.
   b. Among the whole collection, Mary did not find a single object of value.
   c. The whole class lifted the piano.
   d. The whole class got an A.
   e. The whole family saw each other.
   f. John introduced the whole team to each other.

The interaction of part-structure-sensitive perspective shifters with ACC clearly shows that ACC must be purely semantic in nature. In particular, it requires that 'accessible part structure' should be defined in purely semantic, not syntactic, terms. Also, it motivates the relativization of ACC to reference situations, since the function of part-structure-sensitive perspective shifters is to modify an entity in a reference situation.

There is a potential alternative account of perspective shifters that should briefly be discussed. On that account, 'perspective shifters' do not change the perspective of an entity, but rather define a new entity. Thus, *the whole family* would denote a different entity than *the family*, and *the boxes as a whole* a different object than *the boxes*. Let me call this the *ontological account* of perspective shifters.

There are good arguments against the ontological account, however. First, unlike what the ontological account would predict, perspective shifters do not induce plural agreement when modifying a singular count NP in a conjunction:

(33) The family and the whole family has / # have been to France.

If *the family* and *the whole family* denoted different objects, the conjunction in (33) should require plural agreement.

Second, predicates of existence do not apply to NPs modified by a perspective shifter in the way the ontological account would predict:

(34) # The boxes exist, but not the boxes as a whole.

If *the boxes* denotes a different object than *the boxes as a whole*, it should in principle be possible to apply a predicate of existence to one, but not the other, object. But (34) sounds semantically illformed (not merely false).

A more indirect argument against the ontological account is that it is unable to provide a unified account of perspective shifters. In particular, it would not be able to treat the perspective shifter *alone* in (35) in the same way as *together*:

(35) The box alone weighs 100 pounds.

Alone behaves in all relevant respects the same as *together*. But it clearly does not modify an entity inherently; it only modifies an entity in relation to other entities in the relevant situation — namely, as not being part of an integrated whole in that situation. The semantics of *alone* will be discussed in more detail in Chapter 6.

Thus, rather than treating some of the modifiers as defining new entities, they are better seen in a unified way as operators on entities in reference situations. The effect of *as a whole* can then roughly be described as follows: if *as a whole* modifies an NP referring to an entity *x* in a situation *s*, then *s* will be mapped onto a situation *s´* in which *x* is an integrated whole. As a consequence, if the NP is an argument of a predicate *f*, any part-structure-specific semantic selectional requirements of *f* (or a reading of *f*) will have to be satisfied with respect to *s´* and not *s*. Thus, if *x* is specified as an integrated whole in *s´* and if *f* or a reading of *f* imposes ACC, then the sentence will come out as unacceptable (with respect to the relevant reading of *f*), regardless of how *x* is specified in *s*. We will see later that part-structure-sensitive perspective shifters have to do even more than merely change the reference situation.

In order to motivate a more formal treatment of modifiers such as *as a whole*, it is fruitful to undertake an excursus into the semantics of a broader class of expressions whose function is to shift the perspective of an entity, namely expressions such as *as*-phrases like *as a teacher* or *as a prime number*. These expressions shift the perspective of an entity not with respect to its part structure but with respect to a 'dimension' in which the entity may be specified with properties. It is my goal to treat all *as*-phrases in a unified way, in particular *as*-phrases like *as a teacher* and *as*-phrases like *as a whole*, and hence also *together* and *alone* (since *as a whole* has the same semantic function as *together*, and *together* belongs to the same category as *alone*).

3.1.2.2. Excursus: The semantics of perspective shifters involving dimensions

3.1.2.2.1. *As*-phrases specifying dimensions

Perspectives play a role not only in the semantics of constructions involving part structures. They also play a role in a construction that restricts an entity to a specific 'dimension' (in a sufficiently broad sense of 'dimension'). This construction also involves the preposition *as* and is illustrated in (36):

(36) John as a teacher is good.

The phrase *as a teacher* in (36) specifies that John is good regarding his teacher qualities; that is, good in what one may call the 'dimension of teacherhood'. Intuitively, the semantic effect of *as a teacher* in (36) is to put John under the perspective of being a teacher and to restrict the properties one may attribute to John to those he has on the basis of being a teacher. Technically, this means that the reference situation for the evaluation of *John* will be mapped onto one in which

John is a teacher, and the denotation of *John*, construed as a generalized quantifier (i.e., the set of properties that hold of John) will be restricted to those properties that are 'based on' John being a teacher (in the new, shifted reference situation).

The analysis of *as*-phrases that I have just sketched as involving a shift in the reference situation and as restricting the properties of an NP-denotation construed as a generalized quantifier has two rival analyses that have been proposed in the literature. One of them takes *as*-phrases to fill in an additional dimension-argument of dimensional adjectives. The other one takes *as*-phrases (like *as a teacher*) to define a new kind of entity from objects of the usual sort. In the following section, I will briefly discuss the adequacy of such approaches before turning to the technical elaboration of my own account.

3.1.2.2.2. Prior analyses of dimension-specifying *as*-phrases

3.1.2.2.2.1. The dimensional account

The first approach, which can be called the *dimensional account*, has been proposed by Bartsch (1987) (see also Bartsch 1986/7). Bartsch's point of departure is the lexical meaning of dimensional adjectives such as *weak*. Bartsch treats dimensional adjectives as indexicals in Kaplan's (1977) sense; that is, dimensional adjectives have a so-called 'character', a function from contexts (in the sense of Kaplan (1977)) to functions from worlds to sets of entities. Dimensions are indices that form part of the context. Thus, the character of *weak* as in (37a) is a function from contexts containing indices for dimensions to functions from worlds to sets of entities. Modifiers such as *physically* select the dimension to which the adjective applies. Thus, *physically weak* applies to a context <*d*> as in (37b), where *d* is a dimension and *i* a possible world:

(37) a. John is physically weak.
    b. $[John]([physically\ weak]^{d,i}) = weak(d_{physically})\ (i)$

The account straightforwardly applies to *as*-phrases that occur in adverbial position, as in (38):

(38) John is good as a teacher.

As a teacher in (39a) is simply treated as denoting a dimension, yielding (39b):

(39) a. John is good as a teacher.
    b. $good(d_{teacher})(i)$ (John)

This analysis of *as*-phrases can be carried over to nominal occurrences as in *John as a teacher* in the following way. The denotation of *John* is construed as a set of characters. Then, when *as a teacher* modifies *John*, it restricts this set to those characters that John has as a teacher, as in (40):

(40) $[John \; as \; a \; teacher]^i = \{P \mid P(d_{teacher})(i)(John)\}$

However, there is a major probem with the dimensional account of *as*-phrases: it is not general enough in two respects. First, there are *as*-phrases that appear to have the same function as *as a teacher* in (36), but with which the predicate does not in any plausible way involve a dimension. In fact, *as*-phrases seem to go with almost every predicate in an appropriate context:

(41) a. John as a teacher supported the school reform.
      b. John as a teacher agreed.
      c. John as an athlete drinks lots of milk.
      d. Mary as a foreigner has no right to vote.
      e. John as a man in his forties was born before 1960.

In (41a) (and similarly in (41b)), *as a teacher* means that John supported the school reform on the basis of the interest or competence he has being a teacher. In (41c), *as an athlete* means John drinks lots of milk because he is an athlete, and similarly for (41d) and (41e).

These data show that *as*-phrases have a more general function than providing a dimension-argument for dimensional adjectives. They, most generally, have the function of specifying the 'basis' for the application of the predicate, whereby such a basis may take various forms: for example, it may consist in a particular 'dimension' or in reasons for why the predicate holds. I will not define exactly what it means to form a basis for the predicate holding of an argument. This relation seems to be inherently vague, but it certainly is involved in the meaning of *as*-phrases if *as*-phrases should have a unified meaning. The general semantic function of *as*-phrases then can be characterized roughly as follows:

(42) *The semantic function of* as-*phrases*
      If a sentence of the form 'f *as a* g VP' is true, then *g* holding of the referent *x* of *f* constitutes the 'basis' for applying VP to *x*.

The semantic function that the dimensional account attributes to *as*-phrases does not yield a unified analysis of *as*-phrases, and hence is inadequate. But the account seems to be appropriate for other adverbials such as *mathematically* or phrases of the type *as far as . . . is concerned* (to which Bartsch also applies her account):

(43) a. John is talented mathematically / as far as mathematics is concerned.
      b. John agrees as a mathematician / # mathematically.

Note that adverbs like *mathematically* are restricted to the predicate-modifier function, which supports the view that such adverbs specifically involve a dimension-argument of the predicate.[4]

There is yet another respect in which the dimensional account is insufficiently general — namely, it does not allow for a unified analysis of *as*-phrases that specify dimensions and *as*-phrases that specify part structures.

3.1.2.2.2.2. The ontological account

The second approach to *as*-phrases is the ontological account, which was already discussed for part-structure-sensitive perspective shifters. On this account, an NP modified by an *as*-phrase denotes a different kind of object than the same NP without the *as*-phrase. An ontological account has been proposed by Landman (1989), who assumes that referential NPs denote partial objects and *as*-phrases specify particular kinds of partial objects. The ontological account can also be linked to Fine's (1982) conception of *qua*-objects, where an object such as John *qua* teacher is an aggregate of the (usual object) John with the property of being a teacher. (Fine, though, does not make a claim about *as*-phrases, but rather restricts himself to defining a kind of object which, in an ontological approach, could naturally be taken as the denotaton of an NP modified by an *as*-phrase.) On the ontological account, *as a teacher* in *John as a teacher* forms a new object from the ordinary object John by restricting, in some way or other, the set of properties that hold of John.

---

[4] Yet another semantic function is displayed by *for*-phrases as in (1):

 (1) Mary is tall for a gymnast.

Only in some contexts are *for*-phrases equivalent to *as*-phrases:

 (2) Mary as a gymnast / for a gymnast is tall.

Despite the apparent equivalence in (2), *for*-phrases have a different semantic function. They can only be used to specify a comparison set that determines the degree to which the property expressed by the adjective should hold of an entity. A *for*-phrase alone does not specify a dimension; it presupposes that a dimension is already specified. This can be seen from the data in (3):

 (3) a. ?? John is good for a teacher.
      b. John is good at mathematics / as a mathematician for a teacher.
      c. # John supports the school reform for a teacher.

(3a) is funny because the *for*-phrase does not provide the required degree argument for the evaluation of *good*. (3b) shows that *for*-phrases and *as*-phrases can coocur, each with a different semantic function. (3c) is bad, again showing that *for*-phrases differ in semantic function from *as*-phrases, with which the sentence is acceptable. For a discussion of the semantic difference between *for*-phrases and *as*-phrases, see also Siegel (1979).

I will not discuss the proposals by Landman and Fine in detail, but rather only point out some general arguments in favor of and, more importantly, against, the ontological account in general.

A potential argument in favor of the ontological account are sentences like (44) (cited from Landman), where *John as a teacher* and *John as a judge* appear to denote different objects, enforcing plural agreement of the verb:

(44) a. John as a teacher and John as a judge earn different incomes.
     b. John as a teacher and John as a father behave differently.
     c. John as a teacher and John as a father do not resemble each other at all.

However, at closer inspection, this argument appears rather weak. Unlike what the ontological account predicts, *as*-phrases do not always enforce plural verb agreement — for example, they do not in (45):

(45) John as a teacher and John as a father was / # were invited to the party.

Plural agreement in the examples in (46) in fact should be attributed not to the particular semantics of *as*-phrases but rather to the general availability of '*qua*-objects' as referents of NPs. For plural agreement is possible even with apparently coreferential NPs without *as*-phrases as in (46a) (again, cited from Landman 1989) and (46b):

(46) a. The judge and the janitor have different incomes.
     b. The teacher and the father do not resemble each other at all.

Another problem with the ontological account is that it provides a way of treating only adnominal *as*-phrases and has nothing to say about *as*-phrases in adverbial position, as in (47):

(47) John is good as a teacher and bad as a father.

Clearly, adnominal and adverbial *as*-phrases should ultimately be treated in (at least) related ways.

The ontological account of *as*-phrases has already been discussed for part-structure-sensitive pespective shifters, and we have seen similar difficulties arising there.

3.1.2.2.3. A new analysis of dimension-specifying *as*-phrases

The analysis that I will propose treats all *as*-phrases and also *together* and *alone* in a uniform manner, namely as perspective shifters; and it can straightforwardly be carried over to occurrences of such expressions in adverbial position.

Earlier, the general function of *as*-phrases was characterized as specifying the 'basis of application' of predicates in the sense of (42). This is the point of departure of my account. Let us first consider perspective shifters modifying an NP. The phrase *as a teacher* in *John as a teacher* can be analyzed as denoting a function operating on the reference situation associated with the referential NP *John*. The semantic operation associated with *as a teacher* in *John as a teacher* then applies to the relevant reference situation s and maps it onto a reference situation s', which minimally differs from s in that in s' John has only properties that are based on his being a teacher.

However, *as*-phrases do not merely change the reference situation. In addition, they establish a link between the property expressed by the complement of *as* and the predicate. This is seen from the infelicity of sentences such as (48a, b) and (49), where the property expressed by the predicate is unrelated to the property associated with the *as*-phrase:

(48) a. # John as a teacher was born in France.
       b. # John as a teacher is forty years old.
(49) # John as a teacher knocked at the door yesterday.

This link can be captured by construing the NP-denotation as a situated generalized quantifier that in a reference situation s', will contain only those properties which hold of an entity x (in s') based on x having the property associated with the *as*-phrase in s'. Formally, then, *as a teacher* will denote a function mapping a situated generalized quantifier to another situated quantifier (which, in general, is a restriction of the first quantifier). Let BASED ON be the vague relation that holds between two propositions p and q iff p forms a basis (e.g., a reason or evidence) for the truth of q. I will conceive of propositions as the relata of the relation BASED ON as *structured propositions* — that is, in the simplest case, as pairs consisting of a property (in a situation) and an argument (i.e., a pair consisting of an entity and a reference situation). Then, the semantic operation expressed by *as a teacher* is as follows:

(50) Let Q be a situated generalized quantifier.
       For a situation s',
       $[as\ a\ teacher]^s{}'(Q^s{}') = \lambda s \lambda P[Q^s{}'(P^s) = 1\ \&\ (\forall x)(P^s(<x, s'>) = 1$
       $\rightarrow$ BASED ON($<P^s, <x, s'>>, <[a\ teacher]^s{}', <x, s'>>))]$

For *John as a teacher*, (50) yields, for a reference situation s', the function from situations s to properties P such that P holds in s of John relative to s' on the basis of John being a teacher in s'.

The meaning of *as a teacher* can be built in a compositional manner. I will assume that *a teacher* as a complement of *as* is interpreted as the (situated) property expressed by *teacher*. Moreover, I will treat *as* in a syncategorematic fashion in that it will denote the empty set. We then get the following semantic composition for *John as a teacher*:

(51) $[John\ as\ a\ teacher]^s{}' = [as\ a\ teacher]^s{}'([John]^s{}') = [as]^s{}'([a\ teacher]^s{}')$

$([John]^{S'}) = \lambda s \lambda P[[John]^{S'}(P^S) = 1 \ \& \ (\forall x)(P^S<(x, s')> = 1 \rightarrow \text{BASED}$
$\text{ON}(<P^S, <x, s'>>, <[a \ teacher]^{S'}, <x, s'>>))]$

The meaning of *John as a teacher* given in (51) is based on the syntactic relations and semantic operations in (52):

(52) a. *The complement relation for* as
         Let *f* and *g* be constituents in a syntactic structure *S*.
         $<f, g> \in$ *as*-COMPL(*S*) iff *f* = *as* and *g* is an indefinite NP and the
         complement of *as* in *S*.
     b. *The semantic operation for property arguments*
         Let *A* be a situated set, *Q* a situated generalized quantifier, and *s'* a
         situation.
         $prop\text{-}arg(\emptyset, A^{S'})(Q^{S'}) = \lambda P \lambda s[Q^{S'}(P^S) = 1 \ \& \ (\forall x)(P^S(<x, s'>) = 1 \rightarrow$
         $\text{BASED ON}(<P^S, <x, s'>>, <A^{S'}, <x, s'>>))]$
     c. $<as\text{-COMPL}, prop\text{-}arg> \in$ corr

The syntactic relation and semantic operation for perspective shifters (*as*-phrases modifying NPs) then are as follows:

(53) a. *The syntactic relation of* as-*phrase modification*
         Let *f* and *g* be constituents in a syntactic structure *S*.
         $<f, g> \in$ *as*-MOD(*S*) iff *f* is an modifier of *g* and has *as* as its head in
         S, and *g* is an NP in *S*.
     b. *The semantic operation of perspective shift*
         Let *F* be a function mapping situated generalized quantifiers to
         situated generalized quantifiers and *Q* a situated generalized
         quantifier.
         $persp\text{-}sh(F, Q) = F(Q)$ if defined, else undefined.
     c. $<as\text{-MOD}, persp\text{-}sh> \in$ corr.

Given this account of adnominal *as*-phrases, the question arises, How should *as*-phrases that modify predicates be treated? Let us first note a difference between the adnominal and the adverbial use of *as*-phrases. *As*-phrases as NP-modifiers differ from *as*-phrases as predicate modifiers in that, in the first case, the *as*-phrase changes the perspective once and for all in the sentence, whereas in the second case, different *as*-phrases may change the perspective for different predicates:

(54) a. * John as a teacher is good and bad (as a father).
     b. John is good as a teacher and bad as a father.

This difference can be accounted for if *as*-phrases as predicate modifiers apply not to the reference situation of the NP but rather, as is syntactically also most plausible, to the described situations associated with the predicate.

For the predicate-modifier function, syntactic relations and semantic operations similar to those given in (52) and (53) can be used, though I will not spell this out in detail. I will assume that the meaning of *good* is neutral with respect to any specific dimension (unlike in Bartsch's 1987 account); it is simply a situation-dependent property. Then the meaning of *good as a teacher* should be as follows:

(55) For a situation *s*,

$[good\ as\ a\ teacher]^S = \lambda x[[good]^S(x) = 1$ & BASED ON$(<[good]^S, <x, s>>, <[a\ teacher]^S, <x, s>>))]$

The meaning of the conjoined predicates *good as a teacher and bad as a researcher* then can be given as in (56), based on an appropriate semantic operation for conjunction, which can easily be spelled out:

(56) $[good\ as\ a\ teacher\ and\ bad\ as\ a\ researcher]^S =$

$\lambda x[(\exists s')(\exists s'')(s = sum_<(\{s', s''\})$ & $[good]^{S'}(<x, s'>) = 1$
& $(\forall x)([good]^{S'}(<x, s'>) = 1 \rightarrow$ BASED ON$(<[good]^{S'}, <x, s'>>,$
$<[teacher]^{S'}, <x, s'>>))$ & $[bad]^{S''}(<x, s''>) = 1$ & $(\forall x)([bad]^{S''}(<x,$
$s''>) = 1 \rightarrow$ BASED ON$(<[bad]^{S''}, <x, s''>>, <[researcher]^{S''}, <x,$
$s''>>))]$

In the next section, we will see that the same treatment of dimension-specifying *as*-phrases can be carried over to part-structure-specifying *as*-phrases and other part-structure-sensitive perspective shifters.[5]

3.1.2.3. The analysis of part-structure-sensitive perspective shifters

Like all *as*-phrases, I consider the function of *as a whole* and *as a group* as effecting an operation on the perspective of an entity, and so, of course, also for *together*. Formally, they denote functions from relations between generalized quantifiers and situations to relations between generalized quantifiers and situations.

For the present purpose, I will simplify the meaning of these perspective shifters, abstracting from a number of additional meaning components. To see what such additional meaning aspects might consist in, consider the subtle differences between *as a whole*, *together*, and *as a group* illustrated in (57):

---

[5] *As*-phrases may also specify the dimension of integrity, as in (1):

(1) Kurdistan as a cultural unit has more integrity than Kurdistan as a political unit.

As-phrases of this sort can be handled in the same way. I will come to the possibility of integrity being relativized to dimensions in Chapter 6.

(57) a. # The wine, the water and the juice as a group taste good.
      b. The wine, the water and the juice as a whole taste good.
      c. The wine, the water and the juice together taste good.

As a group requires that the entity it modifies be a group of individuals, which is not the case in (57a). Moreover, *together*, unlike *as a whole* or *as a group*, might involve a hypothetical change in the entity — for instance, by dissolving the part structure of the entity in the original perspective. *As a group* and *as a whole*, by contrast, have to preserve the part structure of the entity. Only (57c), not (57b), allows for the 'mixture'-reading.

However, all three modifiers have one thing in common: they all put an entity under a perspective in which it is an integrated whole; that is, they map the reference situation onto a situation in which the entity is an integrated whole and restrict the properties the entity may have to those that are based on the entity being an integrated whole in the new reference situation.[6]

Technically, this means that, like dimension-specifying *as*-phrases, they denote functions from situated generalized quantifiers to situated generalized quantifiers, as in (58) for *as a whole*:

(58) Let Q be a situated generalized quantifier.
      For a situation s',
      $[\text{as a whole}]^{s'}(Q^{s'}) = \lambda s\lambda P[Q^{s'}(P^{s}) = 1 \,\&\, (\forall x)(P^{s}(<x, s'>) = 1$
      $\rightarrow \text{BASED ON}(<P^{s}, <x, s'>>, <\text{INT-WH}^{s'}, <x, s'>>))]$

Note that the meaning of *as a whole* is exactly parallel to the meaning of *as a teacher*. In fact, it can be obtained from the same syntactic relation and semantic operation given in (52) and (53).

As a whole, *as a group*, and *together* may also occur adverbially. However, as adverbials, they yield rather different readings, which I will discuss in Chapter 6. We will see then that the account of *together*, *as a whole*, and *as a group* in adnominal position given in this section can be straightforwardly applied to the adverbial occurrences — once certain additional facts are established about part structures and dimensions.

---

[6] In some languages — Spanish, for example — *together* lacks the second function. That is, it only modifies the reference situation, without restricting the properties the entity has. In Spanish, almost any predicate is acceptable with an NP modified by *together*. Thus, (1), whose English translation is unacceptable, means 'John and Mary took the medicine when they were together' (cf. Sánchez 1994):

(1) Juan y Maria juntos tomaron la medicina.
     'John and Mary together took the medicine.'

I take this as evidence that English *together* does more than only modify the reference situation — it also restricts the generalized quantifier in a certain way.

Whole as an adjectival modifier differs from *as a whole* semantically. *Whole* puts an entity x under a perspective in which x is not an integrated whole (that is, in which the connections among parts do not hold that would define x as an integrated whole). Since *whole* may apply to singular count NPs (which characterize an entity as an integrated whole in the reference situation), it may not only restrict a generalized quantifier but also modify the reference situation the quantifier applies to. In fact, it may change the reference situation to a situation containing less information — namely, a situation in which the relevant entity is not an integratead whole. Moreover, *whole* involves distribution of the predicate over *all* the parts of an entity, and hence implies that all the actual parts of the entity be in the new situation (see also Chapter 6). Formally, *whole* then denotes a two-place function from situated quantifiers and reference situations to situated generalized quantifiers that involve a somewhat different reference situation:

(59) Let Q be a situated generalized quantifier and s' a situation.
$[whole](Q, s') = \lambda s\lambda P[Q^{s''}(P^S) = 1 \ \& \ (\forall x)(P^S(x, s') = 1 \rightarrow \text{BASED}$
$\text{ON}(<P^S, <x, s''>>, <(\neg \text{INT-WH})^{s''}, <x, s''>>) \ \& \ \forall x'(x' < x$
$\rightarrow x' <_S x))]$, where s'' is the situation that differs minimally from s' in
that for all $x \in D(s'')$, $\neg \text{INT-WH}(x, s'')$.

There are a number of other part-structure-sensitive perspective shifters — for example, *individual*. *Individual* as in (60) specifies that the group in question has as its parts in the relevant situation only (essential) integrated wholes:

(60) John likes the individual students.

Each student is an essential integrated whole, but no proper subgroup of the students is. *Individual* specifies that the referent of *the ... students* does not have any subgroups as parts in the reference situation, but only the (essential) integrated wholes that are its group members.

The main effects of *individual* is that of enforcing a distributive reading (distributing down to the group members), as in (61a), and of forcing a part-structure-sensitive predicate to apply to a group with respect to its group members and not its subgroups, as in (61b), as opposed to (61c):

(61) a. John cannot remember the individual students.
      b. John cannot distinguish the individual students.
      c. John cannot distinguish the students.

Example (61a) implies that John cannot remember each single student, though perhaps he can remember the students as a whole. Unlike (61c), (61b) does not allow for a reading in which John is unable to distinguish one subgroup of students from another subgroup of students (for instance, the MIT students from the Harvard students).

These effects of *individual* simply follow from the kind of situated part structure individual specifies — namely, that all the parts of the referent must be essential integrated wholes in that situation. This means that no proper subgroups will be parts in that situation and therefore involved in the evaluation of the predicate.[7]

We have seen that part-structure-sensitive perspective shifters bear in two respects on the way the Accessibility Requirement should be conceived. First, they have made clear that ACC cannot be viewed as a syntactic requirement, to the effect that a predicate syntactically selects only mass or plural, but not singular count, NPs. Modification of an NP by any of the perspective shifters does not change the syntactic category of the NP, but it may influence the applicability of a predicate, reading of a predicate, or semantic operation. Second, part-structure-sensitive perspective shifters have shown that ACC involves not entities themselves but rather entities under a perspective.

3.1.2.4. Potential counterexamples to the Accessibility Requirement

There are two types of potential counterexamples to ACC that need to be discussed. The first consists in plural and mass nouns with *collective adjectival modifiers* which fail to violate ACC, as in the following examples:

(62) a. John counted the heavy stones in his bag.
         ('heavy' as a group, not individually)
      b. Among the heavy stones in John's bag, Mary found a piece of gold.
      c. John counted the many / ten children in the room.

However, the fact that such adjectives apply to an entity collectively does not imply that they define the entity as an integrated whole or presuppose that it already be an integrated whole. They only measure a group or quantity as a whole, without that group or quantity necessarily being an integrated whole.[8]

---

[7] *Single* is a perspective shifter similar in meaning to *individual*, but it occurs only with singular count NPs. Consider (1a) and (1b):

(1) a. A single student can lift this box.
     b. An individual student can lift this box.

Single emphasizes that the student is numerically one in the reference situation, whereas *individual*, redundantly, emphasizes the integrity of a single student.

[8] One might think of an alternative account of the data in (62). Collective adjectives, as in (62a–c), are generally nonrestrictive modifiers. This was observed for collective modifiers of mass nouns by Bunt (1985), and it applies to collective plural modifiers, as well. For, as restrictive modifiers, they should be able to contrast groups and quantities from other groups or quantities; but they do not, as is seen in (1a, b):

(1) a. # John counted the many / ten children, but not the few / five children.
         (in a situation in which there are two salient groups, one consisting of

But there is a case of collective modification that is more problematic — namely, *collective restrictive relative clauses*. The examples in (63) are all acceptable, even though the predicate imposes ACC and the relative clauses certainly characterize the group or quantity as an integrated whole:

(63) a. John counted the people who formed a line, but not the people who sat as a group on the chairs.
b. John found the shirt among the clothing that formed a heap on Mary's bed, but not among the clothing in the basket.
c. John can distinguish the children that are forming a circle, but not the children that are forming a line.

The examples in (63) contrast with those in (64), which only involve a collective noun:

(64) a. # John counted the line of people.
b. # among the heap of clothing
c. # John can distinguish the circle of the children.

In the examples in (63), the relative clauses are restrictive relative clauses which express properties of form. Hence they present a problem for ACC.

There is an explanation, however, for the special behavior of relative clauses. It relies on the role situations play in the evaluation of clauses: relative clauses do not necessarily involve the same situation that acts as the reference situation of the entire NP, but may involve a different situation, which is used only for the evaluation of the relative clauses themselves. This is possible because relative clauses contain a predicate which may be evaluated with respect to a different situation than the reference situation of the entire NP — in the same way as the predicate of an independent sentence is evaluated with respect to described situations

---

many / ten children, the other of few / five children)
b. # John decided to carry the heavy stones, but not the light stones.
(in a situation in which John has the choice between carrying a bag with stones which is heavy and carrying a bag with stones which is light, with individual stones having the same weight)

In Situation Semantics (Barwise/Perry 1983), nonrestrictive relative clauses have been analyzed as restricting not the resource situation but rather the described situation. Generalizing this treatment to all nonrestrictive modifiers implies that the modifiers in (1) attribute integrity to the entities only in the described situation and not in the resource situation, and hence leave their part structure accessible. However, as mentioned in Chapter 2, fn. 1, the function and status of the resource situation is quite different from that of the reference situation. The resource situation only serves to identify the referent of the NP; hence there is no point in evaluating nonrestrictive modifiers with respect to the resource situation. By contrast, reference situations may contain information that may be important in evaluating a predicate. Hence reference situations may very well serve as the basis for evaluating nonrestrictive modifers.

which are independent of the reference situations of the arguments of the predicate. Thus, in (63a), the relative clause *who formed a line* describes a situation in which the people in question are forming a line in front of the store, and this situation may be different from the reference situation of the entire NP in which these people may be only specified as people. In the latter situation, the referent of *the people who formed a line* in (63) may therefore have an accessible part structure. Thus, the denotation of the NP will roughly be as in (65), relative to possibly distinct situations s' and s'':

(65) $\lambda P \lambda s[P^S(sum_{<s'}(\{x \mid [people]^{s'}(x) = 1 \ \& \ [formed \ a \ line]^{s''}(<x, s>) = 1\}), s') = 1]$

NPs not modified by a relative clause, but only by other nouns or adjectives, do not involve predication and hence do not involve another situation besides their reference situation. Thus, *the line of people* in (65a) simply expresses the situated quantifier in (66), relative to a reference situation s':

(66) $\lambda P \lambda s[P^S(\iota x[[line]^{s'}(x) = 1 \ \& \ [people]^{s'}(x) = 1])]$

Thus, the noun *line* specifies the referent of *the line of people* as an integrated whole in the reference situation, which, in the case of (64a), will lead to a violation of ACC.

Let me make the content of the relative clause *who formed a line* in (63a) more explicit. Its denotation can be construed as the function that maps a situation s (relative to a reference situation s') to the following relation, where the meaning of *who* is taken to be a property that holds of an entity x in a situation s iff x is a person in s:

(67) $\lambda x[[who]^{s'}(x) = 1 \ \& \ [formed \ a \ line]^{S}(<x, s'>) = 1]$

The question now is, What is the status of the additional situation that the predicate of a relative clause introduces? Without going into a detailed discussion, I will assume that it simply forms an additional situation argument in the meaning of the entire sentence. Then we get (68) as the denotation of (63a), relative to situations s' and s'':

(68) $\lambda s[(\exists e)([counted]^S(e, John, sum_{<s'}([people]^{s'}])) = 1 \ \& \ [who]^{s'}(x) = 1$
     $\& \ [formed \ a \ line]^{s''}(<x, s'>) = 1)]$

The additional situation argument for relative clauses will complicate the notion of sentence meaning and its composition. But I will refrain from the necessary technical elaborations.

3.1.2.5. The notion of reference situation and related notions

In the analysis of perspective shifters that I have given, the notion of reference situation plays a central role. But not too much has been said about the nature and the status of reference situations. Let me make up for this at this point. In particular, I want to contrast the notion of reference situation with the related and more familiar notion of *common ground* or *context set*.

The notion of reference situation has certain things in common with the notion of context set, the set of presuppositions in a given discourse context (often identified with the common ground of propositions shared by speaker and addressee) (cf. Stalnaker 1979). Reference situations as well as context sets are context= dependent, and both contain information that is not part of what the sentence asserts. Furthermore, there are conditions on the truth or falsehood of a sentence that have to be met with respect to the reference situation or context set — namely, in the first case, part-structure-sensitive semantic selectional requirements and, in the second case, presuppositions in the traditional sense. However, reference situations and context sets differ from each other in important ways. Reference situations are more or less restricted to the information provided by the referential NP (and perhaps a perspective shifter), whereas context sets may carry information that is quite independent of the information provided by any expressions in the sentence.

Another important difference concerns the status of the information contained in the reference situations or context set. The information in the context set is *incremental*: the context set changes when new assertions are made; that is, the new information is obligatorily added to the context set. By contrast, the information in the reference situation is not incremental: reference situations need not change when new information is given. Conversely, reference situations may change even in the absence of new information. Reference situations may be held constant or change regardless of the assertions made in the course of the conversation. This is seen best with the possibility of using perspective shifters. Perspective shifters may change a reference situation regardless of what kind of information has been given earlier in the context, as in (69a). Furthermore, the restriction imposed on a reference situation by a perspective shifter can always be suspended, as in (69b):

(69) a. John as a teacher and John as a father is good.
     b. John as a teacher is good; but John not as a teacher, but as a father, is bad.

The same point can be made with part-structure-sensitive semantic selection. Crucially, semantic selectional requirements like ACC take into account only the information in the reference situation and must sometimes disregard the information in the described situation. For instance, collective predicates that are in predicative position could define the part structure of a plural argument as inaccessible. But in fact, they never define the part structure of an argument as inaccessible for another predicate, as the following examples show:

(70) a. The children formed a circle and were counted by John.
     b. John connected and counted the pearls.

(71) The children formed a circle. Then, they were counted by John.

Thus, reference situations may remain unaffected by information carried by predicates. The notion of reference situation that plays a role in semantic selection hence differs fundamentally from the traditional notion of context set. And on the account that I have given, it is assigned an accordingly different status in a sentence meaning.

The Accessibility Requirement applies to part structures in situations, part structures that are determined by whatever information is contained in these situations, whether it involves essential or accidental properties. A further assumption is necessary regarding such *situated part structures*. The properties an entity x has in a situation s should be more or less confined to those properties that are assigned to x by the conceptual meaning of the expressions that refer to x in s. This is the Minimality Condition on reference situations given in Chapter 2. Reference situations should contain only the information that is given by the expressions used and, perhaps, some contextual information. In this sense, the use of descriptions determines the part structures of entities as construed in the context of communication.

The Minimality Condition can be motivated by elementary assumptions about communication and individuation of part structures in a semantic context. Entities such as groups, which by their own nature do not have a particular part structure, can be conceived with various part structures — for instance, as integrated wholes or as groups consisting of integrated wholes. When part structures are variable in this way, the speaker has to communicate the part structure he has in mind — in the same way as he must with other information which cannot be presupposed or assumed to be common knowledge. Thus, the communication of the intended part structure requires a correct choice of description. As we will see later with the Integrated Parts Requirement, this applies not only to the integrity an entity has as a whole but also to the individuation of its parts.

The referential NPs in a sentence need not be evaluated with respect to the same reference situation; rather, different argument positions may involve different reference situations. A case in point are the two argument positions of identity *be*:

(72) These people are John's circle of friends.

If *these people* and *John's circle of friends* refer to the same entity x, then the first argument position of *is* in (72) involves x under the perspective under which it is a group, but not necessarily an integrated whole, whereas the second argument position involves x under a perspective under which it is an integrated whole. Thus, the function of identity *be* here consists in identifying entities under different perspectives.

There are many other predicates that may involve different reference situations for the same entity in different argument positions — for example, those in (73–75):

(73) a. John likes the people as a whole, but not the individual people.

    b. John weighed the stones as a whole, but not the individual stones.

(74) The people as a whole work better than the individual people.

(75) John compared the students as a a group and / with the individual students (and concluded that the students as a group work much better than the individual students).

Again, the relevant argument positions of these predicates are sensitive to the information contained in the reference situations.

So far, we have seen that reference situations are needed in three ways in lexical semantics. First, every predicate allows for distributive interpretation, which cares about the way a group is divided in the reference situation. Second, a predicate may impose the Accessibility Requirement, which cares about whether an entity is an integrated whole in the reference situation. Third, a predicate may be true of an entity with a particular part structure in one reference situation, but false of the same entity with a different part structure in another reference situation. In the next section, we will see that the second part-structure-sensitive selectional requirement involves reference situations in just the same way as the Accessibility Requirement.

3.2. The Integrated Parts Requirement

3.2.1. The basic data and the generalization

The second part-structure-sensitive semantic selectional requirement involves not an argument as a whole but rather the *parts* of an argument. At first sight, this requirement appears to be the requirement that an argument be a plural, rather than a mass NP. It shows up with almost the same class of predicates that are subject to the Accessibility Requirement. Consider the data in (76)-(80), in which plural NPs are contrasted with mass NPs that possibly refer to the same entities:

(76) a. John cannot distinguish the rice grains.

    b. # John cannot distinguish the rice.

(77) a. John compared / enumerated / counted the clothes.

    b. ?? John compared / enumerated / counted the clothing.

(78) a. Between the chairs, there was a snake.

    b. # Between the furniture, there was a snake.

(79) a. John ranked the paintings in the museum.

    b. ?? John ranked the art in the museum.

(80) a. The rings are indistinguishable.

    b. # The jewelry is indistinguishable.

There are some predicates, however, that are subject to the Accessibility Requirement, but not to the requirement that is responsible for the selection of plural as opposed to mass NPs. Examples are *among, classify, grade,* and *rate,* which allow for mass NPs as arguments. They differ in that respect from the closely related expressions *between* and *rank*, which do not accept mass NPs:

(81) a. The ring was among Mary's jewelry / # Mary's collection of jewelry.
     b. The ring was between # Mary's jewelry / # Mary's collection of jewelry.
(82) a. John classified / graded / rated the art / # the collection of art. (in the sense of classifying, grading, and rating the pieces of art)
     b. John ranked # the art / # the collection of art.

What is the semantic distinction underlying the contrast between *among* and *between* and between *classify, grade,* and *rate* on the one hand and *rank* on the other hand? Let us first look at the difference between *between* and *among*. *Between* locates an entity *x* on some appropriate connection of two distinct parts of another entity *y*. Thus, it involves a binary relation among parts of *y*. *Among* only specifies that an entity *x* is a proper part of another entity y (as in *John is among these children*) or like a part of *y* and located inside *y* (as in *the apple is among the pears*). Thus, *among* does not involve a binary relation among parts of an argument. Whether or not an expression involves a binary relation among parts in fact appears to be the crucial parameter. It is also involved in the distinction between *classify, grade,* and *rate* on the one hand and *rank* on the other hand. *Classify, grade,* and *rate* involve the assignment of absolute values to the parts of an argument, whereas *rank* involves a comparison among the parts of an argument and an assignment of relative values to those parts.

Also all the other predicates in (76)-(80), *distinguish, compare, enumerate,* and *count* arguably involve a binary relation among parts, at least the binary relation that consists in two parts being distinct or distinguished by an agent.

With the new parameter of involving a binary relation among parts, we now have the following ternary classification of predicates:

(83) a. predicates involving parts (but not the whole):
        among, classify, grade, rank
     b. predicates involving a binary relation between parts:
        between, distinguish, rate
     c. predicates either not involving parts or involving the whole:
        in, through, organize

But what exactly does the selectional requirement that favors plural NPs over singular count and mass NPs consist in? As in the case of the Accessibility Requirement, we have to first answer the question whether the requirement is syntactic or semantic in nature. Again, there is the same sort of evidence that the requirement is a semantic requirement. First of all, the fact that the relevant class of predicates is characterized semantically indicates that it is semantic in nature. Second, there are cases in which the requirement is not satisfied by an NP that is syntactically plural, but by a mass NP of a certain sort. However, before presenting and discussing such cases, I will first formulate the restriction to plural arguments as a purely semantic condition.

For this purpose, let us recall the difference between entities that plurals denote (groups) and mass noun referents (quantities). The difference is that plural referents generally consist of parts (the group members) that are themselves integrated wholes in the relevant situation, whereas mass noun referents generally do not have parts that are integrated wholes in the relevant situation. Then the requirement can be formulated as a semantic requirement as follows: predicates expressing a binary relation between parts require that an argument consist of parts that are integrated wholes (in the relevant situation). If an entity consists of parts that are integrated wholes, I will say that it *has integrated parts*. The property of having integrated parts is explicitly defined in (84), and a preliminary version of the Integrated Parts Requirement is given in (85):

(84) *Definition*
An entity *x* *has integrated parts* in a situation *s* (INT-PARTS(x, s)) iff
$(\forall x')(x' <_s x \rightarrow$ INT-WH(x', s)).

(85) *The Integrated Parts Requirement (IP) (preliminary version)*
If a predicate (with the reading R) or semantic operation P involves a binary relation among the parts of an argument, then P can apply to an entity *x* in a reference situation *s* (with the reading R) only if INT-PARTS(x, s).

Like the Accessibility Requirement, the Integrated Parts Requirement has to be satisfied by entities in reference situations, an assumption that will later be supported empirically.

When exactly does an entity have integrated parts? To answer this question, we have to recall the principles for semantically relevant part structures given in Chapter 1 — in particular, those governing transitivity and situated sum formation. The Transitivity Principle allowed a part of a part of an entity *x* that is an integrated whole not to count as a part of *x*; the Restriction on situated sum formation implied that no sum of a proper subset of integrated parts of an entity *x* can be a part of *x*, unless this sum is itself an integrated whole. Taking these principles together means that if an entity *x* has parts that form a covering of *x* and all of these parts are integrated wholes, then these parts may be the only parts of *x*. In particular, the part structure of a plural referent (in the simple case) will generally consist only of group members and will not include any proper parts of group members (unless these parts fall themselves under the relevant singular count concept) or subgroups of group members (unless those subgroups are integrated wholes).

We can now turn to the exact formulation of IP. As in the case of ACC, it is necessary to restrict IP to the initial state of the event described by the predicate. The reason is that mass NPs are possible with predicates like *differentiate* (as a resultative), which involves a relation of discrimination of parts at the end of the process described:

(86) John differentiated the art in the museum.

Should IP, like ACC, also contain a provision against a predicate making reference to the whole of an argument? This does not seem necessary, since (to my knowledge) there is no predicate that involves a binary relation among parts as well as the whole of an argument (unlike predicates just making reference to parts). IP thus is to be reformulated as in (87), which is also formally more explicit:

(87) *The Integrated Parts Requirement (IP)*
     For the n-place denotation P of (a reading of) a predicate or construction
     in English involving a binary relation among parts of its m-th argument
     at the beginning of the process described by P (if applicable),
     if $R^s(x_1, ..., x_{m-1}, <x, s>, x_{m+1}, ..., x_n) = 1$ or 0, then
     INT-PARTS(x, s).

To see how IP can be satisfied in a sentence, consider (80a), repeated here as (88):

(88) The rings are indistinguishable.

Distinguishable imposes not only ACC but also IP. This follows from the fact that *distinguishable* expresses the binary relation of discernability among parts of an argument. The meaning of (88) will be as in (89):

(89) $[the\ rings\ are\ distinguishable]^{s'} = \lambda s[[the\ rings]^{s'}\ ([are$
     $distinguishable]^s) = 1] = \lambda s[[are\ indistinguishable]^s(<sum_{<s}\text{'}([ring]^{s'}),$
     $s'>) = 1]$

IP is then satisfied as follows. A reference situation s' for *the rings* as an argument of *distinguishable* contains an entity x that in s' has the property expressed by *rings*. This means that in s', x has parts that are integrated wholes in s' (the individual rings), and these are the only parts, given the principles mentioned above.

According to (87), IP applies not only to predicates but also to constructions or the semantic operations they are correlated with. Thus, (87) accounts, for instance, for the fact that reciprocals take only plural NPs, not mass NPs, as antecedents:

(90) a.   The rice grains / # The rice resemble(s) each other.
      b.   John connected the rings / # the jewelry with each other.

Reciprocals clearly involve a binary relation between the parts of the antecedent entity. The content of the reciprocal in (90a), for instance, is that any two distinct parts of the rice grains — that is, any two distinct grains — stand in the relation of resemblance (cf. the analysis of reciprocals in Chapter 4). So the semantic operation associated with reciprocals is subject to IP.

IP, when applied to semantic operations, can explain an interesting difference between the antecedent of *each other* and the antecedent of *same* in parallel constructions with quantified antecedents. Consider the contrast between (91a) and (92a) and between (91b) and (92b):

(91) a. # All the water resembles each other.
      b. # All the jewelry is connected with each other.
(92) a. All the water is the same color.
      b. All the furniture belongs to the same person.

The examples in (91) again indicate that the semantic operation for reciprocals cannot apply to entities that do not have integrated parts. *All* in these examples ranges over the subquantities of water or jewelry (cf. Chapter 4), and these subquantities are not specified as having integrated parts. The examples in (92) show that the semantic operation associated with *same* in the internal reading can apply to entities lacking integrated parts — namely, the subquantities of water and the subquantities of furniture.

This difference between reciprocals and *same* can be explained on the basis of IP if the semantics of *same* in the constructions in (92) is properly taken into account. If we paraphrase the meaning of (92a) as 'for any two distinct water quantities x and y, the color that x has is the same as the one that y has', we see the relevant difference between *each other* and *same*. *Each other* involves a *direct comparison* of the parts of the antecedent entity, whereas *same* (in the relevant construction) involves a comparison only between entities that are only related to the parts of the antecedent entity. Thus, in (92a), *same* compares entities that stand in the relation 'is the color of' to parts of the antecedent entity, and in (92b), *same* compares entities that stand in the relation of ownership to parts of the antecedent entity. Since the binary relation that *same* involves does not hold between the parts of the antecedent quantity themselves, the construction with *same* should not be subject to IP. Of course, *same* involves an indirect or derived relation among the parts of the antecedent; but a qualification as to what counts as a relevant relation, which excludes indirect relations, barely weakens the argument.

In the next sections, we will see that IP may be satisfied not only by plural arguments but also in a variety of ways also by mass arguments. This holds both for predicates and semantic operations, and it shows clearly that IP cannot be a syntactic selectional requirement, a requirement according to which certain predicates or semantic operations select only NPs of the category plural.

3.2.2. Constructional satisfaction of the Integrated Parts Requirement

IP can be satisfied by mass NPs in syntactic constructions that have the semantic effect of characterizing the parts of a quantity as integrated wholes. There are two basic types of such constructions: [1] conjunction of mass nouns and mass NPs and [2] modification of mass NPs by conjoined and plural modifiers.

With the same constructions, IP may also be satisfied by plural NPs in such a way that the plural referent is specified as having a part structure which consists of subgroups, rather than group members, and these subgroups will constitute the integrated wholes the predicate or semantic operation will 'compare'.

When discussing the integration of parts by conjoined NPs and nouns in the next section, I will address data that have often been discussed in the literature in the debate on whether there should be groups besides sums. Thus, besides providing new evidence for IP, I will also give arguments for the particular view of groups that I am defending and against possible alternative treatments of the data.

3.2.2.1. Integrated parts with conjoined mass NPs and mass nouns

As was mentioned in Chapter 1, NP-conjunction may involve the same operation of group formation as plurals, allowing for collective predicates:

(93) a. John and Bill met.
     b. The luggage and the furniture weigh 200 pounds.

The crucial observation is that IP can be satisfied with conjoined definite mass NPs and definite mass NPs with conjoined head nouns, as in the following data:

(94) a. The oil and the vinegar are separated.
     b. John compared the honey and the jam.
     c. The honey and the jam are similar.
     d. Mary cannot distinguish the oil and the vinegar.
(95) a. The oil and vinegar is separated.
     b. John compared the honey and jam.

The possibility of group-like part structures of quantities with conjoined definite NPs is predicted by the notion of situated part structure, the notion of *FF*-integrated whole, and the treatment of definite NPs given in Chapter 1.[9] Definite mass NPs,

---

[9] One might object that a conjunction of modifiers modifying a mass NP as in (94) and (95) actually yields a plural, rather than a mass, NP. Evidence for this would be the appearance of plural agreement with conjoined mass NPs, as in the examples (94a, 94c). This, in turn, could be used as an argument that the phenomenon of mass NP conjunction does not show that the selectional restriction of the relevant predicates is a purely semantic matter, but involves the syntactic categories plural and mass. However, plural agreement in the English examples seems to be due to a general fact about English — that it allows for semantically conditioned agreement (cf. Morgan 1972, 1984; Reid 1984). That is, verb agreement in English does not or need not respect the syntactic category of the subject, but rather cares about whether the subject referent has group structure or not. This even allows collective singular NPs to take plural agreement, as in (1):

(1) a. A great number of people were sick.
     b. The committee do not agree. (British English)

Languages without semantically conditioned agreement — German, for instance — do not require (and may even disallow) plural agreement of verbs with mass subjects containing conjoined modifiers. Example (2) illustrates the absence of semantically

on that account, refer to the maximal quantities whose parts satisfy the concept expressed by the head of the NP. So *the oil* refers to the maximal quantity of oil, and *the vinegar* to the maximal quantity of vinegar. Given the interpretation of conjunction of NPs in Chapter 1, the referent z of *the oil and the vinegar* in (94a) will be the sum of two *FF*-integrated wholes, the maximal quantity of oil and the maximal quantity of vinegar. But this means that these two quantities may constitute the only parts of z.

The NP *the oil and vinegar* in (95a) will refer to the maximal entity z that is the sum of a quantity of oil and a quantity of vinegar in a reference situation s'. Maximality has the effect that also the part of z that is oil in s' and the part of z that is vinegar in s' must be the maximal quantities of oil and of vinegar in s'. Hence they are *FF*-integrated wholes in s'. But this means that they may constitute the only parts of the referent of *the oil and vinegar* in s'.

The maximality condition is crucial in these examples, and it manifests itself empirically. With quantifying NPs of the form *all f and g* or *half of the f and g*, the parts described by *f* and by *g* cannot count as integrated wholes, as seen by the following data:

(96) a. # All oil and vinegar is / are separated.
     b. The oil and the vinegar are separated.
(97) a. The wood and the plastic resemble each other.
     b. # All wood and plastic resemble each other.
     c. # Half of the wood and plastic resemble each other.

We can now see that for the satisfaction of IP by conjoined definite mass NPs, the relativization to the relevant situation is important. Not any property that holds of a maximal subquantity x' of a quantity can specify x' as an integrated part, and the same holds for a property that holds of a maximal subgroup of a group. For instance, in (97a), half of the wood and half of the plastic may be the same color; and the other half of the wood and the other half of the plastic may both be a different color. But sharing the color may not define integrated wholes in that context, influencing the application of the predicate *resemble each other*. The only relevant properties for specifying integrated wholes in (97a) are those expressed by the nouns *wood* and *plastic*.

The fact that the satisfaction of IP involves only properties that hold in the relevant situation shows that part-structure-specific semantic selection is sensitive not to entities *per se* but rather to entities as they are represented in the relevant situations.

---

conditioned agreement in German; (3) shows that in German, verb agreement is singular, not plural, with mass subjects containing conjoined modifiers:

(2) Eine große Anzahl von Leuten war / # waren krank.
     'A great number of people was / were sick.'
(3) Das Wasser im Becken und in der Wanne ist / # sind einander ähnlich.
     'The water in the basin and in the tub is similar to each other.'

3.2.2.2. Integrated parts with modifiers of mass NPs

Modifiers of mass NPs such as *cold* in *cold water* generally do not by themselves specify an entity as an integrated whole. In fact, restrictive modifiers of mass NPs must be homogeneous predicates, which generally do not characterize an entity as an integrated whole (cf. Bunt 1985). This was noted earlier in relation to the Accessibility Requirement with data such as (98):

(98)   John carried the heavy sand, but not the light sand.

Heavy in *the heavy sand* in (98) can, when used restrictively, only describe the general quality of the sand (in which case it acts as a homogeneous predicate). It cannot refer to the weight of a specific quantity of sand as a whole (contrasting, for instance, a large amount of sand with a small amount of sand). Thus, it cannot specify a quantity of sand as an integrated whole.

However, in certain constructions, modifiers of mass NPs are nonetheless able to 'integrate' subquantities of the referent. There are two such constructions: [1] conjoined modifiers which ascribe properties to distinct maximal subquantities and [2] plurals modifiers which relate subquantities to independent integrated wholes. The next section will examine both constructions.

3.2.2.2.1. Conjoined modifiers of mass NPs

An example of the first construction is the NP *the water in the swimming pool and in the tub*. Suppose x is the referent of this NP in a reference situation s'. Then the maximal subquantity y of x in s' that is in the pool is an FF-integrated whole in s', and the same holds for the maximal subquantity y' of water in the tub. But then the referent of *the water in the swimming pool and in the tub* may consist of exactly two integrated wholes y and y' in s'. It is hence expected that the referent of *the water in the swimming pool and in the tub* should satisfy IP. This prediction is borne out by the following examples:

(99) a. (?) John compared the water in the swimming pool and in the tub.
      b. (?) John cannot distinguish the water in the swimming pool and in the tub.
      c. (?) The water in the swimming pool and in the tub differ from each other in various respects.
      d. (?) The water in the swimming pool and in the tub are similar.

For some speakers, though, such data, for some reason, are slightly degraded when the conjoined mass NP is the object of a transitive verb, as in (99a) and (99b).

Further examples with PP-modifiers are given in (100); examples with adverbial and adjectival modifiers, which satisfy IP the same way, are given in (101a-b) and (101c-d) respectively:

(100) a. Mary found the information on TV and in the newspaper. indistinguishable.
   b. (?) Mary compared the information on TV and in the newspaper.
   c. (?) The information on TV and in the newspaper contradict each other.
   d. (?) There was a key between the material on the left side and the right side of the table.

(101) a. (?) Mary's excitement today and yesterday were the same.
   b. (?) Between the sunshine this morning and this afternoon, Mary was unable to concentrate.
   c. Bill is unable to distinguish the old and new furniture in this room.
   d. The green and blue wool do not go along with each other.

In order to formally account for the integration of parts by conjoined modifiers, it is necessary to spell out the semantics of conjunctions of modifiers. The conjunction of two modifiers f and g expresses the property that holds of an entity x iff x is the sum of two entities x' and x'' such that f holds of x' and g of x'', as in (102):

(102) *Semantic rule for the conjunction of modifiers*
   For modifiers f and g,
   $[f \text{ and } g]^S = \lambda x[(\exists x')(\exists x'')([f]^S(x') = 1 \ \& \ [g]^S(x'') = 1 \ \& \ x = sum_{<S}(\{x', x''\})]$.

What is important is that if a definite mass NP is modified by a conjunction of two modifiers f and g, it refers to the maximal quantity satisfying the concepts expressed by the N' (in a reference situation s'). This means that it consists of a subquantity x that is maximal in satisfying f and another subquantity x' that is maximal in satisfying g (in s'). x and x' are both *FF*-integrated wholes in s'. Thus, x and x' may count as the only parts of x in s', and in this case, x will have integrated parts in s'. So in a reference situation s', *the water in the swimming pool and in the tub* refers to the maximal quantity x in s' that is water and that is the sum of two quantities x' and x'' such that x' is in the swimming pool in s' and x'' in the tub in s'. Both x' and x'' are *FF*-integrated wholes, and hence may count as the only parts of x.

Note again the importance of (partial) reference situations here. In a context of full information, any property that happens to maximally hold of a part of an entity would define this part as an integrated whole. For instance, in the case of (100a), some of the information on TV may share the property of being about some specific topic with some other information in the newspaper. But the sum of these two amounts of information cannot constitute an integrated whole for semantic purposes. Only *relevant* (partial) information, information as provided by the descriptive content of the NP, can be used for defining integrity.

As in the case of conjoined mass nouns and NPs, maximality is crucial for the satisfaction of IP. This is confirmed empirically by the following examples, which are less acceptable than those in (99)–(101) or at least have a reading different from the one involving two maximal quantities:

(103) a. ?? John compared all water in the swimming pool and in the tub.
b. ?? Mary found all information on TV and in the newspaper indistinguishable.
c. ?? All information on TV and in the newspaper contradict each other.
d. ?? There is a stick between all material on the left side and the right side of the table.

(104) # All blue and green wool on this desk do not go along with each other.

(105) a. # Half of the information on TV and in the newspaper contradict each other.
b. # Half of the blue and green wool on this desk do (does) not go along with each other.

Like the singular count quantifier *every*, *all* with mass NPs ranges over all relevant entities (in this case, quantities) in the extension of the N'. Thus, *all water in the swimming pool and in the tub* ranges over all water quantities which consist of water in the pool and water in the tub. Crucial in this case is that the range of the quantifier *all* contains many quantities of water that do not consist of a maximal quantity in the tub and a maximal quantity in the pool; only one quantity in the range of *all* (the maximal quantity) satisfies this condition. Therefore, for all other quantities in that range, either the subquantity that is in the tub or the subquantity that is in the pool is not maximal and hence does not count as an integrated whole. Therefore, when the predicate applies to those quantities, IP will not be satisfied, which explains the oddness of the data above.

3.2.2.2.2. Modification of mass NPs with plurals

The second way of achieving integrated parts of a mass referent consists in relating subquantities to independent integrated wholes by a one-to-one relation. This way of specifying integrated wholes is operative in modification by genitive plural NPs, as in the following examples (which are acceptable at least for a number of speakers):

(106) a. John compared the wine on the various tables.
b. (?) John could not see any differences between the jewelry of the women at the party.
c. (?) The children's clothing is indistinguishable.
d. (?) The women's jewelry resemble each other.

All examples in (106) involve a relation between a quantity and a group. In (106a), this is the relation denoted by *on*. For (106b)–(106d), I follow the standard analysis in assuming that the relation is some relation R provided by the context. The relation expressed by *on* or the contextually given relation R may then apply distributively, relating the members of the plural referent to different parts of the quantity (and exhausting the quantity that way).

A new principle for specifying parts as integrated wholes is at work in the examples in (106). This principle says that a part of a quantity counts as an integrated whole if it is related by some appropriate (one-to-one) relation R to an independently specified integrated whole. For instance, in (106a), the tables are related by the relation 'on' to different subquantities of the wine, allowing these subquantities to count as integrated wholes. But this means that these subquantities may be the only parts of the wine. In (106d), individual women are related by the relation of possession to different quantities of jewelry. Therefore, these quantities of jewelry count as integrated wholes, and hence may be the only parts of the jewelry owned by the totality of women. Thus, in the examples in (106), subquantities of a mass noun referent are specified as integrated wholes by being related to different integrated wholes. In this way, IP will be satisfied.

Clearly, the principle of integrating parts by one-to-one relations to independent integrated wholes must again be relativized to situations. A mass noun referent may consist of subquantities that, in the actual world, are related in various ways to integrated wholes. But only those relations and integrated wholes that are mentioned in the description are relevant, for only they will be part of the relevant reference situation. Moreover, not just any relation between integrated wholes and subquantities will do — only nontrivial ones will (for example, the relation of difference won't). Thus, the principle is as follows:

(107) *Integrating Parts on the Basis of Relations (IR)*
       For entities x and y, a situation s, and a nontrivial situated one-to-one
       relation R, INT-WH(x, s) & $R^s(x, y) = 1 \rightarrow$ INT-WH(y, s).

From this principle and the other conditions on part structures, we can derive the following corollary, making use of the general part relation < (cf. Chapter 1):

(108) *Corollary*
       If for a situation s, a set X of integrated wholes in s, a nontrivial situated
       one-to-one relation R, an entity x, R is a one-to-one function in s from
       X onto a set of general parts Y of x which cover x, then the elements of
       Y may be the only parts of x (in which case, x has integrated parts).

IR might seem unnecessary as an independent principle of defining integrated wholes. For, alternatively, the integrated wholes in question might be considered *FF*-integrated wholes. For example, the wine on table x is an *FF*-integrated whole for F = the property of being wine on table x. Still, for the wine to be an integrated whole, it is necessary that the table be an integrated whole, which would not follow from the definition of *FF*-integrated whole.

3.2.2.3. The Integrated Part Requirement and higher-order-group formation

In this section, I will show that the same devices that allow mass NPs to refer to quantities with integrated parts allow plurals to refer to groups whose relevant parts are subgroups, not individual members. The data in question constitute the core of a debate in the semantic literature on plurals. At the end of this section, I will briefly address the issues at stake in that debate and argue that the present account meets the objections that have been raised against some other proposals of handling the data.

The relevant phenomenon is illustrated by a particular reading of the following examples:

(109) a. The parents and the children hate each other.
       b. The cats and the dogs are separated.

Example (109a) has a reading in which the hate-relation holds between the group of parents and the group of children, but not among individual parents or individual children. Similarly, in (109b), the separation may hold only between two groups, the group of cats and the group of dogs but not among either cats or dogs. I will call this the *higher-order-group reading* of plurals, since it involves a group consisting of other groups.

This type of group formation was first noted by Link (1983) and has been further discussed by Landman (1989). Stated in terms of situated part structures, conjunction of plural NPs as in (109) may result in the formation of a group of groups (the referents of the conjuncts) which is not identical to the mereological fusion of these groups, having only subgroups as parts, not individuals. The predicate then specifies a relation that holds between the groups denoted by the conjuncts, without holding among the elements of these groups.

Conjunction of definite plural NPs also allows for what one may call the *fusion reading* of plurals, in which only individuals are considered parts of the group. In the fusion reading, the predicate holds among the members of the groups denoted by the conjuncts. For instance, in the fusion reading of (109b), separation holds among dogs as well as among cats. In this reading, the part relation is transitive as regards the members of the conjunct groups.

However, it seems that one reading of conjunctions of definite NPs is excluded. (109b) cannot describe a situation in which two groups consisting of both dogs and cats are separated, but no separation holds within any one of these groups; that is, *are separated* cannot hold of a group that consists of subgroups of members of different conjunct groups. The conjunct groups are the only subgroups that can act as the exclusive parts of the group referent.

The higher-order-group reading of conjoined plural NPs constitutes a well-known problem for an extensional mereological account of the semantics of plurals, by challenging the assumption of transitivity. Link (1983) tries to solve the problem within an extensional mereological approach by postulating an additional formal level of entities — a level of groups — which is distinct from the level of lattice-theoretical sums. This account, however, poses a number of problems, which are discussed in Landman (1989). As an alternative, Landman proposes the reintroduction of sets in addition to lattice-theoretical sums for the formal representation of groups. At the end of this section, I will come to specific objections against Link's and Landman's approaches and argue that the present theory accounts for the relevant data more accurately.

In contrast to the approaches that Link and Landman take, I consider the phenomena of conjunction simply an indication that the part relation that is relevant in semantics is not transitive. Single cats and dogs in (109b) are parts of the group of cats and the group of dogs respectively, but not parts of the group of cats and dogs.

Higher-order-group formation with conjunction of plural NPs is not limited to 'second-order' groups as in (109), but is presumably restricted only by independent cognitive constraints on semantic complexity (see also Landman 1989 and Lønning 1989 for similar considerations). Consider the 'third-order-group reading' of (110) as a statement about father-son and mother-daughter problems:

(110) Fathers and sons and mothers and daughters have similar problems with each other.

The possibility of nontransitive part structures of groups with conjunction seems to be inherent to the operation of group formation and cannot be handled by assuming just one higher level of groups (besides the level of sums), as in Link (1983).

The higher-order-group reading can be accounted for by exactly the same principles and rules as the examples with mass NPs referring to quantities with integrated parts. The conjunct NPs refer to maximal entities satisfying the head nouns. These entities are FF-integrated wholes and hence, by the conditions on part structures, may count as the only parts of the referent of the entire NP. So the entire NP may refer to an entity with integrated parts.

Also the fusion reading is accounted for. If the conjunct NPs refer to subgroups that are integrated wholes, this does not mean that the members of those subgroups could not count as parts of the entire group; it only means that they do not *have* to count as the parts of the entire group. Note also that FF-integrated wholes are integrated wholes only to a weak degree (as was mentioned in Chapter 1), which means that FF-integrated wholes do not generally have a sufficient degree of integrity to count as the only parts of an entity. What appears to be the case is that only if the context provides additional integrity conditions can the subgroups be integrated wholes of a degree sufficient to count as the only parts.

The fact that definite plural and mass NPs refer to maximal entities satisfying the relevant concepts is crucial for the availability of the higher-order-group reading. In quantified NPs with conjoined plural or mass nouns as heads, the conjuncts do not define integrated wholes, as the examples in (111) and (112) show:

(111) a. All parents and children hate each other.
      b. All cats and dogs are separated.
(112) a. Half of the parents and children hate each other.
      b. Half of the cats and dogs are separated.

Here we do not get higher-order-group readings. Example (111a), for instance, lacks a reading in which the entire group of parents stands in the hate-relationship to the entire group of children.

As is expected, higher-order-group readings are possible not only with conjoined plural NPs and plural NPs with conjoined plural head nouns but also when plural NPs are modified by conjoined modifiers or other plural NPs. In the following examples, conjoined modifiers may specify subgroups as integrated wholes and thus as the only parts of the plural referent:

(113) a. The students at MIT and at BU are not comparable.
       b. The people from Europe and from Africa avoid each other.
       c. (?) John compared the people in the pool and in the tub.

Of course, the examples in (113) also allow for the fusion reading.

The availablity of the higher-order-group readings and the fusion readings can be explained in exactly the same way as in the case of conjoined plural NPs and plural nouns.

Again, the definiteness of the complex NP is crucial for the availability of the higher-order-group reading. If the NP is not definite but quantified, the higher-order-group reading is at least significantly harder to get:

(114) a. (?) All students at MIT and at BU are not comparable.
       b. (?) John compared all people in the pool and in the tub.
(115) (?) Half of the students at MIT and at BU are not comparable.

It is difficult to get a reading of the examples in (114) and (115) in which the students at MIT (or the people in the pool) are contrasted with the students at BU (or the people in the tub).

Finally, there is also the case in which higher-order-group readings of definite NPs are due to another plural modifier specifying subgroups as integrated wholes by connecting them to independent integrated wholes. Examples are given in (116):

(116) a. John compared the children at the various schools.
       b. The students in the two departments are competing with each
           other.

In (116a), the parts of the referent of *the children at the various schools* may be exactly the maximal subgroups x of children such that for some school y, every member of x is at y. In this case, we get the reading in which John compared the children according to their schools. Similarly, if (116b) describes the situation in which the students in one department compete with the students in the other department, the part structure of the referent of *the students in the two departments* will consist only of the group of students in one department and the group of students in the other department.

Let me now briefly turn to some objections against the accounts of the higher-order-group reading by Link (1983) and Landman (1989). Schwarzschild (1992a) argues against groups conceived as atoms besides individuals in Link's account and conceived as singleton sets of sets in Landman's approach. The data Schwarzschild uses are similar to those given in this section and in Moltmann (1990a). Schwarzschild argues that there is no way to compositionally get groups in Link's or Landman's sense for the higher-order-group reading, since the NPs may not themselves be conjoined, but modified by conjoined modifiers or plurals. Schwarzschild's own suggestion of how to handle the higher-order-group readings is to let definite plural NPs always denote 'sums' — that is, groups whose parts are the individual members. Higher-order-group readings then are collective readings of the predicate induced by pragmatic information about the linguistically relevant subgroups. Such information has the same status as adverbs like *by age* as in (117):

(117) John compared the cows by age.

Schwarzschild is not explicit how the relevant subgroups come about, but generally attributes the higher-order-group readings to the way predicates apply to sums, rather than to the NP referent itself.

There is evidence, however, that the higher-order-group readings cannot be due to the predicate. Such an account would predict that with the same referent, different conjoined predicates would allow for readings relating to different subgroups. But this is not the case. Consider (118):

(118) John compared and evaluated the ice skaters.

It seems hard to get a reading of (118) in which John compared couples of ice skaters and evaluated individual ice skaters. Such a reading is possible only when the conjunct predicates are modified explicitly by perspective shifters:

(119) John compared the ice skaters as couples and evaluated the ice skaters as individuals.

The present account makes explicit which higher-order-group readings are available on the basis of what kind of information, and it shows that, by the same devices, parallel readings are available for plural and mass NPs. It takes reference situations to be the basis for determining the relevant part structures of groups or quantities. Characteristically, reference situations may be influenced in various ways; but they remain the same for different predicates.

3.2.3. Contextual satisfaction of the Integrated Parts Requirement

If semantic selectional principles like IP are satisfied by information given in the relevant situation, integration of parts should be possible not only on the basis of information expressed by the referential expression but also by information that is given or presupposed independently in the context. There are in fact such cases, though with some of the predicates and semantic operations they are quite hard to get, if not generally impossible. Let me call the cases in which IP is satisfied by information not conveyed by the referential expression cases of *contextual satisfaction* of the selectional requirement. The following examples are generally accepted by speakers:

(120) a. John went from table to table to compare the wine.
       b. At first, Mary could not distinguish John's music from Bill's music. Only after she had talked to both composers for several hours, was she able to distinguish the music.
       c. Mary went to all the nightclubs in this town and found the music very similar.

Thus, the predicates *compare*, *distinguish*, and *be similar* allow for contextual satisfaction of IP. The contexts in the examples in (120) allow for integrated parts by providing one-to-one functions from integrated wholes (tables, composers, or nightclubs) to parts of the quantities in question.

However, *between* and reciprocals, for instance, seem to resist contextual satisfaction completely:

(121) a. # The wine was poured into two glasses that were put on the table, and between the wine Mary put a candle.
       b. # John went from table to table to compare the wine with each other.
(122) a. ?? John took the dust from the sofa and from the floor and found that it was very similar / different.
       b. # John took the dust from the sofa and from the floor and found that it resembled each other.

The difference between these two types of predicates and constructions can be traced perhaps to the fact that *between* and *each other* involve a binary relation to a stronger degree than predicates like *compare* or *distinguish* do.

The general fact that the satisfaction of part-structure-sensitive selectional requirements by nonlinguistic contextual information is highly restricted points to another respect in which reference situations differ from context sets. Context sets allow for accommodation to a much greater extent than reference situations do.

3.3. Other part-structure-sensitive semantic selectional requirements?

In this chapter, we have seen extensive evidence for two semantic selectional requirements involving the part structure of an argumen: ACC and IP. This raises the question whether there are or can be other part-structure-specific semantic selectional requirements. Given the present view of part structures, one might expect a requirement that is the opposite of ACC, namely, one that requires that an argument be an integrated whole and thus, in general, be the referent of a singular count NP. This expectation, however, is not borne out. In English, any predicate allowing for singular count NPs also allows for plural NPs. This, however, follows from the fact that predicates systematically allow for distributive readings (that is, they have disjunctive lexical meanings with one disjunct representing the distributive reading, cf. Chapter 2). Thus, every predicate may take a plural NP as its argument and have its 'literal meaning' applied only to the members of the group referent of that NP.

We have seen that semantic selectional requirements involving the part structure of an argument require that a potential argument have certain properties in the reference situation, a situation that carries partial information about entities, but, crucially, need not carry the information provided by the predicate.

The phenomena of part-structure-sensitive semantic selection constitute strong motivations for the notion of part structure as it was conceived in Chapter 1. First, the semantic selectional requirements involve the notion of integrated whole as a crucial parameter. Second, part-structure-sensitive selectional requirements involve part structures that are relative to situations. As an entity may have different partial representations in different situations, it may have different part structures in different situations; and only the part structure it has in the reference situation will matter for semantic selection. The reference situation contains at least the information given by the description of the relevant referential expressions used, and, in certain cases, it may also contain further, contextually given information. However, the possibility for part-structure-related information not carried by the referential expression to be included in a reference situation is highly restricted — in ways, though, that unfortunately remain mysterious.

4

Part Structures and Quantification

The subject of this chapter is the interaction between part structures and quantification with noun phrases. There are at least three respects in which part structures and quantified NPs relate to each other.

First, there is an indirect connection between part structures and plural and mass quantifiers. The domain of quantifiers like *all men* and *all wood*, as I will argue, consists of all groups of men or all water quantities in — as usual — a contextually restricted domain of quantification. The restrictions on the domain are not arbitrary, though, but rather governed by certain conditions. This chapter will establish that these conditions are exactly parallel to the conditions on part structures introduced in Chapter 1.

The second respect in which part structures bear on quantification with noun phrases is the relation between determiners such as *ten* or *many* and part structures. Given that such determiners may act as cardinality attributes, and given the generalized notion of part, they should act as predicates, counting the parts of a group. This chapter takes the stand that this view can be maintained despite some apparent counterexamples, and it explores an even bolder view — namely, that mass cardinality attributes such as *much* and *little* also act as predicates, counting the parts of a quantity.

The third, and most prominent, way in which quantified NPs and part structures interact involves universal quantifiers ranging over the relevant parts of an entity. Such quantifiers are found in many languages and are exemplified in English by the *all the*-constructions (*all the men, all the wood*). The domains of such part quantifiers consist of situated parts and hence depend on whether relevant entities have been characterized as integrated wholes. Universal part quantifiers involve the notion of integrated whole in two other ways: first, they often impose on the NP they apply to conditions which concern the degree of integrity of the NP-referent; second, they often have secondary functions — for example, as perspective shifters. In this function, they have a lexical meaning involving the notion of integrated whole.

4.1. Quantification with plural and mass NPs

4.1.1. A uniform treatment of plural and mass universal quantification

Plural quantifiers such as *all men* and mass quantifiers such as *all water* are formally parallel to singular count quantifiers such as *every man*. Hence they suggest a parallel semantics, with *all men* ranging over all relevant groups of men and *all water* over all relevant quantities of water.[1] In this section, I want to defend such a view.

The view that *all men* ranges over all (relevant) groups of men, though plausible from a formal point of view, is not unproblematic. In fact, at first sight, the view seems to go wrong for most cases of plural quantification. For example, (1), under natural circumstances, does not quantify over proper groups of men, but only over individuals (i.e., it does imply that any group of men share two legs):

(1) All men have two legs.

However, there are independently motivated principles that can explain why the range of *all men* in (1) need not include proper groups of men. These principles are analogous to the conditions on the part structure of groups and quantities. The latter are responsible for the corresponding phenomenon with quantification over the parts of a group. Thus, in (2), *all* also ranges only over individual men, not subgroups of men:

(2) All the men have two legs.

NPs of the form *all* N' as in (1) differ from NPs of the form *all the* N' in (2) in that the former denote universal quantifiers ranging over groups or quantities in the extension of the N', whereas the latter denote universal part quantifiers ranging over the parts of whatever the definite NP *the* N' refers to (cf. Section 4.4.). This difference manifests itself in the contrasts between (3a) and (3b) and between (4a) and (4b):

(3) a. All men are happy.
     b. All the men are happy.
(4) a. All water is drinkable.
     b. All the water is drinkable.

---

[1] This conforms with a general principle introduced in Chapter 1, the Uniformity Thesis, which states that plural and mass nouns have the same denotation in all syntactic contexts (except for cases of agreement). Thus, plural and mass nouns in quantificational NPs denote sets of groups or quantities in the same way as they do in definite and indefinite NPs. Thus, quantified plural and mass NPs should range over groups and quantities, respectively.

For (3a) to be true, most naturally, all mankind should be happy. In contrast, for (3b) to be true, everyone in a specific group of men should be happy. This means that NPs of the form *all* N' range over whatever entities satisfy the description given by the N', whereas NPs of the form *all the* N' range over the parts of a specific quantity or group (the referent of *the* N').

Let us now turn to the conditions on quantification domains of groups and quantities. Here a general restriction that universally quantified mass NPs impose on the predicate is relevant, a restriction that distinguishes quantified mass NPs from quantified plural NPs. This restriction can best be introduced by contrasting quantified mass NPs with definite mass NPs, as in (5a) and (5b):

(5) a. All water contains salt / # two gram of salt / # the salt.
    b. The water contains salt / two gram of salt / the salt.

The restriction that is responsible for the unacceptable cases in (5a) is what I will call the *Homogeneity Requirement* (cf. Moltmann 1989, 1991b).

It is not a completely trivial task to state the Homogeneity Requirement correctly. Following Bunt (1985) and Lønning (1987), one might take the Homogeneity Requirement to require that universally quantified mass NPs take only homogeneous (i.e., cumulative and divisive) predicates, as stated in (6a), where a homogeneous predicate is defined in (6b) (as in Chapter 1):

(6) a. *The Homogeneity Requirement*
       The predicate predicated of a universally quantified mass NP must be homogeneous.
    b. *Definition (first version)*
       A predicate *f* is *homogeneous* iff [*f*] is cumulative and divisive.

As it turns out, however, the Homogeneity Requirement cannot be as simple as that. *Contains salt* is certainly cumulative, but it is not always divisive, since not any subquantity of a quantity of water that contains salt needs to contain salt. However, all subquantities of a quantity water *may* contain salt, whereas it is impossible that all subquantities of a quantity of water that contains two grams of salt contain two grams of salt. Thus, there is a modal condition distinguishing the predicate *contains salt* from the predicate *contains two grams of salt*. Taking this into account, homogeneity as defined in (6a) (a definition which in Chapter 1 was intended for mass noun extensions) should be redefined, for the present purpose, as follows:

(7) *Definition (revised)*
    A predicate *f* is *homogeneous* iff [*f*] is cumulative, and for any situation *s* and entity *x* such that $[f]^s(x) = 1$, it is possible that for all *y*, $y <_s x$, $[f]^s(y) = 1$.

Let us say that a predicate is *heterogeneous* iff it is not homogeneous in the sense of (7). Then, obviously, the predicate *contains two grams of salt* is heterogeneous. From now on, I will assume the Homogeneity Requirement as in (6a) with the new sense of 'homogeneity' in (7).

The Homogeneity Requirement can be derived if NPs like *all water* are taken to be universal quantifiers ranging over all quantities of water (in the relevant context). The domain of water quantities is itself homogeneous in the former sense and thus requires the predicate to be homogeneous in the new sense.[2]

Turning now to quantified plural NPs, we see that for them the Homogeneity Requirement does not hold. Example (1) showed that the predicate need not be cumulative (since there *all* did not range over proper groups). The following examples, which contain collective predicates, show that it need not be divisive:

(8) a. All students gathered in the street.
     b. All winners of the contest embraced.

The fact that plural quantifiers do not require cumulativity and divisivity of the predicate indicates that plural quantifiers do not generally range over *all* groups of the relevant individuals satisfying the corresponding singular N'. In order to cope with this fact, most semanticists that have endorsed an extensional mereological account of plurals have opted for a special treatment of quantified plural NPs on which such NPs may range over individuals only.[3] I will not opt for such a special treatment, but rather defend the view that quantified plural NPs such as *all men* are exactly parallel to quantifiers such as *all water*. That is, *all men* ranges over all (relevant) groups of men, as *all water* ranges over all quantities of water.[4] The fact that universal plural quantifiers range over a limited set of groups or only over individuals is then explained on the basis of two independent factors that play a role in natural language quantification: [1] the general possibility of quantification domains being restricted in the relevant context, and [2] general and independently motivated principles that govern the individuation of groups.

---

[2] The Homogeneity Requirement with universally quantified mass NPs, though, can be suspended when the context individuates the subquantities appropriately. This was noted by Gillon (1992) with examples such as (1a) and (1b). Another example is (1c) from Roeper (1983), who, not exploiting the possibility of contextually restricted quantification domains, took it as a counterexample against the view that *all phosphorus* ranges over all quantities of phosphorus.

(1) a. All regular mail in Canada is 38 cents.
     b. No furniture on this floor has four legs.
     c. All phosphorus is either red or black.

[3] See the discussions in Link (1987) and Roberts (1987).

[4] This view has also been held by Higginbotham (1981) and Ojeda (1993). Ojeda, however, does not take contextual restrictions of quantification domains into account.

In principle, the quantification domain of an NP can be restricted in any possible fashion. This holds for quantified singular NPs in an obvious way. *Every tree* in (9) may range over any set of trees, as long as this set is the one relevant in the context:

(9) Every tree was green.

Clearly, a contextual domain restriction is possible also with quantified plural NPs. But here, it may have an influence not only on which individuals constitute the domain but also on which *groups* of individuals may be in the domain. Contextual domain restriction even allows the domain of a plural quantifier to contain only individuals (trivial groups), as in (1), and it allows the quantification domain of *all students* in (8a) and of *all winners* in (8b) to contain only certain groups of students or winners (including the entire group).[5]

What is it that determines which groups are in the quantification domain in a particular case? There are principles that influence the constitution of quantification domains with groups that are the same as those responsible for the part structure of groups. One of the effects of those principles is that quantification over subgroups only (to the exclusion of the maximal group) is in general difficult to get, for example in (10):

(10) All students in this class found a solution.

Example (10) could be true in a situation in which only certain subgroups of students found a solution; but it is hard to get such a reading.

Quantification over groups to the exclusion of the individual group members and the maximal group is possible, however, if the background situation individuates these groups appropriately. For example, quantification over certain pairs of people and only those pairs is possible in (11), taken as a description of a party:

(11) All guests at the party danced with each other.

Taking all these data together leads to the following generalization: groups smaller than the maximal group may be included in a quantification domain only if these groups are integrated wholes in the relevant situation — for example in (11), by forming couples. But this simply is the Restriction on situated sum formation, which was introduced in Chapter 1 to block sum formation for situated part structures:

---

[5] The view that universally quantified plural and mass NPs range over contextually determined groups and quantities has also been proposed by Gillon (1992). Gillon, though, does not provide any principles of how the quantification domain is determined, nor does he draw the connection to quantification over parts of groups and quantities.

(12) *Restriction on situated sum formation*
For a situation s, $D(s)$ contains the sum x of a set of integrated wholes in s only if x itself is an integrated whole in s.

This restriction generally does not affect mass domains, since mass nouns do not characterize entities as integrated wholes. Accordingly, quantified mass NPs generally have a quantification domain closed under sum formation and the relation 'is a part of' (i.e., a homogeneous domain). But plurals do characterize the members of groups as integrated wholes; hence the difference between plural and mass quantification.

Given the relativization of the domains of plural quantifiers to situations, sentences such as (1) will formally be analyzed simply as in (13) for a reference situation s':

(13) $\lambda s[\{<x, s'> \mid [men]^{s'}(x) = 1\} \subseteq \{<x, s'> \mid (\exists e)[have\ two\ legs]^s(e,$
$<x, s'>) = 1\}]$

Example (13) can be obtained by exactly the same semantic operation that was introduced for *every* in Chapter 2.

4.1.2. Further predictions of the account

The account of universal plural and mass quantification given so far makes further predictions. If quantification domains are determined by conditions involving integrity, then there should be ways of specifying domains other than by singular count nouns (or nonlinguistic contextual information). And, in fact, there are constructions by which, independently of the mass-count distinction, the constitution of quantification domains can be influenced.

First, relational adjectives or nouns may specify entities as integrated wholes independently of singular count nouns and so allow for universal plural quantification over proper groups, as in (14a) (from Link 1987) and (14b):[6]

(14) a. All competing companies have common interests.
b. All twin babies in this hospital are indistinguishable.

The quantification domain of *all competing companies* in (14a) contains a group x of companies only if each member of x competes with any other member of x.

Furthermore, integrated wholes (both in the plural and in the mass domain) may be defined by relational relative clauses. This may result in a quantification

---

[6] The phenomenon has also been discussed by Roberts (1987), Lønning (1989), Gillon (1992), and Ojeda (1993).

domain consisting only of certain maximal groups of the relevant individuals, as in (15) and (16):

(15) a. All students who are roommates share one bathroom.
     b. All students who had the same hobby formed a club.
     c. All children who were the same age did not fit into one car.
(16) All ink that has the same color was put into the same container.

In (15a), the quantification domain consists of only the maximal groups of students that are roommates, and similarly for (15b) and (15c). In (16), the quantification domain consists only of the maximal quantities of ink that are the same color, allowing a heterogeneous predicate (given a situation in which different quantities of ink were put into different containers).

In these examples, the relative clauses express relational group or quantity properties. For instance, the relative clause in (15a) expresses the property that holds of an entity x just in case any two parts of x are roommates. The relative clause in (15b) expresses the property that holds of an entity x just in case for any two parts x' and x'' of x, the hobby that x' had is the same as the one that x'' had. Similarly for (15c). The relative clause in (16) expresses the property that holds of an entity x in case the colors of any two parts of x are the same. The content of the relative clause in (15a) will formally be as in (17):

(17) $[who\ are\ roommates]^S = \lambda w[(\exists X)\ (X \neq \emptyset\ \&\ w = sum_{<s}(\{x \mid x \in X$
    $\&\ (\forall y)(\forall z)(y <_s x\ \&\ z <_s x\ \&\ y \neq z \rightarrow [roommates]^S(<y, z>) = 1)\}))]$

Given (17), the extension of *students who are roommates* in (15a) includes *all* entities whose parts all stand in the relation expressed by the relative clause, not just the maximal ones.[7] But the quantification domain of *all students who are roommates* consists only of maximal subgroups among whose members or subquantities the relation in question holds. The reason why only the maximal subgroups are selected is that they are R-integrated wholes with R being the relation expressed by the relative clause. This means that the constitution of the

---

[7] Note that in principle, relational nouns and relative clauses may hold also of groups of entities whose parts stand in the relevant relation to each other. The evidence for this is that definite plurals may have a relative clause as a modifier that characterizes the entire group referent in this way, as shown by (1a) and (1b):

(1) a. All the students who were roommates complained about the size of the room.
    b. All the students who found the same solution got the same grade.

Example (1a) has a reading in which the students can be partitioned into subgroups x such that every member of x is a roommate of every other member of x, but not of any other subgroup. In this reading, *all* ranges over the subgroups in the partition (cf. Section 4.2.2.). The same kind of reading is possible for (1b).

quantification domain for (15a) (as well as (15b, c) and (16)) is governed by the Restriction on situated sum formation — not just by the meaning of the relative clause.

In this section, I have argued that plural quantification can be treated in a way exactly parallel to mass quantification. But we have seen that unlike mass quantifiers, plural quantifiers generally do not range over all entities (all possible groups) denoted by the relevant plural N'. Rather, plural quantification generally involves only either individuals or the maximal group or certain subgroups that are contextually or descriptively designated. These facts, however, could be explained on the basis of two independent factors: the general possibility of contextually restricting a quantification domain, and principles governing the formation of subgroups in quantification domains, principles that are exactly analogous to the principles determining the situated parts of groups given in Chapter 1.

The analysis that was given shows more generally how a rather simple semantic account of challenging data can be maintained by invoking independent principles of individuation to explain apparent counterexamples away.

4.2. Existential quantification over groups and quantities

There is a well-established distinction between the function of determiners such as *four, many, much,* and *little* as cardinality or quantity attributes and the same determiners as quantifiers in the proper sense (cf. Milsark 1977). In the first function, the determiners simply act as attributes of groups or quantities, restricting the range of an existential quantifier ranging over groups or quantities.[8] In this section, I will discuss the first function of the quantifiers in question and provide some support for a rather bold view of the content of those quantifiers, a view on which such quantifiers are simply part-structure attributes.

Quantifiers such as *four, many, much,* and *little* do not seem to naturally fit into a semantics based on the generalized notion of part. The plural quantifiers *ten* and *many* seem to always count individuals, and the mass quantifiers *much*

---

[8] To give some diagnostics for this distinction, in the first function, but not in the second, the determiners may occur in contexts imposing the indefiniteness effects such as *there*-sentences:

(1) There was (were) a man / three men in the garden.

In the second function, but not in the first, the determiners can go with NPs in contexts generally not allowing for indefinite NPs, such as the subject position of individual-level predicates like *blond*:

(2) # A woman / OK Three women is (are) blond.

and *little* seem to not involve any notion of part at all but rather measure the extent of a quantity. Despite these seemingly obvious facts, still some support can be given for the view that these quantifiers do in fact involve the generalized, situated notion of part and count the parts in the general sense of an entity.

A characteristic of group or quantity attributes is that they can take collective predicates (or collectively interpreted predicates):

> (18) a. Many / Four children drew a picture.
>   b. The roof was damaged by a lot of storms.
> (19) a. The roof was damaged by a lot of rain.
>   b. A lot of money has spoiled Mary.
>   c. Little money has driven Mary to work hard.

The relevant reading of (18a) is the one on which the group of four or many children drew a picture together, and the relevant readings of (18b) and (19a) are those on which the high quantity of storms or rain was responsible for the damage of the roof.

The question now is, How should the content of such group and quantity attributes be formulated within a semantics based on the generalized situated notion of part? The possibility that first comes to mind is to analyze group and quantity attributes as numerical predicates counting the parts of a group or quantity. The lexical meaning of *four* then would be (20) — that is, the property of having at least four parts in the relevant situation:

> (20) $[four]^s = \lambda x[(\exists^{\leq 4} y)\ y <_s x]$

But (20) seems inadequate for all contexts in which *four* does not mean 'having four parts'.[9] For instance, *four children* in (18a) can never mean 'four subgroups of children' — even if the children are partitioned into four prominent subgroups in the relevant context.

My suggestion is that (20) can nonetheless be maintained, because there are other ways to exclude the impossible readings. Numerals with a meaning such as (20) make reference to parts of an argument and involve the binary relation of distinctness among parts. Therefore, they are subject to the Accessibility Requirement and the Integrated Part Requirement; that is, the numerals can apply only to entities that have an accessible part structure and consist of integrated parts. Given the Accessibility Requirement, it is excluded that *four* with the meaning in (20) applies to collective or other singular count NPs. The Integrated Parts Requirement, appropriately applied, furthermore might exclude numerals applying to mass NPs and to groups in the sense of counting subgroups, rather

---

[9] This sort of problem was discussed by Link (1987), who therefore rejected an analysis such as (20).

than group members. The reason would be that the subquantities and the subgroups are not generally integrated wholes (of a sufficient degree).[10]

Let us turn to vague quantifiers such as *many* (or *a lot* as a plural quantifer) in their function as group predicates. The lexical meanings of *many* can be conceived as a property of groups x in a situation s such that the cardinality of the set of parts of x is greater than the expected cardinality in s.[11] The expected cardinality may depend on the kind of entity that is counted (many books amount to more than many novels) and on the nature of the described situation. Consider (21):

(21) Many guests came to the party.

Example (21) may be true and false with the same number of guests. It may be true in one situation in which the number of guests exceeds the expected number of guests, and it may be false in a different situation in which a greater number of guests is expected. The expectation value that is here appealed to can be conceived of as the value of a function @ applied to the reference situation s.

However, this account of the meaning of *many* is still not adequate. Strict cardinality does not really do the job. For example, among the natural numbers, there are, intuitively, 'few' prime numbers rather than 'many'. Instead of cardinality, therefore, what seems to be involved is some vague function of contextual evaluation of quantity or extent. I take *eval* to be such a function, but leave its further specification open (in particular, since it has no further relevance in the present context). Formally, then, *many* (or *a lot* as a plural quantifier) has the following lexical meaning:

(22) $[many]^s = \lambda x[eval(\{y \mid y <_s x\}) > @(s)]$

---

[10] There is a problem with this account and that is that it is strictly impossible for numerals to count subquantities or subgroups — regardless of how the context individuates the part structure. In this respect, numerals differ from other phenomena involving the Accessibility and the Integrated Parts Requirement discussed in Chapter 2.

Perhaps, numerals require integrated parts to a higher degree than many other predicates subject to the Integrated Parts Requirement. This possibility is not totally implausible, since, as we have seen in Chapter 2 (Section 2.1.2.3.), predicates may differ with respect to how the Accessibility Requirement or the Integrated Parts Requirement may be satisfied by an argument. *Between*, for example, unlike *compare*, also excludes arguments with integrated parts that are based on contextually given whole-properties.

Alternatively, numerals might require not just parts that are integrated wholes, but rather parts that are essential integrated wholes. Only group members can be essential integrated wholes, but not proper subgroups or subquantities of a quantities.

[11] See Westerståhl (1985) for a discussion of *many* and its various readings.

Thus, *many* expresses the property that holds of an entity *x* in a situation *s* iff the evaluation of the contextually relevant parts of *x* exceeds the expected amount in *s*.

Like *four*, *many* with this meaning is subject to the Accessibility Requirement and the Integrated Parts Requirement; and, again, this may exclude the application of *many* to singular count nouns, mass nouns, and plurals (counting subgroups).

The account of cardinality attributes that I have given raises a potential problem, however. It seems to conflict with the treatment of distributive interpretation of predicates given in Chapter 2. Distributive interpretation as it was treated there consists in the predicate literally applying to the relevant parts of the participant. But if (20) and (22) are right, then the evaluation of the cardinality predicate should involve exactly the same parts as the distribution of the predicate. Since cardinality attributes generally count individuals, predicate distribution over proper subgroups only should be excluded. So the following sentences should be unacceptable, with the numeral applying to parts of the group other than the predicate:

> (23) a. The twelve men lifted the piano in groups of four.
>   b. The ten musicians played duets.

Speakers vary somewhat with respect to the acceptability of such examples, though. For those speakers for whom they are acceptable at all, the predicate perhaps is reinterpreted as a predicate that distributes over individuals, without losing its collective sense. *Play duets* in (23b), for example, then holds of an entity *x* just in case *x* is engaged in the activity of playing duets (which involves some other individual as well).

Let me now turn to the lexical meaning of the mass quantifier *much* (or *a lot* as a mass quantifier). The meaning of *much* is more difficult to specify. *Much* cannot count parts in the strict mereological sense, because, for instance, different quantities of water have infinitely many subquantities so that *much* could not distinguish among them (a problem noted by Parsons (1979) in relation to the mass quantifier *most*). Instead it appears that *much* measures the extent of a quantity relative to an expectation value (as suggested by Parsons 1979 for *most*). Thus, *much* would mean 'a great amount of' or 'a great quantity of'. There are some phenomena, however, that indicate that this view is not quite adequate. The view predicts that the *a*-examples and the *b*-examples in (24)–(26) should be equivalent, but, in fact, they are rather different in meaning or acceptability:

> (24) a. John is of great height / weight.
>   b. # John is of a lot of height / weight.
> (25) a. great laughter
>   b. a lot of laughter

(26) a. John has a good / deep insight.
     b. John has too much insight.

Only *great* in (24a) and (25a) and *good* or *deep* in (26a) measure the mere extent of the relevant entity. *A lot of* in (25b) measures the event of laughing by counting its temporally separated subevents or participants, and in (26b) *much* measures the amount of insight by counting distinguishable subunits of the insight.

These data suggest that quantities can be evaluated by *a lot* or *much* only if they have a contextually determined coarse part structure, a part structure that has some degree of discreteness in the relevant situation. It is impossible for entities like heights or weights to have a relatively discrete part structure in any situation; but it is perfectly possible for concrete masses like wood, gold, or even water to be implicitly partitioned into greater subunits in a given context. The function of quantity attributes then simply is to count such contextually determined parts.

If part structures of this sort are at stake, then the problem with treating *much* as a quantifier counting parts need not arise. It is reasonable to assume that for entities of the same type, a contextual partitioning generally yields part structures with more or less equal parts. If such part structures provide the basis for comparative measurement, then *much* and *little* will hold of entities that differ in the number of their parts.

This account, however, makes a strong and maybe suspect assumption — namely, the assumption that a speaker implicitly divides a homogeneous quantity into countable subunits, subunits whose integrity, if present, is entirely contextually determined or only perceived as such. Rather than rejecting the account for such reasons, however, I will leave it as an empirical question whether this strategy is present in the use of quantity predicates or not.

On the proposed account, the lexical meaning of *much* (and *a lot*)is as in (27):[12]

(27) $[much]^s = \lambda x[eval(\{y \mid y <_s x\}) > @(s)]$

The meaning given in (27) is identical to (22). So the difference between *much* and *many* is considered not a difference in meaning but rather a syntactic difference between determiners that are syntactically mass and syntactically count. The apparent semantic difference between mass and count determiners instead can be traced to the differences between the part structure of quantities (which do not have integrated parts) and the part structure of groups (which have integrated parts).

---

[12] There is also a way to remain neutral with respect to the two alternative accounts of quantity predicates (measurement of extent and counting or evaluation of contextual parts). This is to reinterpret the evaluation function *eval* in such a way that applied to a set *A*, it may either count the elements of *A* or measure the 'extent' of the sum of *A*.

To sum up, there is some evidence, though perhaps not conclusive, that the lexical meaning of determiners that are group or quantity attributes consists in properties involving only the generalized situated notion of part. Restrictions against counting certain kinds of parts such as subgroups can be derived from semantic selectional requirements that these quantifiers impose because of their lexical meaning. Evidence for mass determiners counting parts of quantities comes from their contrast with mass attributes measuring mere extensions such as *great*.

So far I have discussed only numerals and upward-entailing vague plural and mass determiners, but not downward-entailing ones such as *few* and *little*. I have postponed the discussion of such determiners because there is a fundamental difference between the two types of determiners. NPs with determiners *many* and *much* or numerals behave like indefinite NPs in relevant respects (cf. Milsark 1977, Higginbotham 1987). Therefore, they should semantically be represented as existential quantifiers ranging over groups or quantities. NPs with the downward-entailing determiners *few* and *little*, however, cannot be treated semantically by existential quantification over groups or quantities. *Few men came* is false in a situation in which a group larger than few men came.[13] NPs with the determiners *few* or *little* therefore should not be treated as indefinite NPs at all. Rather, *few* and *little* share crucial properties with focused *many* and *much*, which have a semantics different from their unfocused counterparts. For this reason, they will be treated together with focused quantifiers in the next section.

4.3. Focused quantifiers

Determiners such as *four, many*, and *much* in their second function as quantifiers can be analyzed on the basis of the same lexical meaning they were given as group or quantity attributes. The difference lies only in their role in a sentence meaning. In both functions, the determiner counts the parts of an entity; but the entity in question is specified in different ways. In the first function, it is specified only by the head N'; in the second function, it is specified both by the head N' and the predicate in the sentence.

One diagnostic for determiners to act as quantifiers is *focusing*. When determiners like *a lot, many*, or *much* are focused, they differ from their

---

[13] These determiners have other properties that distinguish them from determiners like *many* and *much*. For example, *few* and *little* generally cannot occur in positions that exhibit the indefiniteness effect, such as predicative positions as in (1) and pseudocleft constructions such as (2), a fact noted by Higginbotham (1987):

    (1)   a. # They are few students.
           b. # This is little water.
    (2) # What John saw were (was) few children / little water.

unfocused counterparts not only in the general semantic effect of focusing but also in truth conditions. In particular, they may receive a distributive interpretation that is not available otherwise. The contrast shows up in generic sentences, as in (28) and (29), as well as in nongeneric ones, such as in (30):

(28) a. A lot of children disturb John.
     b. A lót of children disturb John.
(29) a. A lot of jewelry fits her well.
     b. A lót of jewelry fits her well.
(30) a. Ten injections last year have harmed John's health.
     b. Tén injections last year have harmed John's health.

Example (28a) suggests that any collection of many children disturbs John, whereas (28b) suggests that each member of a collection of many children disturbs John. Examples (29a) and (29b) exhibit a similar contrast. Example (30a) allows for a reading in which the cumulative effect of ten injections have harmed John's health, whereas (30b) implies that each one of ten injections has harmed John's health.

There are also determiners that act only as quantifiers — *most*, for example. *Most* patterns with focused determiners with respect to whether the predicate is understood distributively or collectively:[14]

(31) a. Most children disturb John.
     b. Most injections last year have harmed John's health.
     c. Most jewelry fits her well.

Turning now to downward-entailing quantifiers, we see that *few* and *little* pattern with *most* (and focused *many* and *much*) with respect to obligatory distributive interpretation. Compare the following *a*-examples and *b*-examples (with the cardinality or quantity attributes *a few* and *a little*):

---

[14] Significantly, *most* does not exhibit the other diagnostics of indefinite NPs such as support of *donkey*-pronouns, occurrence in predicative position, and cleft constructions (cf. Higginbotham 1987) (see also Footnote 13):

(1) a. # Every farmer who owns most donkeys beats them.
     b. # These are most children of Mary.
     c. # What John ate was most cake.

The judgments with focused *a lot, many* and *much* are not decisive in this respect. Focusing only allows, but does not require, a distributive interpretation:

(2) a. Every farmer who owns many donkeys beats them.
     b. These are many children.
     c. What John ate was a lot of cake.

However, I think the conclusion can be drawn that focused *many, a lot*, etc. with distributive interpretation and *most* can be classified together semantically.

(32) a. Few children disturb John.
     b. A few children disturb John.
(33) a. Few injection last year have harmed John's health.
     b. A few injections last year have harmed John's health.
(34) a. Little jewelry fits her well.
     b. A little jewelry fits her well.

So *few* and *little* seem to obligatorily be interpreted like focused quantifiers.

I will propose a treatment of focused quantifiers first with mass quantifiers. Mass quantifiers such as *much*, *little*, and *most* pattern the same way as the corresponding count quantifiers. Mass quantifiers, moreover, impose the Homogeneity Requirement. This is seen in the contrast between (35a) and (35b) and between (35c) and (35d):

(35) a. Too much water contained salt.
     b. # Too much water contained two grams of salt / the salt.
     c. Little water contained salt.
     d. # Little water contained two grams of salt / the salt.

The Homogeneity Requirement should follow from the homogeneity of the extension of mass nouns or the part structure of quantities. But it is not obvious how it can do so within an adequate quantificational analysis. Suppose (35a) is analyzed as in (36):

(36) $\lambda s[(\exists x)([too\ much\ water]^{S'}(x) = 1\ \&\ (\forall x')(x' <_{S'} x \rightarrow (\exists y)([salt]^{S''}(y) = 1\ \&\ [contain]^{S}(x', y) = 1)))]$

Clearly, on this analysis, the Homogeneity Requirement comes out as a consequence of the homogeneity of the quantification domain. However, as was mentioned earlier, downward-entailing quantifiers such as *little* imply a maximality effect, and hence cannot be analyzed as in (36).

A better analysis is (37) with the operation of situated sum formation:

(37) $\lambda s[[little]^{S'}(sum_{<_S'}(\{x \mid [water]^{S'}(x) = 1\ \&\ (\exists y)([salt]^{S''}(y) = 1\ \&\ [contain]^{S}(x, y) = 1)\})) = 1]$

According to (37), *little* is predicated of the maximal entity composed of entities that are water in the reference situation and contain salt in the described situation; *little* holds of such an entity x if x has 'few' parts with respect to a given expectation value @.

But from (37), the Homogeneity Requirement cannot yet be derived. For *little* could apply to the value of $sum_{<_S}$ applied to a heterogeneous set — for example, the set of water quantities containing two grams of salt. What is required is that *little* applies to an entity whose parts form a homogeneous set of quantities of water containing salt.

A way of achieving this is by the following analysis:

(38) $\lambda s[[little]^{S'}(sum_{<_{S'}}(\{x \mid (\forall x')(x' <_{S'} x \ [water]^{S'}(x) = 1$

$\qquad \& \ (\exists y)([salt]^{S''}(y) = 1 \ \& \ [contain]^{S}(x',y) = 1))\})))]$

In (38), *little* is predicated of the maximal entity in the reference situation whose situated parts are quantities of water containing salt. This entity must have a homogeneous part structure, since neither itself nor its parts are specified as integrated wholes in the reference situation. Hence, the predicate must be homogeneous as well.

The same analysis can be applied to count quantifiers such as focused *a lot* in (28b). Intuitively, *a lot* in (28b) evaluates the group of entities satisfying both the head noun and the predicate, as in (39):

(39) $\lambda s[[a \ lot]^{S'}(sum_{<_S}(\{x \mid (\forall x')(x' <_{S'} x \to [child]^{S'}(x') = 1$

$\qquad \& \ (\exists e)[disturb]^{S}(e, x', \text{John}) = 1)\})) = 1]$

The analysis in (39) correctly requires a distributive reading in which the predicate must hold of every single child. But the Homogeneity Requirement will not be imposed. *A lot* in (39) is predicated of a group all of whose situated parts are in the extension of *child* and hence integrated wholes in the reference situation, blocking the formation of (nonmaximal) sums.

Focused count quantifiers not only display a strictly distributive interpretation but also allow for collective predicates. Examples of this sort have been discussed by Schein (1986, 1994), Roberts (1987), and Lønning (1989):

(40) a. A lót of experts agree.
    b. Between mány houses, there stood a tree. (Roberts 1987)
(41) a. Few experts (ever) agree. (Schein 1986)
    b. Few / Most guests danced a waltz.
    c. Few / Most employees collaborate.
    d. Most twin babies love each other. (Roberts 1987)

Without going into a detailed discussion of such examples and the way they have to be understood, let me only indicate how they can be dealt with within the present approach. In order to account for collective predication, the interpretation scheme for focused quantifiers must be revised. The modification necessary is to replace the singular predicate in the definition of the set by the corresponding plural (which, by the way, then also respects the Uniformity Thesis of Chapter 1). As a marginal case, plural predicates may also apply to group members, allowing for strict distributive readings. The first sentence in (41a) is in the relevant respects to be analyzed as in (42):

(42) $\lambda s[[few]^{S'}(sum_{<_S}(\{x \mid (\forall x')(x' <_{S'} x \to [experts]^{S'}(x') = 1$

$\qquad \& \ (\exists e)[agree]^{S}(e, x') = 1)\}), [experts]^{S'}) = 1]$

The analysis in (42) presupposes that in the relevant situation, the experts are divided into groups such that there is agreement among the members of each group. Thus, the analysis crucially relies on the contextual individuation of groups. In the present case, the groups are formed on the basis of the integrity constituted by the relation 'agrees with'.

There are examples, however, in which the difference between the number of individuals and groups in the respective context is more prominent. As was mentioned in the previous section, numerals may count only individuals, not groups. Focused numerals (in the distributive interpretation) hardly go with predicates that are unambiguously collective. Roughly, the following evaluations hold for the examples in (43) and (44):

(43) a. # Ten children sang together a duet.
      b. ?? A lot of / Few / Most children sang together a duet.
      c. ? All children sang together a duet.
(44) a. # Hundred children sang a song in a group of four.
      b. ?? A lot of / Few / Most children sang a song in a group of four.
      c. ? All children sang a song in a group of four.

Examples (43a) and (44a) indicate that an obvious clash between entities counted by the quantifier and entities specified by the collective predicates is not acceptable. Examples (43b) and (44b) indicate that *a lot* and *few* may also count subgroups, unlike numerals. Examples (43c) and (44c) indicate that the quantifier *all* may range over just those subgroups of which the collective predicate holds.

I can now formulate the compositional semantic analysis of sentences with focused quantifiers. For the sake of simplicity, I will formulate the syntactic relations and correlated semantic operation only for the case of quantified subjects of intransitive predicates:[15]

(45) a. *The syntactic relation for focused quantifiers*
          Let f and g be constituents in a syntactic structure S.
          $\langle f, g \rangle \in$ FOC-QUANT(S) iff f is a determiner and g an N', and f is
          a focused quantifier modifying g in S.
      b. *The semantic operation for focused quantifiers*
          Let A and B be situated sets.
          For a situation s',
          $foc\text{-}quant(A, B)(s') = \lambda s \lambda P[A^{s'}(sum_{<s'}(\{y \mid (\forall y')(y' <_{s'} y$
          $\rightarrow B^{s'}(y') = 1 \ \& \ P^{s}(y') = 1)\})) = 1]$

---

[15] The analysis is not yet all accurate. Focused quantifiers are not only associated with a distributive interpretation; they are also associated with the proportional reading. *A lot of children* in (28b) involves the expected proportion of the set of children that disturb John among the relevant set of children. (Note that *most* inherently has the proportional reading.)

      c. <FOC-QUANT, *foc-quant*> ∈ corr

Let me turn to the treatment of *most*. Its inherently proportional reading can be accounted for by an additional argument place in the lexical meaning of *most* (for the set denoted by the head noun). I will suggest a particular lexical meaning for *most* that makes crucial reference to the context-dependent notion of part. Evidence for this will be given shortly. According to this proposal, *most*, as a plural and as a mass determiner, expresses a relation between groups (or quantities) x and sets of groups (or quantities) X (namely the relevant extension of the head noun) such that x is an element of X and is maximal among the elements of X with respect to the relation 'has more parts than'. Thus, *most* expresses the relation in (46), where > is an irreflexive ordering among the values of *eval* with the intended meaning 'is a greater value than':

(46) $[most]^s = \lambda x X[x \in X \ \& \ (\neg \exists z)(z \in X \ \& \ eval(\{y \mid y <_s z\})) > eval(\{y \mid y <_s x\}))]$

According to (46), *most* holds between an entity x and a set X iff x is an element of X and X has no element z such that the parts of z are evaluated as being 'more' than the parts of x — that is, x must be maximal in X with respect to the relation 'has more parts than'.[16]

    The meaning of *most* in (46) presupposes that the part relation applied to groups and quantities is coarser than the strict subgroup or subquantity relation — that is, it involves the situated part relation $<_s$ rather than the general part relation $<$. With $<$, maximal proper subgroups would contain all except one element, which is not in accordance with the meaning of *most*. *Most children* does not mean 'all but one child'. *Most children laughed* may be considered true if fifteen out of twenty children laughed. So if (46) is correct, the group of the fifteen children is a maximal subgroup among the subgroups of children — given a contextually determined part structure of the entire group and the intended meaning of the evaluation function *eval*.

---

[16] Note that since maximal elements are not unique, *most* N' may refer to different groups in the scope of a quantifier, as is possible in (1):

(1) a. Every student solved most problems.
      b. Every student has understood most of the lecture.

For (1a) to be true, each student may have solved a different set of problems; and for (1b) to be true, each student may have understood different parts of the lecture. On the basis of (46) and the analysis of focused determiners in (45), (1a) is to be analyzed as follows:

(2) $\lambda s[(\forall x)([student]^{s'}(x) = 1 \rightarrow [most]^{s''}(sum_{<_s}'(\{y \mid (\forall y')(y' <_s' y$
      $\rightarrow [problem]^{s''}(y') = 1 \ \& \ (\exists e)([solve]^s(e, x, y') = 1)\}), [problems]^{s''}])$
      $= 1)]$

The meaning of *most* supports the general view advocated in this book —
namely, that in the context of natural language semantics, subgroup and
subquantity formation is not strict, but rather contextually determined.

It is worth briefly comparing this account of *most* with the traditional one
within the theory of generalized quantifiers (cf. Barwise/Cooper 1981). There,
most is analyzed as a relation between two sets X and Y such that more than half
of X is included in Y. There is evidence against this account and in favor of the
present proposal. First, intuitively, 'most' seems to be more than 'at least
half'. Secondly, *most* across languages is in general either derived from or
morphologically identical to the superlative of *more*, i.e., *the most*. For
instance, in German *die meisten* means both 'most' and 'the most'. The
meaning of *most*, therefore, should at least be related to *the most*. Consider (47):

(47) John solved the most problems.

The most problems in (47) refers to the group of problems that is maximal with
respect to the relation 'has more parts than'. This group of problems may be
maximal with respect to the subcollections of the set of all problems, or it may
be maximal with respect to a contextually given set of comparison groups of
problems — for example, with respect to the set containing the groups of
problems that Mary solved, the group of problems that Bill solved, and the
group of problems that Ann solved. In the latter case, *the most* is interpreted as a
comparative superlative (cf. Szabolsci 1982, Heim 1985). On the present
account, *most* differs from *the most* only in the comparison set. For *the most*,
the comparison set may be contextually given, whereas for *most* the comparison
set is the set of groups or quantities denoted by the head noun.

To sum up so far, there is syntactic and semantic evidence that the
determiners *most*, focused *a lot, many, much, few*, and *little* are of the same type
and should be given the same semantic analysis based on the contextually
determined notion of part. *Most, few*, and *little* can be considered inherently
focused and thus as belonging to the class of focused quantifiers.[17] Formally,

---

[17] An important issue that I have left out is the treatment of sentence with multiple
quantifiers. There are two two types of quantifier cooccurrences: those exhibiting
scope interactions and those exhibiting so-called *cumulative quantification*. The first
kind is illustrated in (1), where each boy among a majority of boys ate at least two
cakes:

   (1) Most boys ate at least two cakes.

The analysis of *most* given above straightforwardly accounts for quantifier
occurrences with scope interactions. However, the analysis has to be modified for
sentences with cumulative quantification (cf. Scha 1981). Cumulative quantification
is illustrated by particular readings of the following examples, where, for example, in
(2a), *less than ten* counts the total number of boys that ate cakes and *less than twenty*
counts the total number of cakes eaten by boys:

   (2) a. Less than ten boys ate less than twenty cakes.

they were treated on the basis of the same lexical meaning that they were assigned when acting as group or quantity predicates.

4.4. 'Generalized' part quantifiers

I will now turn to a class of quantifiers that has not received much attention in the semantic literature, even though they constitute a widespread phenomenon across languages. These quantifiers, again, support the general notion of situated part structure in which the notion of integrity plays a prominent role. The notion of integrated whole also plays an important role in selectional restrictions the quantifiers are subject to and in secondary meanings of the quantifiers as predicates, as perspective shifters, and in nominalizations.

The quantifiers in question are universal quantifiers ranging over the parts of an entity. They often apply to an entity irrespective of its type or the kinds of parts it has — that is, they range over the parts of an entity, regardless of whether this entity is an individual, a group, or a quantity. The quantifiers are found in many languages — for example, German (*ganz*), Russian (*ves'* and *celyj*), Italian (*tutto*), French (*tous*), and Spanish (*todo*). Since this type of quantifier ranges in principle over all types of entities (individuals, quantities, and groups), it can (though somewhat misleadingly) be called *generalized part quantifier*.

In what follows, I will first draw a distinction between two subtypes of generalized part quantifier before discussing each of those types separately.

4.4.1. Adjectival generalized part quantifiers

A brief view of a variety of languages suggests that there are two types of generalized part quantifier which differ in syntactic and semantic respects. The first type has adjectival form and hence can be called *adjectival part quantifier* (abbreviated *APQ*). It is exemplified in German by *ganz* and in Russian by *celyj*. English *whole* and *entire* are degenerate instances, applying only to singular count nouns. Let me discuss the characteristic properties of APQs with German *ganz*.

The adjective *ganz* has two different functions: it acts either as a *quantifier* or as a *perspective shifter* (as was discussed in Chapter 3). As an adjectival part quantifier, *ganz* can occur in singular count, plural, and mass NPs — though

---

    b. 600 Dutch firms own 1, 000 computers.
    c. Little noise disturbed many people.

On the relevant reading, (2a) basically means that the number of boys that, individually or as a group, ate cakes is less than ten and the number of cakes eaten by a boy or a group of boys is less than twenty. This would require a rather complex modification of the compositional treatment of focused quantifiers — which goes beyond the present interest, however.

with plurals it is somewhat substandard. The following *a*-examples show the quantifier function of *ganz* (where indefinite NPs interact in scope with the universal part quantifier representing *ganz*); in the *b*-examples, by contrast, a definite NP does not contain *ganz* and therefore cannot interact in scope with an indefinite NP:[18]

(48) a. Der Lehrer gab der ganzen Klasse eine Eins.
          'The teacher gave the whole class an A.'
          (implies: individuals evaluation)
      b. Der Lehrer gab der Klasse eine Eins.
          'The teacher gave the class an A.'
          (implies: collective evaluation)
(49) a. Das ganze Wasser enthält Salz.
          (implies: salt is everywhere in the water)
          'The whole water contains salt.'
      b. Das Wasser enthält Salz.
          'The water contains salt.'
          (implies: salt is somewhere in the water)
(50) a. ? Die ganzen Häuser erhielten eine neue Farbe.
          'The whole houses got a new color.'
          (true in case every house got a different color)
      b. Die Häuser erhielten eine neue Farbe.
          'The houses got a new color.'
          (implies: the same color for every house)

Ganz is not equally acceptable with all kinds of NPs, but is subject to certain semantic selectional restrictions. For example, *ganz* generally is degraded with plural NPs such as in (50a). What matters, though, is not the syntactic category 'plural' but rather the kind of entity the plural NP refers to. This is supported by the fact that among different kinds of plural NPs, *ganz* displays different degrees of acceptability. With respect to the acceptability of *ganz* with plurals, the

---

[18] Measure adverbial constructions as in (1) show that also English *whole* may act as a true part quantifier:

(1) John wrote poems the whole night.

The whole night has the semantic characteristics of measure adverbials. Measure adverbials such as *for two hours* and *the whole night* act as universal part quantifiers ranging over the parts of the measuring entity — that is, the parts of the night in *the whole night* or the parts of two hours in *for two hours* (cf. Dowty 1979, L. Carlson 1981, Hinrichs 1985, Moltmann 1989, 1991b).
    But *whole* may also mean 'not just a part' as in (2), acting as a perspective shifter:

(2) John prefers a whole cake (to a cake cut into pieces).

following generalization holds. *Ganz* is best with plural NPs that refer to groups which constitute a natural whole — that is, groups whose members have little prominence in the relation to the whole (for example the houses in a block), and it is worst with plurals referring to groups of entities that have strong individuality themselves and where the groups referred to cannot easily be considered a natural whole. *Ganz* in the quantifier function is quite bad with groups of persons, unless the intended effect is to disregard the individuality. This can be seen in the contrast between quantification with *ganz* in (51a) and (52a) and quantification with *all* in (50b) and (51b), a universal part quantifier of the second type (cf. Section 4.4.2.):

(51) a. ?? Die ganzen Frauen haben eine Tochter.
     'The whole women have a daughter.'
   b. All the women have a daughter.
(52) a. ?? Die ganzen Studenten fanden eine Lösung.
     'The whole students found a solution.'
   b. All the students found a solution.

Significantly, *ganz* improves with groups of entities having less individuality — for example, children or animals:

(53) a. ? Die ganzen Kinder sind gekommen.
     'The whole children have come.'
   b. All the children have come.
(54) a. ? Die ganzen Bienen haben Maria gestochen.
     'The whole bees have stung Mary.'
   b. All the bees have stung Mary.

The selectional restriction governing the acceptability of *ganz* with different kinds of NPs obviously involves the notion of integrity: *ganz* as a quantifier applies preferably to entities whose integrity as wholes is more prominent than the integrity of their parts. The semantic function of *ganz* in all cases then consists in universal quantification over the parts of such wholes.

Let us turn to the second function of *ganz* as a perspective shifter. In Chapter 3, I discussed perspective shifters such as *as a teacher, as a whole, whole*, and *individual*. *Ganz* as a perspective shifter basically patterns like *whole* as an adjectival modifier in English. The function of *ganz* as a perspective shifter is shown in (55). In (55a) and (55b), *ganz* acting as a perspective shifter contrasts with overt simple part quantifiers in (55c) and (55d):

(55) a. Das ganze Bild gefiel Maria.
     'The whole picture pleased Mary.'
   b. Das ganze Bild gefiel Maria nicht.
     'The whole picture did not please Mary.'
   c. Jeder Teil des Bildes gefiel Maria.

'Every part of the picture pleased Mary.'
   d. Jeder Teil des Bildes gefiel Maria nicht.
'Every part of the picture did not please Mary.'

Other examples in which *ganz* may act as a perspective shifter are given in (56):

(56) a. Die ganze Aufregung war dem Mann unverständlich.
       'The whole agitation was incomprehensible to the man.'
     b. Die ganze Oper war ein einziger Erfolg.
       'The whole opera was a unique success.'
     c. Die ganzen Probleme haben Marias Gesundheit ruiniert.
       'The whole problems have ruined Mary's health.'

In (55a) and (55b), *ganz* may roughly have the following effect: it specifies that the totality of the parts of the picture and the way these parts are related to each other pleased Mary. Thus, *das ganze Bild* can be paraphrased as 'the picture in its totality' or 'the picture in the way its parts relate to each other'. With a mass noun as in (56a), *ganz* can mean something like 'the agitation in its full amount' or even 'the agitation in the way its subevents are connected to each other'. With a singular noun as in (56b), *ganz* means something like 'the opera in all its aspects'. Finally, with a plural such as in (56c), *ganz* can mean something like 'the problems in their full collective impact or complex interaction'. In all these readings, *ganz* means always something like 'the totality of the parts as well as the ways the parts relate to each other'. The interrelations among the parts may be more or less explicit as with singular count nouns (*das ganze Bild* 'the whole picture') or implicit as with mass and plural nouns. Implicit integrity with *ganz* usually consists in the function that a group or quantity has in relation to the relevant agent. In (56a), it is the complexity of the agitation as perceived by the man, rather than some external complexity. In (56c), *ganz* specifies the complexity of the group of problems as Mary perceives it, rather than as they may actually be.

These remarks about the semantic function of *ganz* as a perspective shifter should suffice to see the contrast with quantificational *ganz*. Other semantic phenomena involving perspective shifters were discussed in Chapter 3.

Let us return to the function of *ganz* as a quantifier, in particular, to the selectional restrictions it imposes. These restrictions are obviously related to the meaning of *ganz* as a perspective shifter. In both cases, *ganz* implies that the entity has some degree of integrity.

The implication of integrity in fact underlies the following preference scale amongst NPs with which *ganz* and APQs more generally combine. APQs are best with singular count nouns and worst with plurals, whereby mass nouns occupy an intermediate position. This preference scale reflects cross-linguistic distribution as well as language-internal degrees of acceptability. For instance, German *ganz* is only marginally acceptable with plurals, but it is fine with singular count and mass nouns. English *whole* is impossible with plurals and mass nouns, but it is fine with singular count nouns. The preference scale shows that APQs presuppose that the entities they apply to have integrity of a particular degree. Since the referents of plural and mass NPs are not explicitly specified as integrated wholes, APQs are either only acceptable if they are specified implicitly as integrated wholes, or, as in English, not acceptable at all. APQs are least acceptable with plurals, the reason being apparently that plurals have parts with strong integrity, which weakens any integrity the whole may have. The distribution of German *ganz* is governed by the explicit or implicit presence or absence of integrity; in contrast, the distribution of English *whole* and *entire* seems to be governed only by the explicit presence or absense of integrity.[19]

The implication of integrity with APQs can be related to another fact about APQs. Often, APQs have certain secondary meanings when acting as *predicates*. German *ganz* and Russian *celyj* in predicative position have the meaning 'not broken, intact'. An example from German is (57):

(57) Das Glas ist noch ganz.
'The glass is still intact.'

The meaning *ganz* has in predicative position shares with the other meanings of *ganz* a condition on the integrity of the argument.

To sum up, we have seen that adjectival generalized part quantifiers, when they act as true quantifiers, may range over the parts of an object in a generalized sense (parts of an individual, subgroups or members of a group, and subquantities of quantities), and they always involve the notion of integrated whole: first, integrity underlies the scale of acceptability of objects over whose parts adjectival part quantifiers may range; second, integrity is involved in their function as perspective shifters and in the secondary meanings they have when acting as predicates and in nominalizations.

---

[19] Interestingly, with plurals, the integrity presupposition of *ganz* cannot be satisfied by relative clauses with collective content, as in (1a), as opposed to (1b):

(1) a. ?? Die ganzen Studenten, die das Orchester darstellen, passen nicht in den Bus.
    'The whole students that form the orchestra don't fit into the bus.'
   b. Das ganze Studentenorchester paßt nicht in den Bus.
    'The whole student orchestra does not fit into the bus.'

This can be related to the fact that relative clauses do not block the accessibility of the part structure of an argument, as discussed in Chapter 3. The reason given there — that relative clauses involve a situation different from the reference situation of the NP can be invoked here as well. The relative clause in (1a) specifies integrity in a situation different from the reference situation. By contrast, the adjectival modifier *ganz* in (1b) must apply to the reference situation.

4.4.2. Generalized part quantifiers of the type *all*-definite NP

The second type of generalized part quantifier differs from the first type mainly in the role integrity plays in selectional restrictions. Roughly, integrity plays an opposite role in the second type of part quantifier, which exhibits the opposite scale of acceptability amongst the part structures of entities it may apply to.

The second kind of generalized part quantifier appears exclusively in the predeterminer position of a definite NP. Let me call it therefore *pre-NP part quantifier* (abbreviated *PPQ*). It is found, for instance, in Italian (*tutto*), French (*tous*), and Russian (*ves'*). English *all* is a more restricted version.[20]

Let me illustrate the basic properties of PPQs with Italian *tutto*. *Tutto* combines with definite singular count, plural, and mass NPs:

(58) a. Tutta la superficie e coperta di fiori.
          'All the surface is covered with flowers.'
      b. Tutti i bambini sono arrivati.
          'All the children have arrived.'
      c. Tutta l'acqua contiene sale.
          'All the water contains salt.'

Again, like APQs, PPQs exhibit a preference scale, cross-linguistically and language-internally, with regard to the kinds of NPs they combine with. The preference scale of PPQs is inverse to the one of APQs in that PPQs prefer plural and mass NPs over singular count NPs. For instance, in English, the PPQ *all* can modify definite plural and mass NPs, but not definite singular count NPs. In languages such as Italian, where PPQs can attach to singular count NPs, PPQs are restricted to those singular count NPs that refer to entities with weak integrity. *Tutto* is acceptable, for instance, with *superficie*, as in (58a). But it is bad with NPs that refer to entities with strong integrity or individuality. For instance, *tutto l'uomo* 'all the man' is barely acceptable. By contrast, APQs are fine in such cases (such as German *der ganze Mensch* 'the whole man'). Thus, in contrast to APQs, PPQs generally lack the presupposition of integrity. Instead, PPQs seem to presuppose that an entity has a sufficiently weak degree of integrity.

The presupposition of the lack of integrity with PPQs may in some languages — English, for instance — be just a historical motivation for a syntactic restriction of PPQs to plural and mass NPs. But in other languages, such as Italian, it obviously is a semantic selectional restriction.[21]

---

[20] The function of *all* as a general part quantifier has been noted by L. Carlson (1981), who also observed the importance of context-dependent individuation of part strucures in this respect.

[21] The restriction may be considered an instance of the Accessibility Requirement. Universal part quantification by PPQs, being an operation involving the parts of an argument, should require that the argument have an accessible part structure. The

We have seen how integrity plays a role in selectional requirements of part quantifiers in two different ways: the first type of generalized part quantifier prefers entities that have integrity, whereas the second prefers entities that lack integrity. This, again, gives support to the view that the notion of integrated whole plays a fundamental role in natural language semantics.

Generalized part quantifiers involve situated part structures in the same way that part-structure-specific semantic selection, discussed in Chapter 3, does. In particular, the notion of integrated whole plays exactly the same role in part structures for the purpose of part quantification as it does for the purpose of part-structure-specific semantic selection. Also, generalized part quantifiers support the view that the notion of part is a uniform relation applying to all three domains of entities. Generalized part quantifiers range over the parts of an entity, regardless of whether this entity is an individual, a group, or a quantity. Hence it is more plausible that they involve one and the same semantic operation than a family of semantic operations for distinct part relations. Also, the restrictions on the kind of entity that APQs and PPQs may impose often concern the presupposition of integrity independently of the distinction between individuals, groups, and quantities.

Generalized part quantifiers support the role of integrity in situated part structures as discussed in Chapter 1. To take the simplest case, generalized part quantifiers applied to a plural NP may range over the members of the group only. Thus, group members, but not parts of group members, count as the parts of a group. This is due to the fact that group members are integrated wholes and thus block the transitivity of the part relation. Generalized part quantifiers also show that the semantically relevant part relation is not generally closed under sum formation. APQs and PPQs when combined with mass NPs require the predicate to be homogeneous; but when combined with plurals, they allow for heterogeneous predicates. The predicate must be homogeneous also if the part quantifier applies to a singular count NP whose referent has a homogeneous part structure. Consider the following data from German, Italian, and English:

Part quantification with singular count and mass NPs:
(59) a. Auf dem ganzen Boden lagen Teppiche.
   'On the whole floor lay carpets.'
  b. # Auf dem ganzen Boden lag ein Teppich.
   'On the whole floor lay a carpet.'
(60) a. Das ganze Wasser enthält Salz.
   'The whole water contains salt.'
  b. # Das ganze Wasser enthält zwei Gramm Salz / das Salz.
   'The whole water contains two grams of salt / the salt.'
(61) Tutta la superficie e coperta di fiori / # un fiore / # dieci fiori.

Accessibility Requirement, though, would require a much weaker degree of accessibility with PPQs than in the other cases discussed in Chapter 2, because it does not exclude certain singular count nouns (at least in languages like Italian).

'All the surface is covered with flowers / a flower / ten flowers.'
(62) All the water contains salt / # two grams of salt / # the salt.

Part quantification with plurals:
(63) Die ganzen Probleme haben eine Lösung.
       'The whole problems have a solution.'
(64) Tutti gli studenti hanno trovato un errore diverso.
       'All the students have found a different mistake.'

As in the case of part quantifiers with mass NPs, the fact that part
quantifiers with singular count NPs impose the Homogeneity Requirement
follows from the homogeneity of the part structure of the relevant individuals.
The Homogeneity Requirement is enforced whenever a quantifier ranges over a
homogeneous domain. The sum of two parts of a surface is a natural part of the
surface, and so for a part of a part of the surface.

(63) and (64) show that part quantifiers with plurals do not require the
predicate to be homogeneous. The property of having a solution and the
property of having found a mistake are certainly not homogeneous properties.
The absence of the Homogeneity Requirement for part quantifiers with plurals
corresponds to the absence of the Homogeneity Requirement for universal
quantification with plurals, as discussed in Section 1; and the two cases are due
to the same principle — namely, the Restriction on situated sum formation of
Chapter 1.

Let us turn to the formal semantic analysis for sentences with generalized
part quantifiers. The first sentence in (62), *all the water contains salt*, will have
the denotation in (65):

(65) $\lambda s[\{x \mid x <_s ' sum_{<s}' (\{x' \mid [water]^S{}'(x') = 1\})\} \subseteq$
       $\{x \mid (\exists e)(\exists y)([salt]^{S}{}''(y) = 1 \,\&\, [contain]^S(e, x, y) = 1)\}]$

Compositionally, such sentence meanings will be based on syntactic relations
and semantic operations as in (66) (which is restricted to quantified subjects of
intransitive predicates):

(66) a. *The syntactic relation for part quantification*
         Let f and g be constituents in a syntactic structure S.
         $<f, g> \in$ PART-QUANT(S) iff $f = all$ and g a definite NP preceded
         by f in S.
      b. *The semantic operation for universal part quantification*
         For an entity x and a situation s',
         $part\text{-}quant(<\varnothing, <x, s'>> = \lambda P \lambda s[\{x' \mid x' <_s' x\} \subseteq \{x' \mid P^S(x', s')$
         $= 1\}]$

Here, unlike in Chapter 2, the definite NP is treated simply as a referential expression referring to the unique or maximal entity in its extension, and *all* is treated syncategorematically with the empty set as its denotation (cf. Chapter 2).

4.4.3. Further properties of generalized part quantifiers

In this section, I will discuss a number of further phenomena with universal generalized part quantifiers which can be explained on the basis of (66).

As with direct quantification over groups and quantifiers discussed in Section 3.4.1., there are certain ways in which the integrity of parts can be specified independently of the content of singular count nouns, allowing subgroups or subquantities to be integrated wholes. First, relational nouns may characterize subgroups as *R*-integrated wholes. The quantification domain of *all* in (67a) consists of maximal groups of people who are enemies of each other. Similarly, the domain of *all* in (67b) consists of groups that are R-integrated wholes on the basis of the relation 'has a child with':

(67) a. All the enemies sat in front of each other.
b. All the parents agreed to take their child out of school.

A second way of defining integrated wholes is by relative clauses with relational or collective content. Again, such relative clauses may characterize certain subgroups as well as certain subquantities as *R*-integrated wholes, as in (68) and (69):

(68) a. All the files that belonged together were put into the same container.
b. All the children that played together were siblings.
(69) All the jewelry that was in the same box had the same color.

All in (68a) ranges over maximal groups of files that belong together, *all* in (68b) ranges over maximal subgroups of children that played together, and *all* in (69) ranges over maximal quantities of jewelry that was in one box.

Subgroups or subquantities may also receive integrity in the relevant situation just on the basis of the situational context, as in (70) (though not all speakers accept examples with mass nouns such as (70b)):

(70) a. All the guests danced together.
(situation: formal party)
b. All the gold had two grams of copper in it.
(situation: gold in the form of bars)

Such a context may also be suggested or required by the predicate, as in the examples in (71):

(71) a. All the guests are dancing a tango.
      b. All the sugar (on this table) is cubic. (Bunt 1985)

Another phenomenon with generalized part quantifiers concerns a difference between plural part quantifiers and definite plurals. Plural part quantifiers imply a stronger *degree of participation* in the described event than definite plurals. This was noted by Link (1987) with the examples in (72). A similar contrast is given in (73):

(72) a. All the children destroyed the piano.
      b. The children destroyed the piano.
(73) a. All the men gathered in the yard.
      b. The men gathered in the yard.

Example (72a) carries the implicature that every child was involved in the destruction; (72b), by contrast, is fine with some of the children not being involved in the destruction of the piano. Example (73a) carries the implicature that every man was involved in the gathering; (73b) allows for more exceptions.

Thus, the relative amount of exceptions permitted by a predicate applying to a group is lower with universal plural quantifiers than with definite NPs. This can be traced to a condition that *all* generally ranges not only over the whole group but also over (a certain number of) subgroups. Furthermore, it is a plausible condition that if the predicate *gather* holds of a group, then there is a certain amount of admissible exceptions relative to the size of this group. If *all* in (73a) ranges over subgroups, then fewer exceptions are allowed than for the whole group, and thus the number of admissible exceptions for the truth of (73a) is automatically reduced. The predicate *gathered in the yard* is predicated in (73b) only of the whole group and therefore allows for a greater number of exceptions than (73a).

There is an empirical difference between part quantification with plurals and universal quantification with singular count nouns. Strictly heterogeneous predicates are considered slightly less acceptable in the first case than in the second. This is seen in the contrast between (74a) and (74b):

(74) a. ? All the students have discovered a different mistake.
      b. Each student has discovered a different mistake.

Thus, quantification over individuals with plural part quantifers, although not excluded, is worse than with singular count quantifiers. This can be traced to a pragmatically motivated principle that, in addition to individuals, plural quantifiers should range over subgroups:

(75) If a speaker uses a plural part quantifier rather than a singular
      quantifier, then he or she suggests that the quantification domain does
      not consist only of individuals.

The principle in (75) can be explained, in a Gricean fashion, by the fact that the speaker must have some reason to use a plural quantifier rather than the more informative singular count quantifier, which may range only over individuals.

Another interesting phenomenon with part quantifiers consists in a difference between two types of collective predicates with quantified plural NPs. Collective predicates that describe the *formation* of groups or units such as *come together* or *form a circle* (*unit-creating predicates*) allow for plural and mass quantifiers, as in (76a) and (77a); but predicates that describe the *dissolution* of groups or units such as *disperse* or *separate* (*unit-dissolving predicates*) disallow plural and mass quantifiers, as in (76b) and (77b). Both kinds of predicates, though, are equally good with definite NPs, as seen in (76c) and (77c):

(76) a. All the children came together / formed a circle.
     b. # All the children dispersed / went apart.
     c. The children dispersed / went apart.
(77) a. All the wax merged.
     b. # All the wax separated.
     c. The wax separated.

Using quantifiers ranging over the parts of a group or quantity requires the group or quantity to be divided into parts in the relevant context. A predicate that describes the dissolution of a group or quantity as a unit, however, requires that the group or quantity not be divided into parts in the reference situation. In the reference situation, it must be a unit, even though it ceases to be a unit in the described situation. Thus, the domain of the reference situation for the quantified NPs in (76b) and (77b) should contain only the entire group or quantity, but not their parts. Hence nonvacuous part quantification is impossible. In contrast to unit-dissolving predicates, unit-creating predicates allow for reference situations in which the entity is divided into subgroups or subquantities. These subgroups or subquantities have to merge into one unit only in the described situation. Hence nonvacuous quantification over parts is possible, as in (76a) and (77a).

4.5. *Each other, same/different*, and part quantification

Each other and *same/different* are relevant in the present context for two reasons.[22] First, *each other* and *same/different* (in a particular construction) involve universal quantification over parts in the generalized sense. In the case of *each other*, the part quantifier ranges over the parts of the referent of the antecedent NP; in the case of *same/different* (in the relevant construction), it

---

[22] The following is, to some extent, a condensed presentation of Moltmann (1992b), which also contains relevant references on the issue.

ranges over the parts of an event. We will see that the constructions with *each other* and *same/different* involve the same conditions on part structures as the other constructions with universal part quantification discussed in the previous sections. The second respect in which the constructions with *each other* and with *same/different* are relevant consists in the part-structure-specific selectional requirements to which these constructions are subject.

4.5.1. Reciprocals and quantification over parts

Each other involves quantification over parts in the generalized sense, rather than over group members. This can be seen by contrasting *each other* with the *each-the other*-construction in (78):

(78) The women each admire the other.

The *each-the other*-construction clearly involves quantification over group members as in the analysis in (79), where < is to be taken as the relation 'is group member of' and 'other₁' is a three-place relation that holds among x, y and z iff x and y are group members of z and $x \neq z$:[23]

(79) $(\forall x)(x < z \rightarrow (\forall y)(\text{other}(x, y, z) \rightarrow \text{admire(the women}, y)))$

Each other, by contrast, does not necessarily involve quantification over group members, but rather involves quantification over the parts of a group in the generalized sense, parts which may be either subgroups or group members. In this respect, it patterns with plural part quantifiers. Moreover, *each other*, unlike *each-the other*, does not require that every group member stands in the relevant relation to every other group member, and also it allows for collective predication. Consider the contrast between (80a) and (80b):

(80) a. The students communicate with each other.
     b. The students each communicate with the other.

Example (80a) may be true if certain students do not communicate with some other students; but in this situation, (80b) is clearly false. Furthermore, (80b) may be true in a situation in which the students are partitioned into groups and the communication takes place among the groups, rather than among individual students.[24] Such examples show that reciprocals may involve subgroups instead of individuals.

---

[23] This actually is the analysis of the *each other*-construction given in Heim/Lasnik/May (1991).

[24] Examples of this sort have been noted and discussed by Lasnik/Fiengo (1973), Langendoen (1978), Higginbotham (1981), and Moltmann (1990b, 1992b).

For *each other,* the analysis in (79) should be modified by replacing '<' by the generalized, non-transitive part relation $<_s$ and by treating 'other₂' as a predicate that holds among x, y, and z iff x and y are parts of z in the sense of $<_s$ and different from each other (relative to a situation s). So the meaning of (80a) should be as in (81):

(81) $\lambda s[(\forall x')(x' <_s \, sum_{<_s} \, '(\{x \mid [students]^{s'}(x) = 1)\}) \to$
$(\forall y)(other_2(x', y, z, s') \to (\exists e)[communicate]^s(e, x', y) = 1))]$

Example (81) states that, for any relevant part x' of the students, there is another relevant part y such that an act of communication involves x' and y. The analysis of reciprocal sentences in (81) is not yet quite correct, though in ways that need not concern us (cf. Moltmann 1990b, 1992b).

The parts that *each other* quantifies over are specified in the familiar ways. Moreover, as we have seen in Chapter 3, *each other* imposes the Integrated Parts Requirement, requiring the parts of the antecedent group to be integrated wholes. Let us recall the various ways of describing an entity with integrated parts other than by using simple plurals. One way is to specify the parts as maximal entities satisfying the conjuncts of a conjoined plural or mass NP or a conjoined adjectival phrase, as in (82a), (82b), (82c), and (82d), respectively. Another way is on the basis of relational nouns, which may specify subgroups as integrated wholes, as in (82e). Finally, parts may be specified as integrated wholes by a relation to independent wholes, as with the plural modifiers in (82f):

(82) a. The Leitches and the Latches hate each other. (Link 1983)
b. The wine and the vinegar resemble each other.
c. The people here and there hate each other.
d. The water in the tub and in the pool resemble each other.
e. Sue's grandparents hate each other.
f. The jewelry of the various women resemble each other.

Example (82e) has a reading on which Sue's maternal grandparents hate Sue's paternal grandparents; in this case, the universal part quantifier associated with *each other* ranges over groups of elements connected with each other by the relation 'has a child with'. A case in which subgroups are formed in the situational context was already given in (80a).

4.5.2. *Same/Different*, its semantic antecedent, and the part structure of its antecedent

Same/different in a certain function involves universal quantification over the parts of an event. In order to identify this function, it is useful to first list the main constructions in which *same/different* may act. First, *same/different* has an indexical reading, as in (83):

(83) John saw the same tree / a different tree.

Second, *same/different* appears in comparatives, as in (84a), and in relative identity statements, as in (84b):

(84) a. John found the same solution as Mary.
       b. This the same man that we saw ten years before.

I disregard these two readings in the following.

Third, *same/different* may receive a bound interpretation with a quantified antecedent such as a quantified singular count NP, as in (85a), and a quantified mass NP, as in (85b):

(85) a. Everyone saw the same tree / a different tree.
       b. All the furniture is of the same color / of different colors.

Finally, *same/different* may, in a certain way, relate to a plural NP such as *John and Mary* in (86):

(86) John and Mary found the same solution / different solutions.

The semantic function of *same/different* in (86) can be called the *internal reading* following Carlson (1987), who made important observations about this construction. This function is the relevant one for our discussion, but the third function is also of interest.

The first question that arises with the internal reading of *same/different* is, What is the 'antecedent' of *same/different*? In (86), a plural NP seems to be the antecedent. But a broader range of data, first noted by Carlson (1987) and further discussed in Moltmann (1992b), shows that this is not the right generalization. The following examples display the full range of licensing environments for the internal reading of *same/different*: conjoined NPs and plurals as in (87), conjoined verbs and VPs as in (88), and conjoined adverbials as in (89):

(87) a. John and Mary saw the same picture.
       b. The students saw the same picture.
(88) a. The same man / Different men came and left.
       b. John praised and criticized the same person.
       c. The same man / Different men helped Mary and ruined John.
(89) a. The same child slept in the bed and on the floor.
       b. John did different tasks eagerly and grudgingly. (Carlson 1987)
       c. John played the same sonata on his violin and on his piano.

Same and *different* in the examples in (88) and (89) apparently relate not to a group participant but to a group event. In (88a), *same* and *different* compare the men that were involved in the two parts of a complex event, an event consisting in a subevent of coming and a subevent of leaving. In (88b), they compare the persons involved in the two parts of a complex action by John, an action consisting of an act of praising and an act of criticizing. In (88c), they compare the men that are the agents of one of the parts of a complex action (an action consisting of a subaction of helping Mary and a subaction of ruining John). In the examples in (89), again, the participants of a complex event are compared. In (89a), *same* compares the children engaged in the two parts of a complex event consisting of sleeping in the bed and sleeping on the floor. In (89b), the complex event consists of acts that John did eagerly and acts that he did grudgingly. In (89c), it consists of activities of John's playing on his violin and John's playing on his piano.

The examples in (87)–(89) can be reinterpreted in the following way: *same/different* does not compare things related to John and Mary or the members of the group of students, but rather things related to the parts of a complex event that is distributively related to John and Mary or to the individual students. This was suggested by Carlson (1987), and it is in accordance with the account of distributivity given in Chapter 2. (Recall that, according to that account, an event that is related to a group participant may consist of subevents each of which is related to group members or subgroups of the participants by the relation denoted by the verb.) More generally, an event with a group participant (for instance the group consisting of John and Mary) may consist of parts that are each related to a different part of the participant (for instance a part that is related to John and another part that is related to Mary). Thus, in (87a), *same* compares the pictures that are the object of a complex event of seeing (an event, one of whose parts is a perception by John, the other one a perception by Mary). In (87b), the complex event consists of the acts of seeing by the various students. So *same/different* in the internal reading can be treated in such a way that it always relates to the event argument of the verb.

The licensing environments of the internal reading of *same/different* (plural arguments, conjoined verbs or VPs, and conjoined adverbials) have one thing in common: they all specify an event argument as a group event. *Same/different* involves a simple universal quantifier ranging over the parts of the relevant event: the various licensing conditions on the internal reading of *same/different* represent exactly the ways in which parts of an entity x can be specified as integrated wholes and thus as the only parts of x.

In the first environment (conjoined or plural NPs), the subevents are related to different parts of the participant. Since this relation is a one-to-one mapping from subevents to participant parts and the participant parts are themselves integrated wholes, the subevents may count as integrated parts according to the principle of Integrating Parts on the Basis of Relations introduced in Chapter 3. Hence, these subevents may count as the only parts of the event. In the second environment (conjoined verbs or verb phrases), subevents that are maximal events satisfying the event concept expressed by the verbs or the VPs count as *FF*-integrated wholes.

As in the case of the satisfaction of Integrated Parts Requirement with NPs discussed in Chapter 2, maximality is crucial. If the subevents are not maximal

— for instance, if the argument NP quantifies over several participants, as in (90) — the internal reading is harder to get:

(90) a. Everybody read the same book / different books in English and in French.
   b. Everybody created and solved the same problem.

In the only nonindexical interpretation for *same/different* in (90a, b), *everybody* acts as a quantified antecedent. It is difficult to get a reading of (90a) in which books written in English and written in French are compared. As the absence of an internal reading for (90b) shows, this holds even for telic verbs such as *create* and *solve*.[25]

In the third licensing environment (conjoined adverbials), the same principle applies as for conjoined verbs or VPs. In fact, here we have a case exactly parallel to the determination of integrated parts of quantities by conjoined modifiers discussed in Chapter 3.

The internal reading of *same/different* can be analyzed in a way parallel to the analysis of *each other*, as roughly in (91) for (87a):

(91) $\lambda s[(\exists x)([see]^S(e, sum_{<_S}'(\{John, Mary\}), x) = 1 \ \& \ (\forall e')(\forall e'')(e' <_S e$
   $\& \ e'' <_S e \ \& \ e' \neq e'' \rightarrow (\forall x')(\forall x'')(x' <_S '' x \ \& \ x'' <_S '' x$
   $\& \ (\exists y')(\exists y'')(y' <_S ' sum_{<_S}'(\{John, Mary\}) \ \& \ y'' <_S '$
   $sum_{<_S}'(\{John, Mary\}) \ \& \ [see]^S(e', y', x') = 1 \ \& \ [see]^S(e', y'', x'')$
   $= 1) \rightarrow x' = x'')))]$

The denotation in (91) holds of situations in which there is an event *e* of seeing pictures by John and Mary such that for any two distinct proper parts *e'* and *e''* of *e*, the part of the pictures seen in *e'* (by a part of John and Mary) is the same as the part of the pictures seen in *e''* (by a part of John and Mary). Since John and Mary form a group argument of *see*, the event argument of *see* in (87a) may be a group event whose parts have the same or different objects.

An analysis of this sort will also account for the internal reading of *same/different* licensed by conjoined adverbials, verbs, or VPs. Here conjoined adverbials, verbs, and VPs have to be construed as predicates that hold of group events. For instance, *come and leave* will be the predicate that holds of a pair of an event *e* and a participant *x* iff *e* consists of two parts *e'* and *e''* such that *e'* is a coming by *x* and *e''* a leaving by *x*. (See also Chapter 3.) Example (88a) (with *different men*) then has the denotation in (92), which is exactly parallel to (91):[26]

---

[25] This suggests again that telic verbs do not classify with singular count nouns (which characterize an entity as an integrated whole) but rather with mass nouns, as discussed in Chapter 7.

[26] An explicit compositional analysis of sentences with *same/different* in the internal reading is given in Moltmann (1992b).

(92) $\lambda s[(\exists x)([men]^s{}'(x) = 1 \ \& \ [come\ and\ leave]^s(e, x) = 1$
      $\& \ (\forall e')(\forall e'')(e' <_s e \ \& \ e'' <_s e \ \& \ e' \neq e'' \ \& \ (\forall x')(\forall x'')(x' <_s' x$
      $\& \ x'' <_s' x \ \& \ [come\ and\ leave]^s(e', x') = 1 \ \& \ [come\ and\ leave]^s(e'',$
      $x'') = 1 \rightarrow x' = x'')))]^{27}$

Let us now turn to the issue of whether reciprocals and *same/different* impose part-structure-sensitive semantic selectional requirements. Already in Chapter 3, we have seen that *each other* is subject to the Accessibility Requirement and the Integrated Parts Requirement. What about *same/different*? It is expected that *same/different* in the internal reading requires the relevant event to have an accessible part structure, since it quantifies over the parts of the event. Interestingly, this expectation does not quite seem to be borne out. The following examples allow for an internal reading of *same/different*, even though the verb is telic and thus should block accessibility (since telic verbs seem to clearly characterize events as integrated wholes):

(93) a. John built the house under different circumstances.
      b. John wrote the book with the same pencil / with different pencils.
      c. During his illness, John read the same book / different books.
      d. John saw different people when he walked home.

However, as we shall see in Chapter 7, verbs, whether they are telic or not, behave like mass nouns in various respects, and so may not characterize an event as an integrated whole in the relevant sense.[28]

Also it appears that *same/different* does not have to impose the Integrated Parts Requirement, at least not in a strong sense. The events described in the sentences in (93) at least do not have parts with strong integrity. A related phenomenon, already mentioned, is that *same/different* with a quantified antecedent can take mass NPs as antecedents, which do not satisfy the Integrated

---

[27] Note that often the relation between the event and the entities that are compared is not simply a thematic relation expressed by some verb, but is more complex — for instance, in (1):

(1) John and Mary said that different cities were attacked.

In (1), the relation involved in the comparison expressed by *same* is roughly the relation that holds between an event *e* and an entity *x* if *e* is a saying (by John or Mary) that *x* was attacked.

[28] Also the possibility of conjoining telic event predicates to form concepts of group events indicates the mass status of verbs. As will be discussed in Chapter 7, singular count nouns cannot be conjoined to yield group predicates — they only allow for appositional conjunction (as in *the secretary and lover of John*). Only plural and mass nouns can be conjoined to yield predicates of entities that are composed of different kinds of individuals or masses, as in *the women and children* and *the bread and wine*.

Parts Requirement. This was explained in Chapter 3 by the fact that in contrast to *each other*, *same/different* involves not a direct, but only an indirect, comparison of the parts of the semantic antecedent.

5

Metrical and Other Lexical Specifications of Part Structures

On the information-based account of the mass-count distinction, singular count, plural, and mass nouns differ in the manner in which the properties they express relate to parts and wholes. Singular count, plural, and mass nouns describe their referents with different part structures: referents of singular count NPs are described as integrated wholes; referents of plurals, as entities composed of integrated wholes; referents of mass NPs as entities that neither are integrated wholes nor have parts that are integrated wholes. But the semantic conditions associated with the categories 'mass', 'count', 'singular', and 'plural' do not constitute the only way of specifying particular types of part structure. In the previous two chapters, we saw various ways in which part structures may be specified independently of the mass-count distinction — namely, by certain types of constructions. In particular, we saw that entities could be described as having integrated parts even with mass nouns. Hence, even though the syntactic mass-count distinction implies a semantic mass-count distinction, the converse does not hold.

The following question now arises: if part structures can be specified by particular constructions independently of the mass-count distinction, are there also expressions that, independently of the categories 'singular count', 'plural', and 'mass', carry part-structure-specific information? This chapter shows that this is in fact the case. I will discuss two kinds of lexical words that are of the relevant sort: [1] frequency expressions and a certain German metrical determiner and [2] German vague count quantifiers. Both classes of expressions specify part structures with integrated parts, but apply to both mass and count nouns and so classify as plural expressions in the semantic, though not in the syntactic, sense.

In the following, I will first discuss frequency expressions in English, showing that they can function as part-structure attributes. In this function, they specify that an event consists of parts that are separated in time. I will then come to the German metrical determiner, arguing that it differs from frequency expressions only in that it has a more general lexical meaning, expressing separation among parts in some unspecified dimension, not necessarily in time. Finally, I will show that the German vague count quantifiers exhibit a behavior very similar to metrical determiners, which, as I will argue, should also be traced to a particular part-structure-related lexical meaning.

5.1. The lexical meaning of frequency expressions

5.1.1. Frequency expressions as part-structure attributes

The goal of this section is to show that the lexical meanings of frequency expressions such as *frequent(ly)* and *rare(ly)* can be considered properties of part structures — namely, properties of events that imply that the event parts are separated in time. I will restrict the discussion of the lexical meaning of frequency expressions to *frequent(ly)* and *rare(ly)*, though nothing bears on the generality of the point.

The lexical meaning of frequency expressions is most transparent when frequency expressions act as part-structure attributes where they simply ascribe a property to an entity regarding its part structure. But first let me distinguish between different functions in which frequency expressions may be used.

Adjectival frequency expressions such as *frequent(ly)* and *rare(ly)* can function semantically as *event quantifiers* and as *event predicates*. The event-quantifier function is illustrated in (1):

(1) John frequently / rarely wrote a story.

Frequently and *rarely* in (1) quantify over events of John's writing a story, but do not count parts or subevents of an event described as John's writing a story. In this sense, they do not act as event predicates.

As adverbials, frequency expressions can have only the event-quantifier interpretation. The event-quantifier interpretation is also the only interpretation available when frequency expressions modify a certain type of nominalization — namely, a nominalization that preserves the argument structure of the verb, as in (2):

(2) a. The frequent accusation of Mary annoyed John.
b. The frequent transmission of world news was appreciated.

In (2a) and (2b), *accusation* and *transmission* preserve the object argument position from the argument structure of the corresponding verbs. Nominalizations of this sort differ in various ways from nominalizations that do not preserve the argument structure of the verb (cf. Grimshaw 1990). The event-quantifier function is impossible when a frequency attribute modifies an underived noun or a deverbal nominalization that does not preserve the argument structure of the verb. This is seen in the examples in (3), which contain an underived noun (3a, b) or a nominalization in which arguments of the corresponding verbs are missing (3c, d):

(3) a. # John's frequent journey took him all over Europe.
b. # That frequent event amazed Mary.

    c. # The frequent accusation annoys John.
    d. # The frequent transmission was appreciated.

Frequent in the examples in (3) is excluded because *frequent* here must act as an event predicate. It can act as an event predicate modifying a count noun only if the noun is in the plural (a restriction to which I will come back later). Only then can *frequent* properly apply as a part-structure predicate to a group and count its members. The event-predicate function of frequency expressions is illustrated in (4):[1]

---

[1] There are some differences between frequency adjectives and other, nonnumerical adjectives which seem to challenge the analysis of frequency expressions as part-structure attributes. First, as was pointed out to me by Barry Schein, frequency adjectives differ from other adjectives in that they may not occur in predicative position when the subject refers to a particular group of events:

    (1) a. # In Mary's speech, these allusions to John's past were frequent.
         b. # Those car accidents last year were frequent / rare.

Second, frequency expressions may occur only as nonrestrictive adjectives. Like other nonrestrictive relative clauses, as in (2a), relative clauses with frequency predicates may not be extraposed, as seen in (2b) (cf. Guéron 1980, who attributes this to the Name Constraint of May 1977):

    (2) a. # John *e* came [who I know very well].
         b. # Mary pointed out the car accidents *e* in her speech [which were frequent].

Moreover, frequency adjectives cannot be used contrastively:

    (3) # The frequent initiatives were better than the rare initiatives.

These observations could be taken as arguments that frequency adjectives are not predicates of groups of events in the way that adjectives like *recent* are predicates of events. But if this were so, then also quantifiers like *many* and *hundred* should not be treated as group predicates when they act as attributes, rather than true quantifiers, as in (4):

    (4) The hundred men / Many men gathered in the hall.

Numerical expressions like *many* and *hundred* pattern exactly the same as frequency expressions. Example (5a) shows that they are bad in predicative position, and (5b) and (5c) that they may not act as restrictive modifiers:

    (5) a. ?? The guests were hundred.
         b. # Those children played a game who were ten.
         c. # The two children are nicer than the three children.

Thus, the inability of frequency adjectives to occur in predicative position and to act as restrictive modifiers seems to be a general property of group predicates with numerical lexical meaning and not a peculiarity of frequency expressions. Then, of course, an explanation is needed for the special behavior of numerical expressions in general.

(4) a. These frequent changes are bad for John's health.
     b. The frequent / rare games were organized by this company.
     c. The frequent transmissions cost too much.

Frequent and *rare* are possible in (4) as event predicates because the head noun is plural, in which case it denotes a set of groups of events rather than a set of single events. *Frequent* and *rare* can apply to plural nouns since, intuitively, they express properties of event groups. *Frequent*, in first approximation, expresses the property that holds of an event group *e* if *e* has 'many' subevents, and *rare* expresses the property that holds of an event group *e* if *e* has 'few' subevents.[2]

Often, though, *frequent* does not count specific events, but rather specifies that events of a certain type occur with a certain regularity. (Examples (4a) and (4c) plausibly have such a reading.) For the time being, and in particular for the analysis that I will develop, though, I will pretend that the paraphrase I have just given is adequate.

I will present an analysis of frequency *quantifiers* only in Chapter 7. Given this analysis, the semantic relation between frequency expressions that act as event

---

[2] There is one exception to the generalization that frequency adjectives may not modify singular count nouns. Frequency adjectives may modify generic singular count nouns — for instance, kind-denoting nouns, as in (1a) and (1b), and also, arguably, in (1c):

(1) a. This is a rare kind of flower.
     b. The Siamese cat is rare.
     c. This mistake is frequent / a frequent mistake.

This mistake in (1c) sounds more like an NP denoting an event type than an NP denoting a concrete event. Thus, it should be classified as a generic NP. Perhaps, frequency expressions may, derivatively, apply to kinds and in those cases count instantiations of kinds, rather than group members.

Another case in which a frequency adjective modifies a singular count noun is (2), discussed in Stump (1979):

(2) An occasional cup of coffee helps keep John awake.

Sentences of this sort can be paraphrased by sentences with frequency adverbials as in (3):

(3) Occasionally, a cup of coffee helps keep John awake.

The examples that I discuss neither involve kinds nor do they contain frequency expressions acting as adverbials. For instance, there is no way to paraphrase (4) adverbially:

(4) The frequent games were organized by this company.

Furthermore, it is impossible to understand (4) as a claim about a kind. In (4), *frequent* can only be a predicate of event groups.

quantifiers and frequency expressions that act as event predicates is as follows. Frequency expressions in the two functions have the same lexical meaning, a property of event groups, but they differ in their role in the sentence meaning. When frequency expressions act as event predicates, the event property is predicated of an event referent of an NP, whereas when they act as event quantifiers, also quantification over the members of the event group takes place in the sentence meaning.

5.1.2. The lexical meaning of frequency expressions as a part-structure property

Let me now turn to the precise formulation of the lexical meaning of frequency expressions. The most important observation in this respect is that predicative frequency expressions may modify not only plural count nouns but also mass nouns. This is seen in the following *b*-examples (where the mass status of the nouns involved is seen in the choices of determiners in the *a*-sentences and the fact that with frequency modifiers they still take singular agreement):

(5) a. Mary heard little / not too much laughter / * many laughters.
     b. Mary heard frequent laughter.
(6) a. Too much explaining / * A lot of explainings is (are) unnecessary.
     b. Frequent explaining is (* are) advisable if you want your students to understand.
(7) a. Mary got lazy because of too much sunshine / * many sunshines.
     b. Mary was impressed by the frequent sunshine.
(8) a. A lot of drinking / Too much drinking is bad for one's health.
     b. Frequent drinking is (* are) bad for one's health.

The fact that frequency expressions are compatible with mass nouns shows that even though the entity frequency expressions apply to must have a countable or group-like part structure, the condition on the applicability of frequency expressions must itself be independent of the syntactic mass-count distinction. It is only the specific lexical meaning of frequency expressions that implies that an entity must have a countable or group-like part structure. Thus, an entity may have such a part structure independently of whether it is a referent of a plural or a mass noun. But this means that frequency expressions as event predicates must have a lexical meaning that covers both a property of groups and a property of quantities.

Let me first characterize the lexical meaning of *frequent(ly)* and *rare(ly)* as properties of groups and then generalize it to frequency expressions applying to quantities. *Frequent(ly)* as an event-group predicate is similar in meaning to the group predicate *many* (cf. Chapter 4): it specifies that an event group has more members than a given standard or expectation value. In *the frequent deaths*, the numerical specification of *frequent* depends entirely on the circumstances: a certain number of deaths may be frequent in some circumstances, but not in others. However, *frequent* differs from *many* in one crucial respect. Compare (9a) with (9b):

(9) a. # Mary had her frequent inspirations all at the same time.
     b. Mary had her many inspirations all at the same time.

The contrast between (9a) and (9b) shows that *the frequent inspirations* differs semantically from *the many inspirations* in that it may not refer to a group of inspirations that happened all at the same time. *Frequent* implies that the members of the event group have some temporal distance from each other. It is the condition of temporal distance between group members that distinguishes *frequent(ly)* from *many* in lexical meaning. Thus, the lexical meaning of *frequent(ly)* consists in the property informally given in (10):

(10) $\lambda x[x$ has many members and x has only members separated in time]

In contrast to *frequent(ly), many* holds of a group x just in case x has many members.

If the lexical condition of temporal distance between group members is generalized as temporal distance between parts, the same lexical meaning may apply to quantities as well. *Frequent* in *the frequent singing* then specifies that the singing consists of parts that all have a minimal temporal distance from each other and that the cardinality of these parts exceeds a given standard or expectation value. Even though the parts of quantities *per se* are not countable the way group members are, the condition of temporal distance between parts will specify the parts of a quantity as countable. This is because, generally, only a relatively small number of subquantities of a quantity will be specified as being temporally separated and thus as the only situated parts of the quantity.

Note that the same difference between *frequent* and *many* above shows up between *frequent* and the quantity attributes *much* and *a lot*, as in (11) and (12):

(11) a. John's speeches caused frequent excitement.
      b. John's speeches caused a lot of excitement.
(12) a. Mary's frequent nervousness makes her unsuited for continuous work.
      b. Too much nervousness makes Mary unsuited for continuous work.

For (11a) to be true, there must be many events of excitement caused by John's speeches, which are separated in time. But for (11b) to be true, it suffices that many people got excited at the same time during John's speeches. Similarly, for the truth of (12a), it is important that Mary's states of nervousness are distributed over time. But in order for (12b) to be true, it suffices that Mary is very nervous generally or during a single time interval.

Thus, frequency adverbials apply to an event and count the parts of that event, requiring that the parts be separated in time. Since frequency expressions apply to both groups and quantities, they will involve the generalized notion of part, which applies to groups in the same way as it applies to quantities.

This lexical meaning of frequency expressions can now be made explicit formally. The metrical component of the meaning of frequency expressions consists of a function that, applied to any two parts x and y of the event group, must yield a value different from 0. In order to make this precise, I will adopt the notion of metric in the standard mathematical sense, but relativizing all notions involved to a situation:

(13) *Definition*
Let X be a nonempty set. A real-valued function m on $X \times X$ (the Cartesian product of X or the set of ordered pairs of elements in X) and a situation s is a *metric* on X in s (METRIC(m, X, s)) iff (M$_1$)–(M$_4$) for every x, y, and z in X:

(M$_1$) $m_s(x, y) \geq 0$
(M$_2$) $m_s(x, y) = 0 \leftrightarrow x = y$
(M$_3$) $m_s(x, y) = m_s(y, x)$
(M$_4$) $m_s(x, z) \leq m_s(x, y) + m_s(y, z)$

Condition (M$_1$) states that the value of a metric must always be positive or 0. Condition (M$_2$) states that the value of a metric applied to a pair $<x, y>$ (the distance between x and y) is 0 just in case x is identical to y. Condition (M$_3$) expresses the fact that the order of entities in a pair to which a metric applies does not matter. Condition (M$_4$) requires that the value of a metric applied to a pair $<x, z>$ not exceed the sum of the values of the metric applied to the pair $<x, y>$ and the pair $<y, z>$.

The lexical meaning of *frequent(ly)* and *rare(ly)* can now be given formally as in (14), where m is the function of temporal distance and @ the function mapping a situation s onto the expectation value relevant in s:[3]

(14) a. *The lexical meaning of* frequent(ly)
$[frequent]^s = \lambda x[\text{CARD}((\{y \mid y <_s x\}) > @_s \ \& \ \text{METRIC}(m_t, \{y \mid y <_s x\}, s)]$

b. *The lexical meaning of* rare(ly)
$[rare] = [frequent]$ with '<' instead of '>'

----

[3] *Frequent* often has an additional meaning component not represented by (14). *Frequent* often does not count just temporally disconnected subevents, but rather subevents that happen on specific occasions. For instance, in (1), *frequently* counts events among those that are awakenings by John on Mondays:

(1) On Mondays, John frequently wakes up at seven.

Apparently, *frequently* counts those events that form a subset of a certain reference set of occasions. (See de Swart 1991 for a detailed discussion.) This reference set may be treated as another argument place in the lexical meaning of *frequent*. *Frequent* then denotes a relation between entities x and y such that y is the reference group of occasions as specified by the context and x is a part of y.

The notion of metric that I have employed — in particular, condition (M_2) — implies that no two parts of an event e that is modified by a frequency expression may be simultaneous or overlapping in time. Any two simultaneous or overlapping subevents of e must count as one part. This, I think, is adequate.[4]

At the beginning of this section, it was mentioned that the analysis of frequency expressions in which they count the actual parts of a concrete event is not always adequate: frequency expressions often do not count the subevents of a concrete event group, but rather express the fact that a certain event type is instantiated with a certain regularity. Consider, for example, (15):

(15) John frequently goes out.

Frequently in (15) does not count a particular group of events; rather it states that instances of John's going out, whenever they occur, will be found with a certain regularity. It involves a time interval with vague boundaries (as it occurs in a generic sentence) and requires a different analysis of the quantificational force of *frequently*. (For a proposal in this respect see de Swart 1991.)

However, examples such as (15) need not distract from the point to be made, for the metrical requirement imposed by frequency expressions is independent of the way frequency adverbials as quantifiers should ultimately be analyzed.[5]

---

[4] If this consequence is not desired, there is the following alternative way of conceiving of the metrical component: *frequent* does not directly count parts of an event, but rather equivalence classes of parts that are simultaneous. The metric then does not apply to parts directly, but rather to the equivalence classes of parts *modulo* simultaneity.

In order to decide between the two alternatives, one has to look at how the part structure of event groups specified by frequency expressions is actually treated in natural language. One way of testing whether the part structures in question may have simultaneous parts or not is part quantification (cf. Chapter 1). Consider (1):

(1) a. ?? Some of these frequent accidents happened at the same time.
     b. ?? Most of these frequent accidents last year happened at the same time.

Examples (1a) and (1b) sound odd. But they should be good if the group of frequent accidents could have parts that occur at the same time. This constitutes evidence that an event group e specified by *frequent* may have only temporally disjoint parts; that is, all subevents of e that happen at the same time must count as one and the same part of e. Thus, there is reason to prefer the present analysis to its alternative.

[5] De Swart (1991) notes another use of frequency adverbials, *always* in particular, as 'phase quantifiers'. In this function, *always* count not individual events but rather the time interval at which a single event takes place, as in (1):

(1) That is the first time I have lived in France; I always lived in Germany.

Such examples indicate that *always* has a second lexical meaning which does not involve a metrical component.

5.1.3. Implications of the lexical meaning of frequency expressions

The lexical meanings of *frequent(ly)* and *rare(ly)* as given in (14) make sense only if the part relation $<_S$ is neither closed under sum formation nor transitive — and hence corresponds to the notion of part introduced in Chapter 1. Let me show why.

If *frequent(ly)* or *rare(ly)* is predicated of an event e, then the part structure of e need not be closed under sum formation — that is, for any two parts e' and e'' of e, the sum of e' and e'' need not be a part of e. The sum of e' and e'' in fact may not be a part of e if e' and e'' are distinct parts. For then, if e''' is the sum of e' and e'' and a part of e, e' and e''' (as well as e'' and e''') would not be separated in time; and hence, given (14), *frequent* or *rare* would not hold of e. Closure under sum formation also often leads to more parts than are actually counted. A group of ten temporally disconnected events can be evaluated as 'rare', but on the basis of counting ten subevents, not on the basis of the power of ten minus one ('minus one', since there is no zero event).

Frequency expressions furthermore require that the part structure of the modified event is not transitive. Suppose *frequent(ly)* or *rare(ly)* holds of an event e (so that e has temporally separated parts). Then, a proper part e'' of a part e' of e cannot be a part of e. For otherwise, e'' and e' would not be temporally separated.

Thus, whenever a frequency expression is predicated of an event e, e must have a *discrete part structure*, a part structure in which no two distinct parts have a sum and which contains no proper part of any of its elements. Formally, a discrete part structure is defined in (16), where $D(s)$ is the domain of the situation s:

(16) *Definition*
An entity x has a *discrete part structure* in a situation s (DISCR(x, s)) iff for the set A, $A = \{x' \mid x' <_S x\}$, the following holds:
(i) $(\forall A')(A' \subseteq A \ \& \ A' \neq A \ \& \ |A'| \geq 2 \rightarrow sum_{<S}(A') \notin D(s))$
(ii) $(\forall x')(\forall x'')(x' \in A \ \& \ x'' <_S x' \rightarrow x'' \notin A)$.

Thus, we have:

(17) For a frequency predicate f, an event e, and a situation s,
if $[f]^S(e) = 1$, then DISCR(e, s).

The implication in (17) obtains because of the Transivity Principle and the Restriction on situated sum formation of Chapter 1. These two principles apply because frequency expressions specify parts as integrated wholes. For let R be the relation among the general parts of an event e such that $R = \{<x, y> \mid m_{ts}(x, y) \neq 0\}$. Then, a part e' of e is an R-integrated whole just in case e' is the sum of a maximal set of temporally connected subparts. Given the Restriction on Situated Sum Formation, no set of such R-integrated wholes has a sum; for the potential sum could not be an integrated whole itself on the basis of temporal connectedness. Moreover, by the Transitivity Principle, a part of a maximal temporally connected part e' of e need not be a part of e, because e' is an integrated whole.

Thus, the part structure of an event modified by a frequency predicate is that of a group specified only by a plural noun. Without further information, the group referent of a plural has as its situated parts all and only the individuals denoted by the corresponding singular noun and no groups of such individuals. But then, since frequency expressions may modify mass nouns, mass noun referents may be specified with exactly the same sort of part structure as plural referents.

This has implications for the semantic mass-count distinction in general. In particular, it supports the information-based account of the mass-count distinction as opposed to the extensional mereological account. Recall from Chapter 1 that, in the (strong) extensional mereological account of the semantic mass-count distinction, the count domain is characterized by atomicity and the mass domain by both divisivity and cumulativity. On the information-based account, the distinction between mass nouns and count nouns consists in that count nouns express whole-properties, but mass nouns do not. Since the extensional mereological account treats the semantic mass-count distinction as an absolute distinction among extensions, there is no way the distinction could be suspended in a given case. By contrast, the information-based account draws the distinction as a distinction in information and thus as a distinction that can be overruled by other information in a given context. Thus, the set of parts of a mass noun referent must be homogeneous, if there is no information about integrity blocking transitivity and closure under sum formation. Homogeneity for part structures is defined as follows:

(18) *Definition*
      An entity x has a *homogeneous part structure* in a situation s
      ($HOM(x, s)$) iff $<_s$ is transitive and closed under sum formation with
      respect to $\{y \mid y <_s x\}$.

Frequency expressions show that an entity may belong to the extension of a mass noun and still have a discrete part structure — the kind of part structure plural referents usually have. Thus, a quantity has a homogeneous part structure only if there is no information to the contrary — for instance, lexical information as provided by frequency expressions. A quantity specified only by a mass noun has a homogeneous part structure; but if it is, in addition, specified by a frequency expression, it will have a discrete part structure. Hence, the syntactic mass-count distinction implies the semantic mass-count distinction, but not conversely.

There is one other issue concerning the lexical meaning of frequency expressions that is of interest in the present context — namely, the question about the interaction between frequency expressions and *semantic selection*.

It is obvious that frequency expressions impose the Accessibility Requirement. For only events with an accessible part structure can be modified by frequency expressions. This can be seen from the fact that *frequent* does not make sense in the following examples with count nouns, even though possible interpretations are imaginable, as indicated in (19a):

(19) a. # the frequent performance
          (i.e., the performance that had many temporally disconnected parts

or many interruptions)
  b. # the frequent life / speech / dance

The nouns *performance, life, speech,* and *dance* characterize an event as an integrated whole. Hence the part structure of such an event will not be accessible, and *frequent* cannot apply, counting the parts of such an event.

Frequency expressions also impose the Integrated Parts Requirement. Due to the metrical component, *frequent* involves a binary relation between distinct parts of any event it can modify — namely, the relation $R^S = \{<e', e''> \mid m_S(e', e'') \neq 0\}$. Since frequency expressions can modify mass noun referents, the Integrated Parts Requirement will be satisfied merely on the basis of the nonlinguistic context.

The Integrated Parts Requirement interacts with frequency expressions in a more interesting way: a mass NP modified by a frequency expression should be able to satisfy the Integrated Part Requirement. This predication is borne out, as seen in the examples in (20)–(21) (though the data are not completely felicitous for independent reasons):

(20) a. (?) Between the frequent sunshine, Mary did not even notice the occasional rainfalls.
      b. # Between the sunshine, Mary did not even notice the occasional rainfalls.
(21) a. (?) John stopped counting the frequent rain / # the rain.
      b. (?) The frequent agitation / # The agitation was indistinguishable. (and so it seemed as if only one and the same kind of people were involved)

These data also confirm the point that semantic selectional requirements must be satisfied by an entity relative to a given reference situation, not by an entity *per se. The frequent sunshine* in (20a) may certainly refer to exactly the same event as *the sunshine* in (20b). But only (20a) provides the information that the event consists of many temporally disconnected parts. Thus, (20a) and (20b) may be about the same event, but with different part structures under different perspectives (i.e., in different reference situations).

In this section, I have argued that frequency expressions express a part-structure property which holds of an event only if the event consists of temporally disconnected subevents. This property can be attributed even to mass noun referents. An event that has this property has a discrete part structure and can satisfy the Integrated Parts Requirement independently of the syntactic mass-count distinction. This confirms the importance of a semantic mass-count distinction based on the notion of integrated whole, a notion that is independent of the syntactic mass-count distinction.

5.2. German mass quantifiers

5.2.1. The metrical determiner *manche(s)*

5.2.1.1. The readings of *manche(s)*

Metrical components in lexical meanings are found not only with event predicates or quantifiers. For example, there is a German determiner that not only applies to events but also has a more general metrical meaning. This is *manche*, approximately 'several'. *Manche* may be the determiner of NPs other than event-denoting ones, and, correspondingly, the metrical component of *manche* is more general than in the case of frequency expressions. When *manche* does not apply to an event-denoting NP, the metrical component will not be temporal distance, but, for example, spatial distance, or it will be based on a more abstract relation among entities. What kind of metric is involved in a particular case depends on the kind of entities denoted by the head noun and on the context. Thus, *manche*, roughly speaking, expresses the property of having several parts and having only parts that are distant from each other with respect to the contextually given metric. Examples involving a temporal, a spatial, and a more abstract metric are given in (22):

> (22) a. An manchen Tagen war Maria krank.
>   'On several days Mary was sick.'
>   b. Manche Sterne waren sehr hell.
>   'Several stars were very bright.'
>   c. Manche Ideen können sich sehr leicht durchsetzen.
>   'Several ideas affirm themselves easily.'

Example (22a) implies that the days on which Mary was sick are not consecutive days. Example (22b) implies that the stars have a certain minimal distance from each other. Example (22c) implies that the ideas are not closely related in terms of, for instance, content, place of origin, or domain.

In order to see the metrical effect more clearly, let us contrast *manche* with the German determiner *einige*, which lacks a metrical requirement, but otherwise means the same. The examples in (23) differ minimally from the examples in (22):

> (23) a. An einigen Tagen war Maria krank.
>   'On several days Mary was sick.'
>   b. Einige Sterne waren sehr hell.
>   'Several stars were very bright.'
>   c. Einige Ideen können sich sehr leicht durchsetzen.
>   'Several ideas affirm themselves easily.'

Einige, like English *several*, does not have a metrical component as part of its meaning. Thus, (22a) does not imply temporal continuity, (22b) does not imply spatial distance, and (22c) does not imply unrelatedness with respect to content, origin, or domain. Thus, *einige* differs minimally from *manche* with respect to the metrical component.

In the preceding section, we saw that frequency expressions like *frequent* may modify both plural and mass nouns and thus require a lexical meaning that is independent of the mass-count distinction. The same holds for *manche*. *Manche* combines not only with plurals but also with mass nouns, as illustrated in (24):

(24) a. Manches Holz war feucht.
          'Some of the wood was wet.'
      b. Manches Wasser kann man nicht trinken.
          'One cannot drink some of the water.'

Manche, when applied to a mass noun, specifies a quantity as having a discrete part structure, which is due to the metrical component (as determined by the context). Metrical distance among parts as required by *manche* may be achieved in various ways. For instance, (24a) is appropriate in a situation in which the wood quantity is partitioned into spatially disconnected units; (24b) is appropriate when taken as a generic sentence about well-distinguished kinds of water.

Thus, *manche* has the same lexical meaning when it applies to mass nouns that it has when it applies to plurals.

What does the lexical meaning of *manche* exactly consist in? First, *manche*, like English *several*, applies to any group that has at least two members, or more generally, it applies to any entity that has at least two parts. Second, like *frequent*, *manche* imposes a metric on the parts of the entity it applies to. This metric is entirely context-dependent and hence should be construed as a function of the relevant reference situation. Let us take *m* now to be a function mapping a situation *s* to the distance function relevant in *s*. The lexical meaning of *manche* then is as in (25):

(25) *The lexical meaning of* manche
      $[manche]^s = \lambda x[\text{CARD}(\{y \mid y <_s x\}) > 2 \ \& \ \text{METRIC}(m(s),$
      $\{y \mid y <_s x\}, s)]$

There is another expression which shares this lexical meaning with *manche*. This is the adverbial counterpart of *manche*, the frequency adverb *manchmal*, as in (26):

(26) Maria machte manchmal einen Fehler.
      'Mary sometimes made a mistake.'

Even though *manchmal* arguably has the same lexical meaning as *manche,* as an adverbial quantifier, it applies only to events, and its metrical component is restricted to temporal distance. Clearly, the meaning of *manchmal* in a sentence should be the same as the meaning of other frequency adverbials such as *frequently* or *rarely* (see Chapter 6).

The semantic analyses of *frequent(ly)* and *manche* in the preceding and the present section have also shown that lexical meanings with metrical components show up with words of various syntactic categories, such as adverbs, adjectives, and determiners. Words of those categories have rather different semantic functions in a sentence; but their metrical lexical meanings are invariant with respect to the ways they contribute to the meaning of a sentence.

5.2.1.2. Implications of the lexical meaning of *manche(s)*

The lexical analysis of *manche* in (25) makes certain predictions about the semantic behavior of *manche* in a sentence. If *manche* applies to a group x, then x must consist of elements separated from each other in some dimension. Thus, *manche* should not allow for collective predicates implying closeness among the elements in that dimension (in the relevant situation). This appears to be correct. Many speakers get contrasts in the following examples with predicates implying distance in (27a), (28a), and (29a), and closeness in (27b), (28b), and (29b) (at the initial state of the process described):

(27) a. Manche Kugeln sind unverkettet.
       'Several balls are loose.'
     b. ?? Manche Kugeln sind verkettet.
       'Several balls are linked.'
(28) a. Manche Häuser liegen sehr weit voneinander entfernt.
       'Some houses lie far from each other.'
     b. ?? Manche Häuser liegen sehr nahe beeinander.
       'Some houses lie close to each other.'
(29) a. Manche Studenten kamen zusammen.
       'Some students came together.'
     b. ?? Manche Studenten verstreuten sich.
       'Some students dispersed.'

Let me now turn to the semantic analysis of *manche* in a sentence. *Manche* exhibits the characteristics of focused quantifiers and downward-entailing quantifiers such as *few* and *little* (as discussed in Chapter 4, Section 4.3.).[6] Hence, *manche(s)* should be represented in a sentence meaning in the same way as focused quantifiers. Of course, *manche(s)* can be analyzed as a focused quantifier both when occurring as

---

[6] Thus, *manche* is disallowed in predicative positions, as seen in (1a), and does not support *donkey*-pronouns, as seen in (1b):

(1) a. Dies sind # manche / OK viele Fehler.
       'These are several / many mistakes.'
     b. Jeder, der # manche / OK viele Fehler gemacht hat, soll sie verbessern.
       'Everybody who has made several / many mistakes, should correct them.'

See footnotes 13 and 14 in Chapter 4.

a plural determiner and as a mass determiner (cf. Chapter 4). On such an analysis, (22a) has, approximately, the following denotation:

(30) $\lambda s[[manchen]^{S'}(sum_{<_S'}(\{x \mid (\forall x')(x' <_S' x \rightarrow [Tagen]^{S'}(x') = 1 \&$
$(\exists e)([war\ krank]^S(e, \text{Mary}) = 1 \& [an]^S(e, x') = 1))\}) = 1)]$

According to (30), the maximal group of days in the reference situation on which Mary was sick has at least two parts, and all the parts are distinct from each other with respect to — in this case — temporal distance (in the reference situation).

Another important fact about *manche(s)* is that with mass nouns it does not impose the Homogeneity Requirement on the predicate, but allows for heterogeneous predicates — that is, predicates that hold only of certain (distinguished) quantities, but neither of their parts nor their sums. This is illustrated in the examples in (31)–(33), where *manches* is contrasted with *etwas* 'some', which, like *einige*, lacks a metrical component and allows for a homogeneous predicate (when it acts as a quantifier) or a predicate that holds of the entire quantity (when it acts as a quantity attribute):

(31) a. Manches Holz wurde in eine Kiste getan.
          'Some wood was put into a box.'
          (several boxes may be involved)
      b. Etwas Holz wurde in eine Kiste getan.
          (only one box may be involved)
(32) a. Manches Gold wurde in einem südamerikanischen Staat gefunden.
          'Some gold was found in a South American state.'
          (allows for a different state for every unit of gold)
      b. Etwas Gold wurde in einem südamerikanischem Staat gefunden.
          (implies only one state is involved)
(33) a. Mancher Schmuck wiegt höchstens drei Gramm.
          'Several jewelry weighs at most three grams.'
      b. # Etwas Schmuck wiegt höchstens drei Gramm.

Example (31a) with *manches* differs from (31b) with *etwas* (acting as a cardinality attribute) in that it does not require that all the wood was put into a single box, but allows different units of wood to have been put into different boxes. The same difference holds for (32a) and (32b). Example (33a) shows that a mass NP with the determiner *manche* allows for a strictly heterogeneous predicate which is not acceptable with *etwas* as a quantifier, as in (33b).

These facts are predicted by the analysis of the lexical meaning of *manche*, according to which *manche* specifies quantities as having discrete part structures. Analyzing *manches* and *etwas* as focused quantifiers yields (34a) as the analysis of (31a), and (34b) as the analysis of (31b):

(34) a. $\lambda s[[manches]^{S'}(sum_{<_S'}(\{x \mid (\forall x')(x' <_S' x \rightarrow [Holz]^{S'}(x') = 1 \&$
          $(\exists y)(\exists e)([Kiste]^{S''}(y) = 1 \& [wurde\ getan\ in](e, x', y) = 1))) = 1]$
      b. $\lambda s[[einiges]^{S'}(sum_{<_S'}(\{x \mid (\forall x')(x' <_S' x \rightarrow [Holz]^{S'}(x') = 1 \&$

$$(\exists y)(\exists e)([Kiste]^{s\,{''}}(y) = 1 \ \& \ [wurde\ getan\ in]^{s}(e, x', y) = 1))) = 1]$$

Example (34a) holds of a situation *s* iff the maximal entity whose parts (in *s*´) are units of wood (in *s*´) that were put into a box (in *s*) has at least two parts (in *s*´) and has only parts (in *s*´) that are distant from each other in *s*´ with respect to the contextually relevant metric (most naturally, spatial distance). Because of the metrical condition, the parts constitute integrated wholes in the reference situation and hence allow for the heterogeneous predicate *wurde in eine Kiste getan*.

By contrast, (34b) holds of a situation *s* just in case the maximal entity has sufficiently many parts (in *s*´) whose parts (in *s*´) are units of wood (in *s*´) that were put into the box (in *s*). Since *einiges* imposes no metrical requirement on the parts and since the parts are not otherwise characterized as integrated wholes, they form a homogeneous set and hence disallow the heterogeneous predicate *wurde in eine Kiste getan*.

5.2.2. German vague count quantifiers and the mass-count distinction

5.2.2.1. Syntactic and semantic mass-count distinctions among German vague quantifiers

German vague quantifiers have a property that is important not only for the issue of semantically relevant part structures but also for the issue of the mass-count distinction.

Vague quantifiers in German exhibit a semantic mass-count distinction which is independent of the syntactic mass-count distinction: German vague count quantifiers not only combine with plural nouns but can systematically apply to mass nouns as well, while maintaining the semantics of count quantifiers. When modifying mass nouns, they contrast with the proper mass quantifiers, which apply only to mass nouns and have semantically 'mass character'.

Thus, German vague quantifiers divide into two types. The first type applies to both mass nouns and count nouns, but acts semantically like a plural quantifier. Because of their semantics, let us call these quantifiers *count quantifiers*. The second type applies only to mass nouns and has semantically 'mass-character'. Let us call them *pure mass quantifiers*. Quantifiers of the first type are listed under (I), quantifiers of the second type under (II):

(35)   (I)   (II)
    viele(s)   'many'   viel   'much'
    wenige(s)   'few'   wenig   'little'
    einige(s)   'several'   etwas   'some'

The following examples illustrate the application of count quantifiers to mass nouns and show how they contrast semantically with pure mass quantifiers:

(36) a. Viele Kunst wurde ausgestellt.

'A good deal of art was exhibited.'
  b. Viel Kunst wurde ausgestellt.
    'Much art was exhibited.'
(37) a. Maria probierte einigen Schmuck an.
    'Mary tried on a good deal of jewelry.'
  b. Mary probierte etwas Schmuck an.
    'Mary tried on some jewelry.'

Kunst in *viele Kunst* in (36a) is a mass noun syntactically as well as semantically. In particular, it maintains its conceptual meaning as a mass noun and differs semantically from the plural of *Kunst* (as a count noun) —*Künste* — as in *viele Künste* 'many arts, many kinds of art'. Similarly, *Schmuck* in (37a) is conceptually still a mass noun and differs semantically from *Schmuckstücke* 'pieces of jewelry'. *Viele Kunst* in (36a) refers to many units of some amount of art, whereby these units must somehow be well-distinguished from each other in the context. *Einigen Schmuck* in (37a) refers to several well-distinguished units of jewelry. In contrast, *etwas Schmuck* in (37b) refers to an undifferentiated quantity of jewelry (consisting perhaps only of one piece).

A count quantifier applied to a mass NP requires that the quantity the NP refers to be structured into well-distinguished subunits — that is, subunits that are integrated wholes. Thus, it carries a particular presupposition regarding the part structure of the entity it applies to. This presupposition says that the parts of the entity must be individuated as integrated wholes in the relevant context — that is, they must be assigned whole-properties in the reference situation. The condition that an entity be structured into parts that are integrated wholes is part of the lexical meaning of such count quantifiers and can be formulated as a condition on the reference situation. The lexical meaning of *viele(s)* will then be as follows:

(38) *The lexical meaning of* viele(s)

$$[viele(s)]^{s'} = \lambda x[\mathrm{CARD}(\{y \mid y <_s' x\}) > @_s' \, \& \, (\forall y)(y <_s' x$$
$$\rightarrow \mathrm{INT\text{-}WH}(y, s'))]$$

Like *four, many,* or *much,* count quantifiers may act both as attributes and as quantifiers. In the first function, they may be preceded by a definite article, as in (39a). The second function is illustrated in (39b):

(39) a. Das viele Gepäck ist zu schwer.
    the many luggage is too heavy
    (collective interpretation)
  b. Vieles Gepäck ist zu schwer.
    many luggage is to heavy
    (distributive interpretation)

Given the lexical meaning and the two possible functions of count quantifiers, two predictions are made concerning the occurrence of count quantifiers in mass

NPs: [1] in the quantifier function, count quantifiers should suspend the Homogeneity Requirement and allow for heterogeneous predicates; [2] in the function as attributes, count quantifiers should make the NP which they modify satisfy the Integrated Parts Requirement. In these two respects, count quantifiers should pattern exactly the same as the metrical quantifier *manche(s)*. Metrical quantifiers differ from count quantifiers basically only in the following respect: in contrast to entities modified by metrical expressions, entities modified by German count quantifiers may have overlapping parts, since the situated parts of such entities are individuated not on the basis of metrical distance but on the basis of qualitative specification. In the next section, we will see that the two predictions regarding German count quantifiers are borne out.

5.2.2.2. Implications of the lexical meaning of German vague count quantifiers

The Homogeneity Requirement does not hold for mass NPs with vague count quantifiers. *Viel Mobiliar* 'much furniture' and *viel Kunst* 'much art', like all mass NPs with indefinite or focused quantifiers, require either a collective predicate (when *viel* acts as a cardinality predicate) or a homogeneous predicate (when *viel* acts as a quantifier). By contrast, *viele Kunst* and *vieles Mobiliar* allow for heterogeneous predicates applying only to the subunits of art individuated in the context. This is seen in (40) and (41):

(40) a. Viel Kunst wurde von einem europäischen Künstler geschaffen.
          much art was by a European artist created
          'Much art was created by a European artist.'
      b. Viele Kunst wurde von einem europäischen Künstler geschaffen.
          many art was by a European artist created
          'A good deal of art was created by a European artist.'
      c. Viel Kunst wurde von europäischen Künstlern geschaffen.
          much art was by European artists created
          'Much art was created by European artists.'
(41) a. Viel mittelalterliche Kunst hat Hans beim Schreiben seines
          Romans inspiriert.
          much medieval art has inspired John at the writing his novel
          'Much medieval art has John inspired at writing his novel.'
      b. Viele mittelalterliche Kunst hat Hans beim Schreiben seines
          Romans inspiriert.
          many medieval art has inspired John at the writing his novel
          'A good deal of medieval art has inspired John when writing his
          novel.'

Given the analysis of focused quantifiers of Chapter 4, (40a) has the denotation in (42a), (40b) the one in (42b), and (40c) the one in (42c):

(42) a. $\lambda s[[viel]^S{}'(sum_{<_S}{}'(\{x \mid (\forall x')(x'<_S{}'x \to [art]^S{}'(x')$
& $(\exists e)(\exists y)([europäischen\ Künstler]^S{}'(y) = 1$ & $[wurde\ geschaffen$
$von]^S(e, x', y) = 1))\})) = 1]$

b. $\lambda s[[viele]^S{}'(sum_{<_S}{}'(\{x \mid (\forall x')(x'<_S{}'x \to [art]^S{}'(x') = 1$
& $(\exists e)(\exists y)([europäischen\ Künstler]^S{}'(y) = 1$ & $[wurde\ geschaffen$
$von]^S(e, x', y) = 1))\})) = 1]$

c. $\lambda s[[viel]^S{}'(sum_{<_S}{}'(\{x \mid (\forall x')(x'<_S{}'x \to [art]^S{}'(x') = 1$
& $(\exists e)(\exists y)([europäischen\ Künstlern]^S{}'(y) = 1$ & $[wurde$
$geschaffen\ von]^S(e, x', y) = 1))\})) = 1]$

The analyses (42a), (42b), and (42c) account adequately for the acceptability of (40a), (40b), and (40c) in a situation *s* in which, among a given quantity of art, there are many objects, each of which has been created by a different artist. Given (42a), (40a) comes out as unacceptable in *s*. The reason is that the part structure of the quantity of art specified only by *viel* and by *Kunst* must be homogeneous, because neither *viel* nor *Kunst* characterizes subquantities as integrated wholes. But *wurde von einem europäischen Künstler geschaffen* is a heterogeneous predicate in *s*.

In contrast to (40a), (40b) may correctly describe *s*. Given (42b), the quantity of art has a heterogeneous part structure in the reference situation because *viele* requires it to consist of parts that are integrated wholes in that situation.

Also (40c) may describe *s*. The reason is that the predicate *wurde von europäischen Künstlern geschaffen* is a homogeneous, in particular, a cumulative, predicate. Hence it can apply to the parts of the homogeneous part structure of the quantity specified by *viel* and *Kunst* in the reference situation.

The examples in (41) are to be analyzed in similar ways. The interpretations of (41a) and (41b) differ in the following way. Example (41a) preferably has a collective interpretation: a quantity of a lot of art, collectively, was the source of the inspiration. Example (41b), by contrast, can have only a distributive interpretation; that is, it can describe only a situation in which different units of medieval art individually triggered some inspiration. This difference follows from the fact that the part structure of the art in (41a) is homogeneous (preventing a reasonable distributive interpretation), but in (41b) it is heterogeneous.

Like frequency expressions, German vague count quantifiers interact with semantic selectional requirements in certain ways. Clearly, German vague count quantifiers impose the Accessibility Requirement — that is, they may not apply to singular count nouns:

(43) a. # das viele Bild
the many picture
(i.e., the picture with the many well-distinguished parts)
b. das viele Essen
the many things (mass noun) to eat
c. # das viele Mahl

the plenty of dinner (count noun)

Furthermore, mass NPs with count quantifiers satisfy the Integrated Parts Requirement. For example, in (44a) and (44b), a mass NP modified by *vieles* can act as the argument of reciprocals with predicates of comparison, which require arguments with integrated parts:

(44) a. Hans kann den vielen Schmuck / # den Schmuck nicht
         voneinander unterscheiden.
         John can the many jewelry / the jewelry not from each other
         distinguish
         'John cannot distinguish the hight amount of jewelry / the
         jewelry from each other.'
     b. Hans war zu müde, um den vielen Schmuck / # den Schmuck zu
         vergleichen.
         John was too tired to compare the many jewelry / the jewelry
         'John was too tired to compare the high amount of jewelry / the
         jewelry.'

The satisfaction of the Integrated Parts Requirement with *viele(s)*, again, shows the importance of the reference situations for semantic selection. *Viele(s)* does not necessarily express an essential part-structure property; it may characterize an entity as having only an accidental part structure in the reference situation — that is, a part structure in which the parts are only accidental integrated wholes. But even then it does influence the satisfaction of semantic selectional requirements.

5.2.2.3. Count and pure mass quantifiers in other functions

In German, pure mass quantifiers contrast with count quantifiers not only when occurring in the determiner position of a mass NP but also in other contexts that in German require a mass category. Let me briefly illustrate the effect of count quantifiers in those contexts and thereby illustrate the range of abstract dimensions in which the integrity of parts presupposed by count quantifiers may be manifested. There are two such contexts.

In the first context, the count quantifier is the determiner of an NP headed by an adjective. In German, adjectives can be the head of an NP, and in this function, they may receive a rather abstract, nonanaphoric interpretation, referring to anything the adjective may characterize. Adjectives that form the head of an NP are classified as mass nouns. In such NPs, count and pure mass quantifiers can both appear as determiners, but with different semantic effects. Consider the examples in (45):

(45) a. Anna erfuhr viel Neues.
         Ann learned much new
         'Ann learned much news.'
     b. Anna erfuhr vieles Neue.
         Ann learned many new

'Ann learned many news.'

In (45b), *vieles Neue* refers to a group of well-distinguished units of news. In (45a), *viel Neues* refers to a quantity of news which need not be structured into distinct units. This indicates that the additional lexical component of count quantifiers, which specifies parts as integrated wholes, may apply to any kind of abstract entity denoted by the adjective.

In the second context, the count quantifier acts as a prosentential or propredicative pronoun. In German, the class of prosentential and propredicative pronouns (and also pronouns that refer to events, cf. Chapter 7) is identical to the class of mass pronouns. The class of mass pronouns includes *das* 'that', *dies* 'this', *was* 'what', and all mass quantifiers such as *alles* 'all', *nichts* 'nothing', and vague mass quantifiers (vague pure mass quantifiers as well as vague count quantifiers). The semantic contrast between pure mass quantifiers and count quantifiers shows up even in such abstract domains as the domain of propositions, commands, and properties, as in (46)–(48):

(46) a. Maria sagte viel.
  'Mary said much.'
  b. Maria sagte vieles.
  'Mary said many (things).'
(47) a. Anna befahl ihrem Mann viel.
  'Ann ordered her husband much.'
  b. Anna befahl ihrem Mann vieles.
  'Ann ordered her husband many (things).'
(48) a. Anna blieb viel, was sie nicht sein wollte.
  'Ann remained much of what she did not want to be.'
  b. Anna blieb vieles, was sie nicht sein wollte.
  'Ann remained many (things) of what she did not want to be.'

Examples (46b), (47b), and (48b) imply that the relevant group of propositions, commands, or properties is structured into well-distinguished units. The corresponding *a*-sentences do not have this implication.

The application of count quantifiers to such abstract domains as the extensions of adjectival nominalizations, propositions, properties, and commands confirms the context-dependent nature of the kind of integrity count quantifiers require.

5.3. Conclusions

German vague count quantifiers, like frequency expressions, show that besides the syntactic mass-count distinction, there is an independent semantic mass-count distinction. Entities belonging to the semantic count domain have whole-properties themselves or consist of parts that have whole-properties. Entities belonging to the semantic mass domain are not ascribed any whole-properties by the mass nouns that are used to refer to them. But whole-properties ascribed to an entity in a situation can have three independent sources: [1] they may be properties encoded in lexical meanings (as in the case of plurals); [2] they may belong to an indexical argument of a specific lexical expression (as in the case of frequency expressions, German *manche(s)* and German vague count quantifiers); and [3] they may be part of contextual (nonlinguistic) information. The first two sources play an important role in the satisfaction of semantic selectional requirements and in the determination of the domain of part quantifiers. The third source may influence quantification over parts and semantic selection only in much more restricted ways.

6

Dimensions of Parts and Wholes and the Part Structure of Events

6.1. Multidimensional part structures of objects and events

In the preceding chapters, I discussed two sorts of linguistic information that may induce a perspective on an entity: [1] part-structure-related information (as expressed, for example, by phrases like *as a whole* or metrical determiners) and [2] information about dimensions (as expressed by phrases like *as a teacher*). In this chapter, I will discuss phenomena in which these two kinds of information interact in a certain way. This interaction consists in that part structures themselves may be relativized to a dimension. Such a relativization is possible both for the integrity and for the parts an entity may have: an entity may constitute different kinds of integrated whole in different dimensions, and it may have different sets of parts in different dimensions.

Examples of the relativization of integrity and parts to dimensions can already be construed with the object language expressions *integrity* and *part* — namely, simply by using *as*-phrases like *as a cultural unit* or adverbs like *spatially*, as in (1) (relativizing integrity) and in (2) (relativizing parts):

(1) a. Kurdistan has more integrity as a cultural unit than as a political unit.
    b. Kurdistan has more integrity culturally than politically.
(2) (?) This opera has more parts spatially than temporally.

The constructions that I will discuss in this chapter involve part structures relativized to a particular dimension in more indirect ways.

Both *objects* and *events* may have part structures in different dimensions. For objects, this is seen in the examples in (1) and (2). Events exhibit multidimensional part structures in a much more general and more differentiated way than objects. An entity that is not an event — that is, an object — usually has parts (in the relevant sense) and integrity only in *one* dimension. A chair, for instance, has only spatial, not temporal, parts; and it is an integrated whole only in the dimension of space.

This corresponds to the fact that quantifiers ranging over the parts of an object (be it an individual, a group, or a quantity) range only over spatial, not temporal, parts. Events, by contrast, may have temporal as well as spatial parts. The set of the temporal parts and the set of the spatial parts of an event each constitute a different part structure of the event. Moreover, an event may have integrity with respect to time (by being a temporally continuous event separated from other events of a similar type), but not with respect to space (for instance, when participants in the event are scattered in space), and, of course, conversely. Besides having different part structures in the two dimensions of time and space, events may also have different part structures because of the ways they depend on other entities. Unlike objects, events are entities that generaly are ontologically dependent on other entities — for example, the entities undergoing a change in the event or, more generally, the participants in the event. As a consequence, events may have part structures correlating with the part structure of different sorts of participants involved in the event. Thus, an event may have a part structure correlating with the parts of an object consumed in the event and another part structure corresponding to the parts of a group agent in the event.

Thus, there two reasons why events naturally have multiple part structures: because events may have part structures in both space and time and because events are ontologically dependent on other entities, which may induce different part structures of the event. For both ways of having multiple part structures, I will use the term *dimension* (thus extending the use of the term from the familiar dimensions of space and time to more general aspects with respect to which an entity may be specified). Each part structure in a particular dimension in this sense may have its own degree of integrity (corresponding to the connections holding among the parts in the relevant 'mereological dimension').

Multidimensional part structures of events show up in a number of interesting linguistic phenomena; in particular, they show up in constructions expressing quantification over the parts of an event. As a general observation, quantificational expressions ranging over the parts of an event display systematic apparent ambiguities. For example, they may display readings in which the quantifier seems to range either over participants, sublocations, subdurations, or subevents as specified by an event type. These readings do not constitute ambiguities of the quantifier, however, but rather should be traced to different part structures that an event may have in different dimensions — for instance, a part structure related to some event participant, to the event locations, to the event duration, or to the event type. As expected, the ambiguities increase with the number of event types, participants, and locations involved in the description of the event.

6.2. Integrity in different dimensions

Integrity and dimensions relate to each other in that integrity may depend on a particular dimension. For example, a family whose members are separated in space is an integrated whole not based on the relation 'being spatially close', but rather based on relations involving kinship. In this case, the object is an integrated whole in the 'dimension' of kinship relations, but not in the dimension of space. In the following, I will consider the case in which one and the same entity with one and the same set of parts may be an integrated whole in different dimensions when that entity occurs in different *situations*.

The possibility of being an integrated whole in different dimensions relative to different situations plays a central role in the semantics of part-structure modifiers such as *together, as a group*, and *individually* when they occur *adverbially*. Part-structure modifiers specify whether an entity or its parts are integrated wholes or belong to an integrated whole in a particular situation. It is characteristic of adverbial part-structure modifiers that they display a variety of different readings — for example, a spatiotemporal proximity reading or a group-action reading. I will argue that these readings should be reduced to the fact that different dimensions are relevant in different situations, rather than attributed to multiple (though perhaps related) lexical meanings of part-structure modifiers (as has been proposed by Lasersohn 1990).

6.2.1. Adverbial and adnominal part-structure modifiers

In Chapter 3, I discussed part-structure modifiers such as *as a whole, as a group, together, individual,* and *alone*, when they occur in *adnominal* position. In that position, they acted as *perspective shifters*, modifying the reference situation of an entity and restricting the acceptable properties in a generalized quantifier. One of the main functions of adnominal perspective shifters was to influence part-structure-sensitive semantic selection — in particular, the availability of distributive interpretations.

This chapter is focused on the semantics of part-structure modifiers in *adverbial* position. The readings that part-structure modifiers have in that position are very different from the ones they have in adnominal position. I will give an account on which part-structure modifiers have the same lexical meaning in both positions, and the differences in the readings arise simply from the fact that the situations to which the part-structure modifiers apply are different. As adverbials, part-structure modifiers exhibit a variety of readings, depending on the nature of the predicate. The reason for this, on my account, is that predicates yield different situations for the part-structure modifier to apply to, and the way these situations differ from each other resides in the dimensions in which integrity can be established.

Let us first look at the semantic differences among adverbial and adnominal occurrences of the various part-structure modifiers, starting with part-structure-sensitive *as*-phrases. *As*-phrases in general occur both adverbially and adnominally, as in (3a) and (3b):

(3) a. John is good as a teacher.
 b. John as a teacher is good.

'Dimension-specifying' *as*-phrases of the sort *as a teacher* have basically the same semantic effect in adnominal and adverbial position. By contrast, part-structure-modifying *as*-phrases have very different semantic effects in the two positions:

(4) a. The stamps as a whole cost 100 dollars.
     b. # The stamps cost 100 dollars as a whole.
(5) a. # John and Mary as a group have lifted the piano.
     b. John and Mary have lifted the piano as a group.

As a whole in adnominal position in (4a) simply prevents a distributive reading of the predicate, whereas in adverbial position in (4b), it is unacceptable. *As a group* in adnominal position in (5a) is unacceptable, whereas in adverbial position in (5b), it specifies that John and Mary did the piano-lifting collectively.

Such semantic alternations in fact arise with all part-structure modifiers in fully systematic ways. For example, in one and the same sentence, *together* and *alone* in adverbial position may be acceptable, as in the examples in (6) and (7), but in adnominal position unacceptable, as in the examples in (8) and (9):[1]

(6) a. John and Mary have lifted the piano together / alone.
     b. John and Mary thought about the problem together / alone.
(7) a. John and Mary sat together / alone.
     b. John and Mary took the exam together (in different cities).
(8) a. # John and Mary together / alone have lifted the piano.
     b. # John and Mary together / alone thought about the problem.
(9) a   # John and Mary together / alone sat.
     b. # John and Mary together / alone took the exam.

In (6a), *together* means that John and Mary performed a collective act of lifting the piano (*group-action reading*), and *alone* means that John and Mary lifted the piano without the help of others. In (6b), *together* means that John and Mary interacted with each other when thinking about the problem; *alone* means that John and Mary did not interact with others when thinking about the problem (*coordinated-action reading*). In (7a), *together* means that John and Mary were sitting close to each other; *alone* that they were sitting separated in space and time from others (*spatiotemporal proximity reading*). In (7b), *together* has a reading in which John took the exam at the same time as Mary (*temporal proximity reading*).

Also the converse holds — that is, in one and the same sentence, adnominal *together* and *alone* may be fine, but adverbial *together* and *alone* less acceptable, as in (10a, b):

(10) a. The boxes together / alone weigh 200 pounds.
      b. ?? The boxes weigh 200 pounds together / alone.

As was discussed in Chapter 3, the main function of *together* in adnominal position is to enforce a collective reading on the predicate, and the main function of *alone* is to prevent a (marginal) partitive reading. Unlike adnominal *together*,

---

[1] Note that the examples in (8) and (9) with *alone* are acceptable if *alone* means 'only'. Then, (8a) means 'only John and Mary lifted the piano'. For the reading of *alone* as 'only', see Moltmann (1994).

adverbial *together* is possible also with obligatorily distributive predicates as in the examples in (6b) and (7a, b).

A parallel semantic contrast between adverbial and adnominal occurrences is found with the part-structure modifier *individual(ly)*. *Individually* is the adverbial counterpart of *individual* as an adjectival modifier, which, as we saw in Chapter 3, can act as a perspective shifter. Adjectival *individual* has the function of enforcing a distributive reading, as in (11a) and (12a), a function that is impossible in (13a); by contrast, adverbial *individually* specifies individual activity, as in (11b) and (12b), a function which is bad in (12b):

(11) a. John showed the individual children their room.
     b. John showed the children their room individually.
(12) a. John likes the individual students.
     b. ?? John likes the students individually.
(13) a. ?? The individual students studied the problem.
     b. The students studied the problem individually.

Unlike *together* and *alone*, however, *individually* does not allow for a spatio-temporal separation reading:

(14) a. The children together / # individually sat on the floor.
     b. The cups are standing together / # individually on the shelf.

The absence of the spatiotemporal separation reading, though, appears to be a peculiarity of *individually* in English. The corresponding expression in German *einzeln*, for example, allows both for the individual-action reading and for the spatio-temporal separation reading:

(15) a. Die Kinder saßen einzeln auf dem Boden.
        'The children sat individually on the floor.'
     b. Die Tassen standen einzeln auf dem Schrank.
        'The cups were standing individually on the board.'

I will come back to such cross-linguistic differences later.

Also the perspective shifters *whole* and *entire* have adverbial counterparts — namely, *wholly* and *entirely*. And, again, the semantic effect of *wholly* and *entirely* in a sentence is quite different from the one of *whole* and *entire*. In the same sentence, *whole* and *entire* may be acceptable in adnominal position, but not in adverbial position, as seen in (16). And, conversely, they may be acceptable in adverbial position, but not in adnominal position, as seen in (17):

(16) a. The whole / entire collection is expensive.
     b. # The collection is expensive wholly / entirely.
(17) a. The clouds have wholly / entirely disappeared.
     b. # The whole / entire clouds have disappeared.

As discussed in Chapter 3, the semantic function of *whole* and *entire* is to let the predicate apply distributively to an entity otherwise specified as an integrated whole. The semantic function of adverbial *wholly* and *entirely*, by contrast, is to specify that every part of the relevant participant is involved in some subevent of the described event.

Keeping these data concerning adverbial part-structure modifiers in mind, we can now turn to the formal semantic analysis of adverbial part-structure modifiers. One central problem is how to account for the multiple readings of adverbial part-structure modifiers (the group-action reading, the cooperative-action reading, the temporal-proximity reading, and the spatiotemporal-proximity reading). One approach is to attribute the different readings to different, though perhaps related, lexical meanings, an approach which has been taken by Lasersohn (1990). I will not go into a detailed discussion of analyzing part-structure modifiers based on ambiguity (such as Lasersohn's account); rather I want to only give some general arguments against the assumption that the multiple readings are due to an ambiguity — the *ambiguity assumption*, for short.[2]

First, the ambiguity assumption implies that the group-action reading and the spatio-temporal-proximity reading should always both be available. But this is mostly not the case. For instance, in the examples in (14), only the group-action reading is possible; in the examples in (15), only the spatio-temporal- proximity reading is. Generally, action verbs enforce the group-action reading, whereas stative verbs or verbs expressing individual movement enforce the spatio-temporal proximity reading.

A second argument against the ambiguity assumption is that it makes stronger predictions about the separation of the two readings of part-structure modifiers than are confirmed by the facts. It appears that a spatio-temporal- proximity reading usually implies some amount of group action. For example, *together* in (18) not only means that the children sat close to each other; it also strongly suggests some social interaction among the children:

(18)   The children sat together on the floor.

But if one of the readings of *together* sometimes implies the simultaneous presence of some other reading, then the two readings differ from standard cases of lexical ambiguity. In standard cases of lexical ambiguity, different readings are completely independent of each other. For example, the two readings of *light* in English ('light' as opposed to 'dark' and 'light' as opposed to 'heavy') are independent of each other in that one reading of *light* never suggests the presence of the other reading. There is no implication that an object that is light in color also needs to be light in weight.[3]

---

[2] For a detailed discussion of Lasersohn's account, see Moltmann (1994).

[3] Furthermore, *together* in the spatial-proximity reading usually requires that the objects in question be not only spatially close but also similar in kind, as is seen in the different degrees of acceptability of the following data:

So the multiple readings of adverbial part-structure modifiers must constitute a different phenomenon than a lexical ambiguity. Most plausibly, the different readings arise from the same general meaning's being instantiated in different ways in different semantic contexts. The challenge for the semantic analysis of adverbial occurrences of part-structure modifiers then is to derive the various readings from a single meaning, given the semantic context in which the modifiers occur. Another challenge, of course, is to derive such readings from the same meanings that were assigned to part-structure modifiers in adnominal position. My goal in the next section is to meet both of these challenges.

6.2.2. An account based on relativized integrity and perspectives

On my account, part-structure modifiers have the same lexical meaning in adnominal and adverbial position. Moreover, they have the same lexical meaning and semantic function when displaying the various readings in adverbial position. This account is based on exactly the same lexical meanings of part-structure modifiers that they had in adnominal position, as discussed in Chapter 3 — namely, situation-dependent properties involving the notion of integrated whole. Thus, *together*, *as a group*, and *as a whole* always express the property of being an integrated whole in the relevant situation, *alone* always expresses the property of not being part of an integrated whole in the relevant situation, *individual(ly)* always expresses the property of having only essential integrated wholes as parts in the relevant situation, and *whole* and *entire* always express the property of not being an integrated whole in the relevant situation and of consisting of all actual parts in that situation.

    Central in my account is that an object may be an integrated whole or lack integrity in different dimensions (relative to different situations). For example, a group may be an integrated whole with respect to space and time if the group members are close to each other spatially and temporally in the relevant situation (spatio-temporal proximity reading); or it may be an integrated whole with respect to an action *e* if the group members form a collective agent of *e* or cooperate in doing *e* (group-action and coordinated-action reading).

    Two additional assumptions are important for this account:

---

(1) a. The books lay together on the floor.
     b. ? The book and the needle lay together (OK close to each other) on the floor.
     c. # The book and Mary lay together (OK close to each other) on the floor.
(2) a. The cup and the plate can be found together.
     b. ? The chair and the plate can be found together (OK next to each other).
     c. # The chair and John can be found together (OK next to each other).

In (1), *together* is best with objects of the same kind (books), worse with objects that are both inanimate, but are otherwise different in kind (book and needle), and worst with objects one of which is inanimate, the other animate. Similar contrasts hold among the examples in (2).

1. Situations determine the relevant dimensions in which integrity is established.
2. The information content of the situations to which adverbial part-structure modifiers apply is given by the descriptive content of the event predicate.

In Chapter 3, adnominal *together* was analyzed as a perspective shifter, denoting a function from situated generalized quantifiers to situated generalized quantifiers ranging over entities whose properties are based on being an integrated whole in the reference situation. In first approximation, adverbial *together* (when modifying an intransitive verb) maps a situation *s* to a set of entities *x* such that *x* is an integrated whole in *s* in the dimension relevant in *s*. Given this preliminary formulation, three questions have to be answered: [1] What is a dimension? [2] When is a dimension relevant in a situation? and [3] How is integrity established in a dimension?

Concerning the first question, I will identify dimensions, for the present purposes, simply with sets of properties or relations. For example, the dimension of space will be identified with the set of spatial properties and relations and the dimension of color will be identified with the set of color properties. I will use the variables D and D' for dimensions.

The second question receives the following answer: a dimension D is relevant in a situation *s* just in case an entity is specified positively or negatively with a property in *s* that belongs to D, more precisely:

(19) *Definition*
  A dimension D is *relevant* in a situation *s* iff there is an entity x and
  a situated property A such that $A \in D$ and $A^s(x) = 1$ or $A^s(x) = 0$.

Descriptively speaking, the following correlations between contents of predicates and ways of establishing integrity hold. If the predicate describes an action e, then the integrity of the group x will consist in that x is the collective agent of e. If the predicate describes a group of activities e, then the integrity of x may consist in the parts of x cooperating in doing a subactivity of e. If the predicate describes a state or location, then the integrity of x will be established in the dimension of space-time (i.e., the parts of x must be close to each other in space and time in the relevant situation). Finally, if the predicate describes individual activities, then the integrity of x may also be established in time (i.e., the parts of x should participate in the activities at the same time in the relevant situation). So the following correlations hold between predicate types and dimensions for specifying integrity:

(20) *Possible dimensions for integrity in the described situations*
  action predicate:
  integrity based on 'being (co-)agents of the same action'
  individual-activity predicate:
  integrity based on 'cooperating in performing a particular type of action' or
  integrity based on 'being at the same time'
  location predicate:
  integrity based on 'being spatially and temporally close'

These correlations hold because, in each case, the dimension of integrity is exactly the dimension in which the event is specified by the predicate. This dimension is obligatorily present in any situation described by the sentence.

However, *together* does not modify *any* situation the sentence describes. For such a situation may be too large. For example, in a situation *s* in which any of the examples in (6)–(7) is true, John and Mary may be specified in many different dimensions, and every such dimension is relevant in *s*. But this means that, in the case of *together*, John and Mary would have to constitute an integrated whole in every such dimension. But John and Mary need to constitute an integrated whole only in the dimension for which the event is specified. In order to get this effect, *together* should apply not to the described situations but rather to a very small subsituation of any described situation — namely, the subsituation that contains only information *about* the event. Following Devlin/Rosenberg (1993), I will call this situation the *oracle* of the event. It is defined as the maximal subsituation in which only those properties that involve the event as one of their arguments specify entities negatively or positively:

(21) *Definition*
For a situation *s* and an event *e*
s_e (*the oracle of e in s*) = the maximal subsituation of *s* such that for
any *n*-place situated relation R, if $R^s(x_1, \ldots, x_n) = 1$ or $R^s(x_1, \ldots, x_n) = 0$, then $x_i = e$ for some i $\in \{1, \ldots, n\}$.

We can now turn to the third question — namely, How is integrity established in a dimension? For the semantics of part-structure modifiers, a particular notion of integrated whole, the notion of *R-integrated whole* introduced in Chapter 1, basically suffices. Recall that an entity *x* is an *R*-integrated whole if all the parts of *x* are connected by the transitive closure of *R*, and no part of *x* is connected that way to an entity *y* that is not part of *x*. If for a situation *s* the dimension is constituted by a single action *e*, then *R*-integrity will be established for *R* = 'is coagent of *a* in *s* together with'; if the dimension is constituted by a group of actions *e*, then *R*-integrity may be established for *R* = 'cooperates in performing a part *e´* of *e* in *s* with'; if the dimension is space-time, *R*-integrity will be established for *R* = 'is close in space and time in *s* to'; if the dimension is time, then *R*-integrity will be established for *R* = 'is close in time in *s* to'. Such relations *R* can be obtained systematically from the properties for which the event is specified in its oracle — that is, integrity must be established in a dimension *D* such that for some *n*-place property R in D, $R^s(x_1, \ldots, e, \ldots, x_n) = 1$ or $R^s(x_1, \ldots, e, \ldots, x_n) = 0$.

Concerning their semantic status, I will assume (though not too much hinges on it) that *together* and *alone* simply have the syntactic function of depictive secondary predicates (cf. Moltmann 1994). For adverbial part-structure modifiers modifying intransitive verbs, the associated syntactic relation then is as in (22a) and the correlated semantic operation as in (22b):

(22) a. *The syntactic relation for adverbial part-structure modifiers*
          (modifying intransitive verbs)
          For constituents f and g in a syntactic structure S,
          $\langle f, g \rangle \in$ SEC-PREDS) iff f is a depictive secondary predicate
          with respect to the second argument place of g in S.
      b. *The semantic operation for adverbial part-structure modifiers*
          Let R be a situated property and R' a situated relation between events
          and entities.

          $sec\text{-}pred(R, R') = \lambda s \lambda ex[R'^{S}(e, x) = 1 \,\&\, R^{S}e(x) = 1]$.
      c. $\langle$SEC-PRED, $sec\text{-}pred\rangle \in corr$

(6a) (with *together*) will now have the following analysis:

(23) $\lambda s[[\textit{John and Mary}]^{S'}(s)(\lambda x[(\exists e)([\textit{lifted}]^{S}(e, x) = 1 \,\&\, [\textit{together}]^{S}e(x) = 1)]) = 1]$

This analysis can be carried over to the other part-structure modifiers in a
straightforward way. Let us discuss them in turn.

Individual expresses the property of not being an integrated whole and having
only essential integrated wholes in the relevant situation (cf. Chapter 3). If we take
'INT-WH' as a one-place (situation-independent) predicate to express essential
integrity, then we have:

(24) $[\textit{individual(ly)}]^{S} = \lambda x[\neg\text{INT-WH}(x, s) \,\&\, (\forall x')(x' <_{s} x \rightarrow \text{INT-WH}(x'))]$

If *individually* applies to an entity x in the oracle s_e of an activity e, then x may not
be an integrated whole in s_e, and every part x' of x in s_e must be an essential
integrated whole. Since the group members of x' are the only essential integrated
wholes, it follows that no proper subgroup may be an integrated whole in se. Given
the definition of 'integrated whole' and the definition of 'oracle', this means that x
should not stand in the relevant thematic relation R to an integrated subevent of e
(and e should not be an integrated whole itself). Moreover, every part x' of x should
stand in the relevant thematic relation to some subevent e' of e, but not to any
subevent e'' of e so that some other part x'' of x stands in R to e''. In general, we
then have the following implication:

(25) $[\textit{individually}]^{S}e(x) = 1$, then for no thematic relation R such that
      $R^{S}e(e, x) = 1$, FF-INT-WH(x, s_e) for $F = \lambda x[R^{S}(e', x)]$ for some
      integrated subevent e' of e (or $e' = e$ if e is an integrated whole) and for
      every $x', x' <_{s} x$, $R^{S}(e', x') = 1$ for some subevent e' of e and
      $\neg R^{S}(e'', x') = 1$ for any subevent e'' of e such that for some x'', $x'' \neq$
      x', $R^{S}(e'', x'') = 1$.

Whole, wholly, and *entire(ly)* express the property that holds of an entity x iff x is
not an integrated whole in s and s contains all actual parts of x, as in (26):

(26) $[entire(ly)]^s = \lambda x[\neg \text{INT-WH}(x, s) \& (\forall x')(x' < x \rightarrow x' <_s x)]$

Note that here the use of the general part relation < ('is an actual part of') is crucial (cf. Chapter 1). *Entirely* involves a comparison between the actual parts of an entity and its situated parts in the oracle of the relevant event. When *entirely* holds of an entity x in the oracle s_e of an activity e, then x may not be an integrated whole in s_e. This means that e should not be an integrated whole, that is, x should not collectively participate (in the way relevant in s_e) in e (or some subevent of e). Moreover, every actual part of x must be in s_e. By the definition of s_e, this means that every actual part x' of x must participate in some subevent e' of e in the way relevant in s_e — that is, x' must stand in the relevant thematic relation to e'. So we have:

(27) $[entirely]^s e(x) = 1$, then for no thematic relation R such that $R^s e(x, e)$
$= 1$, $FF\text{-INT-WH}(x, s_e)$, for $F = \lambda x[R^s(e', x)]$, with e' a subevent of
e and an integrated whole (or $e' = e$ if e is an integrated whole), and
for every x', $x' < x$, there is some e'', $e'' <_s e$, such that $R^s(x', e'') = 1$.

On this account, all adverbial part-structure modifiers involve the same syntactic relation and semantic operation. Their semantic differences are located only in the different lexical meanings they involve.

Some restrictions, though, may be imposed on the dimensions in which integrity can be established. As we have seen, *individually* does not allow for a spatiotemporal-proximity reading, in contrast to German *einzeln*. The contrast between German and English indicates that individual lexical items that express integrity or the lack of it may restrict the potential dimension in which the object may have or lack integrity. These restrictions to particular dimensions should, in some way, form part of the lexical content of the expressions.

This variation among lexical items along part-structure-related dimensions corresponds to the possibility of language-specific variation among *dimensional adjectives*. A dimensional adjective may be restricted to a certain dimension in one language, but not in some other language. Thus, *light* in English may apply both to the dimension of hue and the dimension of weight. In contrast, German has two expressions corresponding to *light* — *hell* and *leicht* — which are restricted to the dimensions hue and weight, respectively.[4]

---

[4] There are other types of semantic variation among part-structure modifiers across languages. For example, part-structure modifiers may differ in how explicit the relevant dimension should be in the linguistic context. Thus, German *zusammen* 'together' differs from English *together* in that it requires an explicit spatial adjunct for the spatial-proximity reading:

(1) a. Hans und Maria saßen zusammen *(auf dem Boden).
     'John and Mary sat together on the floor.'
   b. Hans und Maria standen zusammen *(in der Ecke).
     'John and Mary were standing together in the corner.'

Let me, at the end of this section, address a few further questions that arise with this treatment of adverbial part-structure modifiers. One question is, If, as this analysis seems to imply, integrity systematically holds relative to a dimension, should integrity also for adnominal part-structure modifiers be relativized to a dimension? If so, this dimension should be the dimension relevant in the reference situation. But what dimensions can a reference situation provide? Clearly, in general, this is not a dimension of any manifest — for example, spatial or qualitative — relations among entities. Rather, the only dimension generally available in a reference situation is the dimension of merely conceived relations among entities. Thus, *together*, when applied to a reference situation, generally specifies an entity as a merely conceived integrated whole — i.e., an *R*-integrated whole with *R* being the relation 'is conceived as belonging together with'.[5]

Another question that has to be addressed is, Need there be a unique dimension in a situation with respect to which integrity will be established? The integrity requirement imposed by *together* may have to be satisfied with respect to more than one dimension, as in (18), where the children are specified as an integrated whole both in space and with respect to social interaction. The first dimension is the one specified by the predicate; the second, it appears, is implied by the nonlinguistic context. Both dimensions will be relevant in the situation *together* applies to. Thus, the integrity conditions expressed by part-structure modifiers should be satisfied in *all* dimensions relevant in the situation in question.

A final issue that should briefly be addressed concerns the semantics of *together* as a *resultative secondary predicate*. In this function, *together* describes a state of an object as an integrated whole resulting from the event that is described. Usually, in this resulting state, the object is an integrated whole in space, as in (28a, b):

(28) a. The people came together.
      b. John moved the chairs together.

Formally, resultative *together* can be treated as a predicate modifier with the same lexical meaning it has in the other functions. Thus we have (29), where resultative *together* serves to form a complex event predicate:

(29) $[came\ together]^S = \lambda ex[(\exists e')(\exists e'')(e = sum_{<S}(\{e', e''\})\ \&\ [came]^S(e', x) = 1\ \&\ [together]^S e''(x) = 1)]$

According to (29), *came* and *together* form a complex event consisting of a subevent of coming and a resulting state in which the agent of the event is an integrated whole (in the relevant dimension, i.e., the dimension of space).

With this I conclude the discussion of expressions of integrity and dimensions. There is certainly a lot more to be said in this area. This section has only given a rudimentary semantic analysis of adverbial part-structure modifiers and has left out

---

[5] For a discussion of some exceptional cases in which even the reference situation does provide a particular dimension, see Moltmann (1994).

numerous issues of more subtle nature. Its main goal, though, was to outline a new approach to the core data with adverbial part-structure modifiers, which relies on the idea that integrity may be established in a particular dimension, depending on the information given in the relevant situation. Central in the analysis was the fact that which dimensions are available for establishing integrity or the lack of it depends on the situation that is 'about' the event described by the predicate.

6.3. Parts in different dimensions

6.3.1. Multidimensional part structures of objects

Not only may an entity have integrity in different dimensions; it may also be structured differently into parts in different dimensions. For instance, the natural parts of a book may be considered its chapters in the dimension of content and its pages in the dimension of material form. The parts of a word as a phonological unit may be considered its phonemes, but the parts of the word as a morphological unit may be considered its morphemes. A familiar device that can be used to specify different dimensions of part structures is the adnominal *as*-construction, as in (30):

(30) a. The word as a phonological unit has many parts.
     b. The word as a morphological unit has few parts.

As in the case of dimensions for adjectives and for integrity, the *as*-construction expresses most directly the dependence of part structures on situations.

The dimension relativity of part structures plays a role in natural language also in more indirect ways, and this is what this section is about. The main point to be established is that whenever an expression makes reference to the parts of an entity, apparent ambiguities may arise, due to the fact that the entity to which the expression applies has more than one part structure. This general thesis is stated in (31):

(31) *The correlation between multiple part structures and multiple readings*
     of expressions involving parts
     Whenever an expression f makes general reference to the parts of an argument, and an entity x has n part structures in a situation s, then f applied to x in s yields n readings.

As an example, consider the part-structure-sensitive predicate *distinguish*. In Chapter 3, we saw that the lexical meaning of *distinguish* makes reference to the parts of an argument in object position and requires that the argument have integrated parts. Now an entity can be attributed a part structure with integrated parts in various ways. Also, it can be attributed several such part structures simultaneously — for example, by conjoined modifiers expressing different kinds of properties. In such a case, multiple readings arise, as in (32a, b):

(32) a. John cannot distinguish the green and the red chairs in the living room

and in the kitchen.
   b. John cannot distinguish the green and red furniture of Sue and Mary.

Example (32a) has two readings: what John cannot distinguish is either the green chairs from the red ones or the chairs in the living room from the ones in the kitchen. Similarly, (32b) has two readings: what John cannot distinguish is either the green furniture from the red one or the furniture of Sue from the furniture of Mary.

   I will argue that the two readings of (32a) and of (32b) are due not to a syntactic or semantic ambiguity but rather to the fact that the group of chairs in (32a) and the furniture in (32b) have two different, simultaneous part structures. On one reading, one of the part structures has been selected; on the other reading, the other part structure was chosen. In (32a), one part structure of the chairs consists of the maximal set of green chairs and the maximal set of red chairs; the other part structure consists of the maximal group of chairs in the living room and the maximal group of chairs in the kitchen. The first part structure is associated with the dimension of hue, the second part structure with the dimension of spatial location.

   This account of the phenomenon, however, requires a modification of two notions: [1] the notion of part structure and [2] the notion of reference situation.

   First, the assumption that the chairs in (32a) have two part structures in different dimensions requires a modification of the notion of part structure. A part structure in the old sense involved all whole-properties that an entity or its parts have in the relevant situation. But this cannot be so for the new notion of part structure that is required. The new notion requires that the relevant set of whole-properties be restricted to properties that belong to a particular dimension; that is, there should be a dimension D to which all the whole-properties in the part structure belong.

   But when does a set of parts belong to a dimension D? Clearly, when the parts are distinguished from each other by properties in D. Thus, in example (32a), the parts in the part structure in the dimension of color are distinguished by color, and the parts in the spatial part structure are distinguished in spatial location.

   A part structure in a dimension can be defined as follows:

(33) *Definition*
   $(s, (D(s), <_s), (E, <))$ is a *part structure in a dimension D* in the situation s iff
   a. $(s, (D(s), <_s), (E, <))$ is a part structure in the familiar sense.
   b. For any situated n-place relation R, if for entities $x_1, \ldots,$ and x_n,
      $R^s(x_1, \ldots, x_n) = 1$, then $R \in D$.

The multidimensional part structure of an entity in a situation s then can be considered the set of all part structures the entity has in some dimension for a maximal subsituation of s:

(34) *Definition*
The *multidimensional part structure* of an entity x in a situation s is
the set of all part structures $(s', (D(s'), <_{s'}), (E, <))$ in some
dimension D for a maximal subsituation s' of s.

An expression making reference to a part structure will not apply to all part
structures an entity has; rather it must select exactly one part structure. How does
this selection come about? Clearly, it is not a matter of choosing an arbitrary part
structure. In order to evaluate (32a), for example, the addressee has to know which
part structure the speaker has in mind. The part structure that will be selected is the
one that is relevant in the intended situation. The selection of a particular part
structure can formally be conceived in exactly the same way as in the case of
adverbial part-structure modifiers like *together* and *alone* — namely, by applying a
function mapping the relevant situation to a subsituation that is restricted to a
particular dimension:

(35) *The dimensional restriction of a situation*
For a situation s, $D(s)$ = the maximal subsituation s' of s such that
for any entities $x_1, ...,$ and x_n and any situated n-place relation R, if
$R^{s'}(x_1, ..., x_n) = 1$, then $R \in D$.

All expressions making reference to parts of an entity now should be evaluated with
respect to some dimensionally restricted subsituation. Again, the dimension-
selection function will constitute an additional index in the sentence meaning. Then,
the denotation of (32a) will be as in (36):

(36) $\lambda s''sD\lambda s[[John]^{s''}([the\ green\ and\ the\ red\ chairs\ in\ the\ living\ room$
$and\ in\ the\ kitchen]^{D(s')}([distinguish]^s)) = 0]$

The possibility of multiple part structures raises two other important questions:
When does an entity have a particular part structure in a situation? and What are the
possible dimensions for part structures and how are they determined in a situation?

The first question can simply be reduced to the question about simple part
structures. For groups and quantities, part structures are usually made available on
the basis of the description — for example, by different conjoined modifiers in (32a)
and (32b). Only in certain cases may multiple part structures also be available on
the basis of the nonlinguistic context. This should be possible in exactly the cases
that allow for contextual specifications of simple part structures. One such case
discussed in Chapter 3 was examples of contextual satisfaction of the Integrated
Parts Requirement — for instance, with the verb *distinguish*. In fact, in such a case,
we may also get multiple readings due to multiple part structures. The two readings
of (32a), in fact, are available also in (37):

(37) John cannot distinguish the chairs.

Example (37) can describe situations in which John is only unable to distinguish
the chairs belonging to one subgroup of the chairs (defined by either color or

location) from the chairs belonging to another subgroup of the chairs (also defined by either color or location) (though he may be able to distinguish individual chairs in one subgroup).

Let us turn to the second question raised above. Here I will only make two general remarks. First, the dimension in which an entity may have a part structure depends, obviously, on the kinds of properties the entity itself is specified with. An entity that is specified in the dimension of color cannot have a part structure in that dimension. Second, in one and the same dimension, an entity may have several part structures corresponding to several ways of defining whole-properties. Consider (38):

(38) John cannot distinguish the orange and red and blue and green balls.

Example (38) has two readings. On the first reading, John cannot distinguish four kinds of balls; on the second, John cannot distinguish two kinds of balls, namely the orange and red balls from the blue and green balls. These two readings can be reduced to different kinds of property formations (and ultimately a syntactic ambiguity). In the first reading, the part structure will involve the whole-properties

$$\lambda x[x = sum_{<s}(\{y \mid [orange]^S(y) = 1\}]$$
$$\lambda x[x = sum_{<s}(\{y \mid [red]^S(y) = 1\}]$$
$$\lambda x[x = sum_{<s}(\{y \mid [blue]^S(y) = 1\}]$$
$$\lambda x[x = sum_{<s}(\{y \mid [green]^S(y) = 1\})$$

In the second reading, the whole-properties are

$$\lambda x[x = sum_{<s}(\{y \mid [orange\ and\ red]^S(y) = 1\})]$$
$$\lambda x[x = sum_{<s}(\{y \mid [blue\ and\ green]^S(y) = 1\})]$$

So far, we have seen some simple examples in which *objects* had part structures in several dimensions. In the next section, I will show that multidimensional part structures play an even more important role with respect to *events*. We will see that multidimensional part structures are responsible for a broad range of different readings that arise with event part quantifiers.

6.3.2. Multidimensional part structures of events

In the preceding section, we have seen examples of a group having different part structures in which it was divided into subgroups in various ways — for instance, with respect to space and with respect to qualities. However, as was mentioned earlier, generally, objects (such as houses, groups of houses, or quantities of water) do not easily have multiple part structures in a given situation. One reason is that objects do not have parts in the temporal dimension.[6] This can be seen from the fact that universal part quantifiers never range over temporal stages, but only over spatial parts of an object. *All of the house, all of the houses,* or *all of the wood* does not range over temporal parts of a house, of a group of houses, or of a quantity of wood, but only over spatial parts, disallowing temporal predicates:

(39) # All of the house / All of the houses / All of the wood was (were) in the
       last decade.

Another reason is that objects usually are ontologically independent — that is, their identity conditions generally do not involve other entities.

Events differ in these two respects from objects and hence naturally have parts in several dimensions. This, it seems, is also the reason why it is less clear what the parts of an event are than in the case of objects. A significant amount of philosophical literature is devoted to the question concerning the parts (and the identity) of events.[7] Rather than going into that discussion, however, let me restrict

---

[6] This at least holds for the semantically relevant notion of part. I do not want to exclude the possibility that there may also be a useful notion of part according to which objects have temporal parts.

[7] Bennett (1988), who gives an overview of the philosophical debate, distinguishes two senses in which an event may have parts: [1] a part of an event may correspond to the entire space-time the event occupies (*nonzonal fission*); [2] a part of an event may correspond to only a part of the space-time of the event (*zonal fission*). As an example of the first kind of part, an event of killing John may have as its nonzonal part an event of pulling the trigger. As an example of the second kind, an event of walking two kilometers has as its part an event of walking one kilometer, or a revolution affecting an entire country may have as its part an uproar in some village. Similarly, for sums of events. Two events that occupy the same space-time may have a sum that is also an event, and two events occupying a different space-time may have a sum that is an event.

Philosophers disagree with respect to the possibility of nonzonal fission and fusion, and they also disagree about the possibility of zonal fission and fusion. Some philosophers allow any spatial or temporal part of an event to be an event again; some do not or allow for it only under certain conditions. Zemach (1970), for example, holds the view that events have only temporal parts, not spatial parts. Some philosophers allow any two events that differ in space-time to have a sum; others allow for this only under certain conditions. Whatever the arguments for one or the other position may be, the relevant question in the present context is, How does natural language treat parts of events? Looking at relevant data, it appears that the parts of an event may be zonal as well as nonzonal parts, but subject to certain restrictions. Furthermore, fusion of events seems to be unlimited. The part quantifier *whole* ranges over zonal parts with respect to time in (1a) and space and time in (1b), and (1c) may be an example where *whole* ranges over nonzonal parts:

(1) a. The whole utterance was uncomprehensible.
     b. The whole performance was great.
     c. The whole moment was incredible.

the present concerns to the question of what role the notion of integrated whole plays in the part structure of an event.

The crucial observation is that the ways in which the part structure of events is specified on the basis of information about integrity correspond exactly to the ways it was specified in the case of objects. We have seen this already in Chapter 4 with the antecedent of *same/different* in the internal reading, which was identified with the event argument of the relevant verb. Let me recall this now with the event quantifier *both*. *Both* can act like a 'floated quantifier' ranging over the parts of an event described by a verb; it requires that the event have integrated parts (since it carries the preupposition that the event has exactly two (distinct) parts). What the relevant parts of the event are depends on the description. In (40), the relevant parts are maximal subevents satisfying the conjunct verbs, that is, they are *FF*-integrated wholes:

(40) John sang and danced, both at the same time.

The same principle of individuating event parts in a situation is at stake in the case of conjoined modifiers, as in (41):

(41) John danced slowly and fast / with Mary and with Sue, both at the same time.

The relevant parts may alternatively be subevents that stand in a relation to independent integrated wholes, as in the case of conjoined or plural NP-arguments in (42):

(42) John and Mary / The two children danced, both at the same time.

In this case, the principle of Integrating Parts on the Basis of Relations given in Chapter 3 is at stake.

Thus, the relevant parts of an event are specified by the description in the same ways as are the semantically relevant parts of objects. Moreover, the part relation applies to events in exactly the same way as it applies to objects. This is in accordance with a tradition in linguistic semantics which carries over the mereological account of plurals originating with Link (1983) to events (cf. Hinrichs 1985; Krifka 1989, 1990; Lasersohn 1990; Moltmann 1989, 1991b, 1992a). There

---

The possibility of fusion of events can best be seen with conjunction that is interpreted by group formation. The following examples show that both zonal and nonzonal fusion is possible:

(2) a. The beginning and the end of the performance resembled each other.
     b. Mary's performance was the beginning and the end of a carreer.

As a conclusion, no general restriction should be imposed on zonal or nonzonal parts of sums of events in the context of natural language.

are some differences, though. The part structure of an event seems to be tied much more closely to the description of the event than is the part structure of objects. I will come to such differences at the end of this chapter.

With these preliminaries regarding the part structure of events, we can proceed to the main issue of this chapter — the interaction between part structures and dimensions. Let me first make more explicit intutitively what part structures an event may have. First of all, an event may have both *spatial* and *temporal part structures*. For example, the parts of a revolution include both the temporal stages of the revolution (which make up its temporal part structure) and the subevents that take place at the subregions of the region affected by the revolution (which make up the spatial part structure). Second, participants whose parts are appropriately involved in the event — for instance, groups of agents or affected objects — may impose another part structure on the event, a part structure that I will call a *participant-related part structure*. Participant-related part structures are part structures in which the event parts correspond to parts of an event participant. The event parts may correspond, for instance, to individuals if the participant is a group of agents or affected objects; or they may correspond to parts of individuals if the participant is a totally affected individual. The event described by *John and Mary laughed*, for example, has a part structure with two parts corresponding to John and Mary, respectively. The event of John's destroying the chairs has a participant-related part structure with as many parts as there are chairs. The event of John's building a house has a part structure in which the event parts may correspond to the functional parts of the house. This part structure need not coincide with the temporal part structure. For instance, John might have built two parts of the house at the same time.

There are still other dimensions in which events may have parts. Events may have part structures corresponding to certain *event qualities*. An event of playing a sonata carefully and sloppily, for instance, has two event parts in the dimension of event qualities: a subevent of playing the sonata carefully and a subevent of playing the sonata sloppily. These two parts need not be natural temporal parts, since they may be discontinuous (and thus do not form integrated wholes in the temporal dimension). Such part structures can be called *quality-related part structures*.

Finally, it is necessary to distinguish the temporal part structure of an event from the part structure that is determined by the *event type* described by the verb. An event of maturing may have temporal parts that are not part of the event as an event of maturation — namely, temporal parts in which no change takes place. I will call this an *event-type-related part structure*.

In the following, we will see that, as in the case of objects discussed earlier, multidimensional part structures of events give rise to apparent ambiguities. That is, whenever an expression makes general reference to the parts of an event and the event has a part structure in more than one dimension, the application of the expression to the event leads to multiple readings. For instance, quantifiers ranging over the parts of an event often display systematic apparent ambiguities where either the temporal parts of the event or the parts of a participant determine the quantification domain. Again, the application of an expression involving parts to an event with more than one part structure requires that exactly one part structure be selected for the evaluation of the expression.

There are some cases, however, in which an expression may fail to display all apparent ambiguities in an otherwise appropriately rich descriptive context. There are two reasons for such failure. First, the expression makes reference to a specific part structure of the event (in which case, usually, reference is made to the temporal part structure). Second, the expression imposes general conditions on part structures which delimit the range of possible apparent ambiguities — for instance, conditions on whether the part structure is determined by a participant, by space, or by time, and conditions on the degree of integrity of the part structure.

There are two different types of expressions that make reference to the parts of an event:

1. Expressions that make reference to the parts of an *abstract event* (*expressions of completion*):
completely, totally, partly, halfway
2. Expressions that make reference to the parts of a *concrete event* (*concrete event quantifiers*):
same/different (in the internal reading), *simultaneously, similarly, differently, one at a time, independently, one by one, in groups of four*, and *all, each*, and *both* (as 'floated quantifiers' ranging over events)

Expressions making reference to the parts of a concrete event display the first type of constraint; expressions making reference to an abstract event exhibit the second type.

Before examining and analyzing these event expressions, it is helpful to give a first example of a multidimensional event part structure in a familiar empirical domain — namely, vague quantifiers such as *a lot* and *little* when they range over events.

6.4. Apparent ambiguities with vague event quantifiers and frequency expressions

Multiple readings of event part quantifiers can be illustrated by contrasting frequency adverbials and vague event predicates or quantifiers such as *a lot* and *little*. *A lot* and *little* as in (43) and *viel* in (44) may have two sorts of readings, which correspond to two different sets of event parts that are counted ((44) being from German because of the impersonal passive, which does not require an explicit agent):

(43) a. a lot of laughter
     b. John faced a lot of expectation.
     c. In this town, one can hear little music, even though in one club, there is music all day and night.
(44) Es wurde viel gelacht.
     it was a lot laughed
     'They laughed a lot.'

In (43a), *a lot* may count either the number of temporal subevents of an event of laughter or the number of participant-related parts. With the participant-related reading, (43a) may refer to a laughing event that is very short in time and hence has only 'few' temporal subevents, but nonetheless counts as 'a lot' because of the number of event participants. In fact, (43a) may refer to an event of laughter that is brief enough not to have any distinguishable temporal subevents at all. The same holds for the German example (44). Here, *viel* 'a lot' may count either participant-related parts of a laughing event or temporal parts (in the same way as *a lot* in (43a)). In (43b), *a lot* can only refer to participant-related parts, since states such as states of expectations do not have well-distinguished parts inherently. In (43c), *little* does not specify that the music in the town has few temporal parts, but rather that it has few spatial or, perhaps, participant-related parts.

A lot and *little* are neutral with respect to what kind of parts they count. This is captured by the lexical meaning of *a lot* and *little* given in Chapter 4, according to which *a lot* and *little* simply count parts without further specification. Thus, in order for *a lot* and *little* to apply to an event-denoting expression, one of the part structures of the described event has to be selected. Which part structure will be selected clearly depends on the speaker's intentions. For the addressee has to know which part structure the speaker has in mind in order to understand a sentence with *a lot* or *little* correctly.

A lot and *little* contrast with frequency expressions and adverbials with *times*. The latter involve only temporal parts of an event; they may never involve participant-related parts. This is seen from the possible readings of the examples in (45):

(45) a. the frequent laughter (of the many children)
     b. The two children laughed twice.

Frequent in (45a) and *twice* in (45b) may count only temporal units of laughter; they cannot count, for instance, subevents of laughter each of which involves a different child. This restriction on frequency expressions and adverbials with *times* follows from their lexical meaning as given in Chapter 5, which makes explicit reference to parts separated in time (the metrical component) and hence to the part structure in the dimension of time.

Expressions with neutral reference to event parts may select any one of several part structures of the event and hence may display apparent ambiguities. But expressions making reference to temporal parts will target only the temporal part structure of the event and hence fail to exhibit apparent ambiguities.

A lot and *little* exhibit multiple part structures of events in rather subtle ways. By contrast, the various event expressions of the two types that I will discuss now display multiple readings related to different part structures in a much more obvious and differentiated way.

6.5. Apparent ambiguities with adverbs of completion

6.5.1. The part-quantificational account
of adverbs of completion

The first type of event-part-related expression consists of adverbs like *completely, totally, halfway, partly,* and *partially,* which can be called *adverbs of completion.*[8] In the account I will propose, the semantic function of adverbs of completion can be described as follows:

(46) Adverbs of completion specify to which extent the parts of a concrete
         event instantiate the parts of a given abstract event.

I will call (46) the *part-quantificational account* of adverbs of completion. To see how the account goes, consider (47):

(47) John completely agreed.

Given (46), *completely* in (47) specifies that John's concrete act of agreeing instantiates an abstract event of agreement to the maximal extent — or, making quantification over parts explicit, specifies that each part of the abstract event of agreement expressed by *John agreed* is instantiated by some part of John's concrete act of agreement.
     The part-quantificational account also applies to adverbs of completion such as *partly* or *halfway* in (48):

(48) John partly / halfway agreed.

Partly in (48) means that the activities by John that the sentence describes instantiate a part of the abstract event described by *John agreed.*[9]

---

[8] A predecessor of this and the following section is Moltmann (1990b).

[9] English *partly* has another function, which relates to the entire situation in question, rather than only the described event, as in (1):

(1) John partly played with Mary.

Example (1) can mean that part of what John was doing was playing with Mary. In this function, *partly* is not a VP-internal adverbial (as it is when it relates to the described event), but rather a VP-external sentence adverbial. This can be seen by from the usual tests for sentence adverbials:

(2) a. # John played with Mary partly.
      b. (?) Partly, John played with Mary.
      c. John (partly) has (partly) been playing with Mary.

Adverbs of completion sometimes appear to have a somewhat different semantic function with stative predicates. With stative predicates, *completely* seems to apply to a scale of properties along a dimension, as in (49), where *completely* measures the degree of darkness of the room:

(49) The room is completely dark.

In (49), *completely* specifies that the room instantiates all degrees of darkness.

The effect of *completely* in (49) can be captured by the part-quantificational account as well. But one additional assumption is necessary for carrying the part-quantificational account over to (49) — namely, the assumption that the following inclusion relation obtains among degrees of darkness: if an object x is dark to a degree d, then x is dark to any degree d' where $d' < d$. I will call this the *assumption of scalar inclusion*:

(50) *The assumption of scalar inclusion*
   For any scalar property P, if an object x is P to a degree d, then x is
   P to the degree d', for any $d' < d$.

For the formal analysis of adverbs of completion, I will use the variables E, E', . . . for abstract events, and the variables $e, e', . . .$ for concrete events. I is the relation of instantiation so that *'e I E'* means that e instantiates E. I will assume a function h which maps the semantic value of a verb (and, if applicable, its modifiers) as a situated relation between concrete events and participants to a situated relation between *abstract events* and participants:

(51) *Definition*
   Let R be an $(n+1)$-place situated relation between events and n
   participants and s a situation.
   $h(R^s) = \lambda E x_1 \ldots x_n [\forall e (R^s(e, x_1, \ldots, x_n) = 1 \rightarrow e\ I\ E)]$.

What is an abstract event? For the present purpose, I will restrict myself to only two assumptions about abstract events: abstract events need not have occurred, and they may be specified with the same properties as concrete events. In particular, abstract events may have concrete participants and may be specified for a particular time and location; more importantly, they may have part structures in the same way as concrete events.

Adverbs of completion relate the parts of the concrete event that the sentence is about to the parts of the abstract event described by the predicate. Thus, they denote relations between abstract events and concrete events. The lexical meanings of *completely* and *partly* then are as follows:

(52) *The lexical meanings of* completely *and* partly
   a. $[completely]^s = \lambda E e [(\forall E')(E' <_s E \rightarrow (\exists e')(e' <_s e\ \&\ e'\ I\ E'))]$
   b. $[partly]^s = \lambda E e [(\exists E')(E' <_s E\ \&\ e\ I\ E')]$

A sentence with completely such as (47) will then semantically be analyzed as follows:

(53) $\lambda s[(\exists e)[completely]^{s}(\iota E[h([agreed])(E, <John, s'>) = 1], e) = 1]$

In order to build such a sentence meaning in a compositional way, *completely* can be associated with the following syntactic relation and semantic operation:

(54) a. *The syntactic relation for adverbs of completion*
Let *f* and *g* be constituents in a syntactic structure *S*.
$<f, g> \in$ ADV-COMPL(*S*) iff *f* is an adverb of completion and *g* a verb (together with its modifiers if applicable) modified by *f* in *S*.

   b. *The semantic operation for adverbs of completion*
Let *R* be a two-place situated relation between concrete events and abstract events, and *R′* an *n*-place situated relation.
For a situation *s*,
$adv\text{-}compl(R^{s}, R'^{s}) = \lambda ex_{1} \ldots x_{n}[R^{s}(\iota E[h(R'^{s})(E, x_{1}, \ldots, x_{n})], e)]$

   c. $<$ADV-COMPL, *adv-compl*$> \in$ corr

The operation *adv-compl* basically inserts the abstract event formed from the event-argument position of an $(n+1)$-place relation (with *n* participants) into the second argument position of a three-place relation between concrete events and abstract events, yielding an $(n+1)$-place relation between a concrete event and *n* participants. This operation is applied to (47) in (55):

(55) $[agreed\ completely]^{s} = \lambda ex[[completely]^{s}(\iota E[h([agree]^{s})(E, x)], e) = 1]$

Verb arguments now enter the relation of argumenthood to the verb modified by *completely* (which requires appropriate changes in the relation of syntactic argumenthood given in Chapter 2). For (47), we have (56a), so that the semantic operation of argument satisfaction applies as in (56b):[10]

(56) a. $<John, completely\ agreed> \in$ ARG$^{2, 3}$(*S*)

   b. $arg2,3([John]^{s'}, [completely\ agreed]) =$
$\lambda s[(\exists e)[completely](\iota E[h([agreed])(E, <John, s'>)], e) = 1]$

---

[10] On this analysis, adverbs of completion syntactically modify the verb, not the sentence or the VP. This seems correct: adverbs of completion always have to be VP-internal and follow auxiliaries, negation, and sentential adverbs; thus, they must be in a position governed by the verb:

(1) a. * Completely John has eaten the cake.
   b. * John completely has eaten the cake.
   c. * The cloud completely probably disappeared.
   d. * The cloud has completely not disappeared.

This analysis of adverbs of completion can be applied also to adverbs of completion like *half* modifying *adjectives*, as in (57), and to adjectives of completion modifying *nouns* (including object-denoting nouns), as in (58):

(57) a. The bottle is half full.
     b. John is half asleep.
(58) a. the complete destruction of the city
     b. the complete edition of the novel

In (57a), *half* yields a participant-related reading and in (57b) an event-type-related reading. *Complete* in (58a) yields a participant-related reading; *complete* in (58b) displays a reading related to an abstract object. In the latter two cases, the same semantic operation given for *completely* in (54b) applies.

In order to carry (54) over to adverbs of completion modifying adjectives, as in (57a,b), it is necessary to assume that adjectives also have an additional Davidsonian event argument place, namely for states. Furthermore, adjectives (or, better, adjective phrases) express abstract states which can be instantiated in part or in whole by concrete states. The same meaning of *completely* given in (52) can be carried over to abstract objects (as opposed to abstract events). Example (58b) then will have the denotation in (59) for a reference situation s':

(59) $\lambda x[[complete]^{s'}(\iota X[h([edition]^{s'})(X, \text{the novel}) = 1], x) = 1]$

6.5.2. The multiple readings of adverbs of completion in English

After these preliminaries concerning the semantics of adverbs of completion, let us turn to the apparent ambiguities of adverbs of completion and to the role of multiple part structures of events.

Adverbs of completion in English have essentially two readings, both of which can be traced to different part structure of the abstract event that is described. In the first reading, the degree of completion of the concrete described event is measured relative to the *event type* expressed by the verb or adjective. This reading can be called the *event-type-related reading* of adverbs of completion. It is the only available reading of *completely* and *partly* in the following examples:

(60) a. John is completely drunk.
     b. John completely ruined Mary.
     c. John completely upset Mary.
     d. John has partly answered the question.

Intuitively, in (60a), *completely* means that John reached the highest degree of drunkenness. In (60b) and (60c), it means that John made Mary reach the highest degree of being ruined or upset. In (60d), *partly* means that the answer John gave does not satisfy the question to the highest degree.

Generally, there are two kinds of event-type-related readings of *completely*: one in which the described concrete event instantiates the highest degree of an abstract state expressed by the verb or adjective, as in (60a), and one in which it instantiates an extreme culmination of an abstract event expressed by the verb, as in (60b) and (60c). In both cases, *completely* means that the concrete described event instantiates every part of the abstract event described by the verb or adjective, whereby the parts must include an extreme degree or a culmination.

The second reading of adverbs of completion in English relates the described event to the parts of a *participant* of a certain kind. It can therefore be called the *participant-related reading*. It is illustrated in the examples in (61):

(61) a. John has completely eaten the cake.
      b. The room was completely dark.
      c. The mice have completely disappeared.
      d. The information was partly new.
      e. The wall became partly wet.
      f. Mary partly wrote the sonata.

Completely in (61a) specifies that John ate every part of the cake. In (61b), it specifies that every part of the room was dark. In (61c), it specifies that each of the mice has disappeared. *Partly* in (61d) specifies that some of the information was new. In (61e), it specifies that some parts of the wall became wet. In (61f), it specifies that Mary wrote part, but not all, of the sonata.

Note that the participant-related reading is possible with participants with any kind of part structure. It is possible with individuals, as in (61a), (61b), (61e), and (61f), with groups, as in (61c), and with quantities, as in (61d).

There are also contexts in which both the event-type-related and the participant-related readings are possible. For example, in the sentences in (62), both event-type and participant-related readings are available — at least for many speakers:

(62) a. The paint completely covered the picture.
      b. John completely erased the writing.
      c. The clouds have completely disappeared.
      d. John partly opened the bundle of presents.
      e. The tulips have partly bloomed.

Notice, again, that the participant-related reading may involve individuals, as in (62a) and (62d), quantities, as in (62b), and groups, as in (62c) and (62e).

In (62a), *completely* has two readings which are associated with distinct truth conditions. On the first reading, (62a) means that every part of the picture was covered (to some extent) by paint. On this reading, (62a) is false in a situation in which a part of the picture, however small, was not covered by paint. However, with this reading, (62a) is still true in a situation in which every part of the picture is only weakly covered by paint (possibly leaving the picture transparent). In the second reading, (62a) means that the paint covers the picture to the highest degree. In this reading, (62a) may be true in a situation in which not every part, but only some significant part, of the picture was covered by paint. However, in the second reading, (62a) is false if the part of the picture that is covered by paint is not covered to the highest degree (the covering being opaque). Thus, one reading excludes the other. The same two readings are exhibited by (62b–e). Example (62b) may mean either that John erased (to some extent) every part of the writing or that he erased (a significant part of) the writing without leaving any traces. Example (62c) means either that every single cloud has disappeared (though, perhaps, still being weakly visible) or that the clouds have disappeared in such a way that no traces are left. Example (62d) may mean either that John opened some, but not all, of the presents (whereby each present was completely opened) or that he opened each of the presents to some extent, but not completely. Example (62e) means either that some of the tulips are in a state of bloom or that every tulip is in a state that is not yet a state of full bloom.[11]

Also, states may have multidimensional part structures. This is seen in the apparent ambiguities of the following examples with adjectives:

(63) a. The apple is half rotten.
     b. The door is half open.
       (the door being a Dutch door)

Example (63a) means either that half of the apple is rotten or that the apple (or at least most of it) is halfway rotten. Example (63b) means either that one of two parts of the door is open or that (both parts of) the door is (are) in a state that is in between closed and open.

6.5.2.1. The source of the multiple readings of adverbs of completion

Before presenting my proposal (on which the multiple readings of adverbs of completion are due to different part structures of the event), let me first discuss some alternative accounts of the different readings on which they are due to a syntactic or semantic ambiguity. In the course of this discussion, the following two generalizations about the multiple readings will be established:

1. The multiple readings are independent of the *syntactic position* of the adverb of completion.
2. The multiple readings are independent of any particular *argument position* of the participant yielding the participant-related reading.

---

[11] The English adverb of completion *halfway* has a strong preference for an event-type-related, as opposed to a participant-related, reading. (1), unlike (62d) in the text, is unambiguous, allowing only for the event-related reading:

   (1) John halfway opened the bundle of presents.

Evidence that the availability of the two readings is independent of the possible syntactic positions of adverbs of completion is that adverbs of completion generally allow for exactly the same readings in all VP-internal positions. Thus, in (62a) and (62d), where the adverbs of completion occur VP-finally, the same two readings are available as in the following examples, where the adverbs of completion occur VP-initially:

(64) a. The paint covered the picture completely.
      b. John opened the bundle of presents partly.

In the examples in (61a, f) and (62a, b, d), the object referent is responsible for the participant-related reading. But the same generalization holds for cases in which the subject referent 'generates' the participant-related reading. Thus, in both (65a) and (65b), the event-type related and the participant-related readings are available:

(65) a. The clouds completely have disappeared.
      b. The clouds have disappeared completely.

The multiple readings of adverbs of completion are also independent of the syntactic position of the NP yielding the participant-related reading. At first sight, it seems as if the participant-related reading is syntactically always associated with direct (deep) objects, as in the examples (61a, c, f), (62a, b, c, d, e), and (65); agentive subjects and indirect objects hardly yield a participant-related reading:

(66) a. # The book has completely influenced John.
      b. # The food was given completely to the crowd.
          (in the reading 'everyone received food')

But there is sufficient evidence that the participant-related reading is not restricted to direct objects. First, there are cases in which subjects may yield participant-related readings, not only subjects of unaccusative predicates, as already in (61c, f) and (62c, e) and as in (67a) but also subjects of adjectival predicates, as in (61b, d, e) and (67b). Moreover, as (67c) shows, there are also direct objects which do *not* allow for a participant-related reading:

(67) a. The ice has completely melted.
      b. The floor is completely dirty.
      c. # John completely invited the children.

The question now is, What exactly are the conditions on the availability of a participant-related reading? That is, what conditions must an argument meet in order to allow for a participant-related reading?

A first possibility one might consider is that the argument must be a *totally affected argument*, a thematic role that an argument x has with respect to an event e if every part of x is involved in a subevent of e which is of the same type as e (cf. Krifka 1989, Tenny 1987). This relation is typically associated with direct objects (cf. Tenny 1987). The condition of total affectedness would be satisfied, for example, in (61a, b, c, e, f) and (62a, b, c, d). But it does not generally hold. It is both too weak and too strong. For instance, the subject of *bloom* in (62e) is not really a totally affected argument. Also, in (68a) and (68b), the objects do not classify as totally affected objects. Moreover, a totally affected object does not always allow for a participant-related reading — for example, *partly* in (68c) (at least for many speakers):

(68) a. John helped the children partly.
    b. John completely / partly changed the situation.
    c. # John partly played the sonata.

These data suggest a second possible condition. In (62e) and (68a, b), the arguments are not totally affected, but they are *directly involved* in the event. The objects of *invite* in (67c) and of *play* in (68c), by contrast, are not necessarily directly involved.

Direct involvement, however, turns out to be too weak a condition. An argument of *touch* is certainly directly involved in the event; nonetheless it does not allow for a participant-related reading — in contrast to the verb *smear*:

(69) a. # John partly touched the painting / wood.
    b. John partly smeared the painting / the wood.

What appears to be at stake is not whether an argument is directly involved in the event but rather whether it undergoes or induces a *change* in the course of the event. Alternatively, in the case of adjectives and statives, it may also be sufficient that the argument instantiate the relevant quality, as in (61d) and (67b). So the following semantic constraint holds for *completely* and *partly*:

(70) *Semantic constraint on* completely *and* partly
    Completely and *partly* can apply to the part structure of an event (or a state) e induced by a participant x only if x undergoes a change in e or exhibits the quality associated with e.

This constraint is satisfied in all the other examples, but not, for instance, with the object of *play*.

The only problematic cases for the constraint may be the objects of *understand*, *analyze*, and *read*, which all can induce a participant-related reading. But even here, one may argue that the object induces a change — namely, a change in the mental state of the agent. I will come back to the general parameters that govern restrictions on adverbs of completion later.

To sum up, the availability of the various readings of adverbs of completion seems to be determined neither by the syntactic position of the adverb of completion nor by the syntactic position of the argument leading to the participant-related reading. This motivates a purely semantic treatment on which the different readings of adverbs of completion are due simply to different part structures of the abstract described event. In the next section, I will present such a treatment in detail.

6.5.2.2. A treatment of the multiple readings of adverbs of completion based on multidimensional part structures

On my proposal, the apparent ambiguity between the event-type-related and the participant-related reading is a matter of part-structure selection and in this sense a matter of 'ontology' and context-dependency, rather than semantic ambiguity. This proposal thus extends the treatment of the apparent ambiguity of the earlier examples with *distinguish*, which involved the part structure of a group.

The proposal allows for a uniform treatment of both readings of adverbs of completion, and it reduces the apparent ambiguity to the fact that events may have multidimensional part structures. Adverbs of completion are interpreted by one and the same semantic operation, which consists in quantification over the parts (or a subset of the parts) of an abstract event (with respect to one of its part structures) and in the association of these parts with parts of the concrete described event. In the event-type-related reading, the quantifier involves an event-type-related part structure; in the participant-related reading, it involves a participant-related part structure. Since one and the same adverb of completion in a sentence may allow for both readings, one of the part structures of the abstract event must be selected prior to the application of this operation.

This account requires some modification of the semantic analysis of adverbs of completion given earlier. The analysis will now involve a function r, which selects the relevant part structure in a situation so that the meaning of *completely* will be as in (71):

(71) *Modification of the lexical meaning of* completely
$$[completely]^S = \lambda E e[(\forall E')(E' <_{r(s)} E \rightarrow (\exists e')(e' <_{r(s)} e \,\&\, e' I E')]$$

Given this account, a question still to be answered is, How do the various part structures of an abstract event come about? A general restriction on the availability of a reading relating to a particular part structure consists in the dependence of the part structure on the description. That is, adverbs of completion may yield a reading based on the part structure of an abstract event E in the dimension D only if E has been described as having a part structure in D. This can be seen in the contrast between (72a) and (72b):

(72) a. # John completely ate.
     b. John completely ate the cake.

Only (72b) allows for an object-related reading — the reason, obviously, being that the object is explicitly mentioned.

The description-relatedness of the readings of adverbs of completion is a phenomenon not exactly of the same nature as the situation-dependence of part structures in general. An abstract event is defined totally in terms of the property expressed by a particular event description; there is no way for it to have a part structure on the basis of nonlinguistic information only.

The account of *completely* and *partly* so far is not yet complete. An important question that still has to be addressed is, Why do *completely* and *partly* not allow for more readings than they actually do? An abstract event may have more part structures than those induced by affected participants and by the event type. Consider (73), where the description specifies the abstract event with a temporal location and spatial location and hence with a temporal and a spatial part structure:

(73) # The children completely played in the garden yesterday.

In (73), *completely* does not allow for a reading relating to either one of these part structures. That is, (73) cannot mean that the children played everywhere in the garden or that they played at all times yesterday.

We will see, however, that this is a restriction specific to adverbs of completion in English. There are expressions of completion in other languages that allow for more, and even the full range of, possible part-structure-related readings. But first, I want to say some more about the restrictions on the possible part structures of events to which *completely* in English may apply.

6.5.2.3. Constraints on the possible readings of English adverbs of completion

There are a number of constraints that delimit the part structures that English *completely* may relate to. Earlier, we saw that the participant-related reading of adverbs of completion in English is constrained by the requirement that the relevant participant be involved in a change brought about by the event. There are other parameters that restrict the potential readings of adverbs of completion in English.

Most importantly, the availability of a participant-related reading depends on the part structure of the argument. For example, it depends on whether the argument is an individual, a group, or a quantity. The following examples show that in certain contexts, a participant-related reading is possible only with individuals or quantities, not with groups; the reverse case, a participant-related reading being available only with groups but not with individuals or quantities, does not seem to occur:

(74) a. John has destroyed the house / the chairs / the material completely.
      b. Mary has dyed the dress / the clothes / the clothing partly.

Completely applying to *the house* or *the material* in (74a) specifies that John destroyed every part of the house or every part of the material; but when applying to *the chairs* in (74a), it can only mean that John destroyed each one of the chairs completely; it cannot mean that John destroyed every one of the chairs, but some of them perhaps not entirely. Thus, *completely*, when applied to *the chairs* in (74a), involves the parts of individual group members, rather than the parts of the group argument itself. In this case, the predicate *destroyed completely* receives a distributive interpretation, distributing over the individual chairs. A distributive interpretation is the only way for *completely* to be semantically acceptable with *the chairs*. The same kinds of interpretations are available or not available for *partly* in (74b).

The examples in (75) show that certain contexts allow for a participant-related reading with individuals, but not with quantities or groups:

(75) a. The lake / The lakes / # The orange juice have (has) dried up completely.
b. The floor / The clothes / # The wood is (are) completely dry.

As in (74a) with *the chairs*, *completely* applied to *the lakes* in (75a) can only mean that each one of the lakes dried up completely (with a distributive interpretation of the predicate); it cannot have the reading on which all of the lakes dried up. *Completely dry* applied to *the floor* in (75b) yields both an event-type-related and a participant-related reading; applied to *the clothes*, it can have only a participant-related reading involving the individual clothes, not the whole group of clothes. With *the wood*, *completely dry* is unambiguous and can only have an event-type-related reading.

So *completely* is subject to another semantic constraint of the following sort:

(76) *Semantic constraint on* completely
Completely can apply to a part structure of an abstract event only if this part structure has integrity of a sufficient degree.

Clearly, (76) still requires clarification of what the required degree of integrity should be. But the present goal was simply to indicate what kind of constraints there are on the interpretation of adverbs of completion.

6.5.3. German *ganz*

We have seen that English *completely* is subject to certain constraints regarding the part structures it can apply to. However, these constraints are not universal. We will now consider an expression of completion that allows for more readings than English *completely*, though it still does not allow for all possible readings. This is the German adverb of completion *ganz*.

6.5.3.1. The possible readings of *ganz*

German adverbial *ganz*, as in (77a) and (77b), though slightly substandard, is an adverb of completion that is formally related to the adjectival quantifier *ganz* 'whole' discussed in Chapter 3:

(77) a. Franz hat den Apfel ganz aufgegessen.
'Franz has eaten the apple (singular count noun) completely.'
b. Anna hat das Holz ganz verbraucht.
'Ann has used the wood (mass noun) completely.'

At first sight, *ganz* in (77) looks like a floated quantifier with a singular count NP in (77a) and a mass NP in (77b) as antecedents. But adverbial *ganz* cannot be a floated quantifier. An indication for this is that, unlike *ganz* as an adnominal quantifier modifying a plural NP, *ganz* in adverbial position cannot take a plural antecedent. This is seen in the contrast between (78a) and (78b):

(78) a. # Die Kinder sind ganz gekommen.
       'The children have completely come.'
     b. Die ganzen Kinder sind gekommen.
       'The whole children have come.'

In contrast to (78b), in (78a), *ganz* cannot have a participant-related reading. With adverbial *ganz*, such a reading, apparently, is subject to the condition that the participant be either an individual or a quantity, but not a group.

Adverbial *ganz* allows for various event-type-related readings. One such reading may consist in the participant instantiating the highest degree of a state or quality, as in (79a–c), or in the event reaching an extreme effect on its participant, as in (80a–b), or else in the event reaching an extreme point of culmination, as in (81a–d):

(79) a. Hans wurde ganz rot.
       'John became completely red.'
     b. Das Wasser ist ganz heiß.
       'The water is totally hot.'
     c. Maria ist ganz nervös.
       'Mary is totally nervous.'
(80) a. Hans hat Maria ganz eingeschüchtert.
       'John has completely intimidated Mary.'
     b. Maria hat Hans ganz verunsichert.
       'John has made Mary completely insecure.'
(81) a. Die Rose ging nicht ganz auf.
       'The rose did not completely unfold.'
     b. Unter diesen Umständen wird das Haus bald ganz verfallen.
       'In these circumstances, the house will ruin completely.'
     c. Diese Sprache wird Hans nie ganz beherrschen.
       'This language, John will never completely master.'
     d. Franz wird dieses Gedicht nie ganz begreifen.
       'Franz will never comprehend this poem totally.'

For (81b)–(81d) participant-related readings are possible as well.

There is another adverb of completion in German that exhibits a similar range of readings as *ganz* but has a different quantificational force. This is *halb* 'half', as in (82):

(82) Der Baum ist halb vertrocknet.
     'The tree is half dried out.'

Example (82) can either mean that half of the tree is dried out, or that the tree has reached 'half' of the degrees of dryness.

Ganz and *halb* also impose restrictions on the part structures they may apply to; however, as we will see in the next section, these restrictions are weaker than with *completely*, and thus a broader range of part structures is allowed.

6.5.3.2. Restrictions on the possible readings of *ganz*

Like English adverbs of completion, the two readings of *ganz* and *halb* are generally associated with two restrictions on the participant and on the event type which measure the completion of the concrete event.

One of these restrictions was already mentioned — namely, the participant that measures the completion must be an individual or a quantity and may not be a group. More accurately, if it is a group, it enforces a distributive interpretation (with the completion of the event being achieved by the individual group members), as in (83a) and (83b):

(83) a. Marias Augen sind ganz rot.
          'Mary's eyes are completely red.'
      b. Die Äpfel sind ganz rot.
          'The apples are completely red.'
          (in the sense that each apple is completely red — not the apples
          are all red)
      c. Das Holz / ?? Die Luft ist ganz trocken.
          (in the sense that the entire air is dry)
          'The wood / The air is completely dry.'

It appears that with quantities, as in (83c), the participant-related reading is degraded the more homogeneous the quantity is. (For example, air is more homogeneous than wood, which has some internal structure.) This is another instance of the restriction we have found with English adverbs of completion — namely, that the completion of the event by a participant can be achieved only if the participant is, to a certain degree, an integrated whole. The constraint on the participant-related reading of German *ganz*, thus, is of the following sort:

(84) *Restriction on German* ganz
      The completion of the event by a participant or an event type is
      possible only if the participant or event type is an integrated whole
      (of a sufficient degree).

An event is a complete whole only if one of its part structures can be matched with the part structure of an integrated whole of a sufficient degree. Even though this constraint also holds for English *totally* or *completely*, not all expressions of completion are subject to it, as we will see later.

German *ganz* differs from *completely* in interesting ways. German *ganz* (for many speakers) allows for a further reading not available with English *completely*.

This is a reading in which the completion relates to a path, as in (85a). Another potential reading, however, is excluded — namely, a reading that relates to the *location* of the event, as in (85b):

(85) a. Maria ist nach Hause ganz gelaufen.
          'Mary has completely walked home.'
      b. # Die Kinder spielen ganz im Garten.
          'The children play all over the garden.'

Example (85a) means that Mary walked all the way home. But (85b) is impossible with the meaning indicated in the English translation.

There is no need to say much about the formal semantic analysis of the adverbs of completion *ganz* and *halb*. It should basically be the same as for English *completely* and *partly*, the only difference being that *ganz* and *halb* allow the selected part structure to have a weaker degree of integrity.

In the next section, we will turn to expressions of completion that do not impose *any* condition on the integrity of the part structure they can apply to — namely, quantifier preverbs in Warlpiri.

6.5.4. Warlpiri quantifier preverbs

Warlpiri (a language spoken in Australia) has expressions of completion that do not have the form of adverbs but rather have the form of so-called *quantifier preverbs*. Warlpiri as described by Hale (1989) has five quantifier preverbs; but in order to show the relevant generalizations about Warlpiri quantifier preverbs, I will restrict myself to the universal quantifier preverb *muku-*.

With *muku-*, event completion is possible with part structures related to the event type and with part structures related to a participant (as with English *completely* and German *ganz*). Example (86a) exhibits an event-type-related reading, and (86b), a participant-related reading:

(86) a. Ngula-jangka-ji   ka   rangkarrka-nyi-rni   muku.
          that-POST-TOP   PRES   dawn-NPST-CENTRIP   UNIV
          'The dawn breaks fully.'
      b. Maliki-rli nyampu-ju   muku-yarlku-rnu.
          dog-ERG   this-TOP   UNIV-bit-PAST
          'The dog bit this (book) all up.'

However, Warlpiri is much more liberal than English or German with respect to the possibilities of event completion. Warlpiri allows completion without any restrictions regarding group participants, as seen in (87a) and (87b) and regarding participants that are quantities, as seen in (87c). In all three cases, the corresponding sentences in English with *completely* are uninterpretable or only marginally acceptable:

(87) a. Kala   urlpulypa ngula ka   muku-pali.
         but   embers   that   PRES   UNIV-die (-NPST)
         'But those embers all die.'
     b. Nantuwu-ku O-nra-lu   warrka-rnu   muku.
         horse-DAT   PERF-1s-PL   mount-PAST   UNIV
         'We all got on the horses.'
     c. Ma-nta   yali   janyungu   ngula-O
         get-IMP that   tobacco   COMP-PERF
         payipi-ngirli   muku-wanti-muku-wanti-ja.
         pipe-EL   UNIV-fall-PAST
         'Pick up all that tobacco that fell out of the pipe.'

Warlpiri *muku-* also allows completion by the path of an event, which, as we have
seen, is possible also with German *ganz*:

(88) Watiya ka-lu   yirdiyi-rla   muku-rra-karri-mi.
     tree   PRES-3pspl   road-LOC   UNIV-CENTR-stand-NPAST
     'Trees stand all along the road.'

However, *muku-* also allows completion with respect to the spatial location of the
event, a possibility not available for German *ganz*:

(89) Warlu ka   yarlu-ngka   muku-janka-mi
     fire   PRES   plain-LOC   UNIV-burn-NPAST
     'The fire is burning all over the plain.'

In this case, the event is completed in the sense that every part of the location
matches with a part of the event in the spatial dimension.

These phenomena show that *muku-* does not require the participant that
'completes' the event to be an integrated whole. Thus, Warlpiri *muku-* on the one
hand, and German *ganz* and English *completely* on the other hand, differ in that
muku- allows the completion of the event to be achieved by any entity (whether it
is an integrated whole or not), whereas *completely* and *ganz* require an integrated
wholes of some degree. Quantifier preverbs in Warlpiri have exactly the same
semantic function as adverbial quantifiers like *completely* and *ganz*, except that for
the completion of the event more 'completing entities' — that is, more dimensions
of event part structures — are available. The dimension in which the event may
count as completed may be any dimension in which the event is specified as having
parts, and the entities that may measure an event being complete may be entities
with any kind of part structure: individuals, groups, or quantities.

Other quantifier preverbs of completion in Warlpiri behave the same way as
muku-, for instance the quantifier preverb *puta-*. *Puta-* specifies partial completion
of the event in some dimension. It allows for exactly the same range of readings as
muku-. An event-type-related reading is illustrated in (90a) and a participant-related
reading in (90b):

(90) a. Prli   nganta yi-rna   ma-ntarla; wiri-lki
         stone SUPP COMP-1ss lift-IRR; big-LKU
         O-rna   puta-ma-nu.
         PERF-1ss   PART-lift-PAST
         'I was to pick up the stone, but as it was big I failed to pick it
         up.'
     b. Ngapa O-ju   puta-nga-jna.
         water   PERP-1so   PART-drink-IMP
         'Just drink some of my water (not all of it).'

Given that the differences between the English and German adverbs of
completion and Warlpiri quantifier preverbs are only a matter of different conditions
on the part structure of the abstract event, the semantic analysis of the universal and
partitive quantifier preverbs of Warlpiri should be exactly parallel to that of *ganz* and
halb. That is, the semantic operation for the universal quantifier prefix *muku-*
should be the same as for *ganz*, and the semantic operation for the partial quantifier
prefix *puta-* should be the same as for English *partly*, the only difference being that
in Warlpiri no condition on the integrity of the part structure of the abstract event is
imposed.

6.5.5. Parameters governing the restrictions on the possible readings of expressions of completion

I now want to discuss in more detail the parameters that govern the restrictions on
the available readings of expressions of completion across languages.
We have seen one parameter that governs the restrictions on *completely* and
ganz — namely, the degree of integrity of the selected part structure. Recall that
individuals, generally, are integrated wholes; quantities, generally, are not integrated
wholes; groups, generally, do not themselves have integrity; but they have parts
(the group members) that are integrated wholes. As a general principle, the integrity
of the parts reinforces the lack of integrity of the whole in the case of groups, and so
groups have a weaker degree of integrity than quantities. The part structure of
participants that are involved in an event in a certain way arguably induces a part
structure on the event that has the same degree of integrity as the participant itself.
Thus, the differences between expressions of completion in English, German, and
Warlpiri can — at least in part — be formulated as differences in the degree of
integrity that the selected part structure of the event must exhibit. The part structure
of an event that is determined by an individual has the highest degree of integrity,
followed by a part structure that is determined by a quantity, followed by a part
structure determined by a group.
English *completely* requires the highest degree of integrity of the selected part
structure; German *ganz* requires a weaker degree; and Warlpiri *muku-* requires no
degree of integrity. *Ganz* and *muku-* furthermore allow for readings relating to paths
or locations. German *ganz* also allows for readings relating to paths, but it does not
allow for readings relating to spatial locations.

What is the relevant difference between paths and spatial locations? Paths differ from connected spatial locations in that they have integrity in two dimensions: they are connected in space and in time. By contrast, spatial locations are connected only in space. Measuring integrity across dimensions, this means that paths have a stronger degree of integrity than spatial locations. German *ganz* then differs from Warlpiri quantifier preverbs in that it does not allow for part structures with the weaker degree of integrity determined by locations.

Summarizing, we get the following scale of part structures of an event relative to their integrity:

(91) *Scale of event part structures according to the degree of integrity*
     part structures determined by
     individual
     quantity
     group
     path
     spatial location

The different restrictions imposed by expressions of completion in English, German, and Warlpiri raise the general question of what the status of such restrictions is. There are three possibilities:

1. Restrictions that have the status of general language-dependent or culture-dependent principles of individuation
2. Restrictions that are systematically associated with quantifier types in a given language
3. Restrictions that are associated with particular lexical items in a given language.

Let us consider the first possibility. As we will see, event quantifiers of the second type in English can apply to part structures not available for *completely*. Given this, it is clear that the restrictions on English *completely* are not restrictions of the first type — that is, restrictions on the individuation of multidimensional part structures involved in the use of English. For otherwise, all event quantifiers in English would exhibit the same range of possible readings.

Can the restriction on English *completely* be a restriction of the second type — that is, a general restriction on English expressions of *completion*? On such a view, one might assume that quantifiers of the first type are associated with a very general restriction in a given language. This restriction would be strongest in English, looser in German, and totally absent in Warlpiri. However, there is clear evidence that this cannot generally be the case. Different adverbs of completion in the same language are sometimes subject to different restrictions. A case in point are the two German adverbs of completion *ganz* and *völlig* (both meaning 'completely'). *Völlig* displays a narrower range of readings than *ganz*; in fact, it seems to be subject to the same restrictions as *completely* in English. For example, unlike *ganz*, it excludes a path-related reading:

(92) Hans ist nach Hause ganz / # völlig gelaufen.
 'John has completely walked home.'

Thus, the restrictions on expressions of completion may be associated only with particular lexical items in a given language. But this means that the restrictions must be of the third type.

6.6. Apparent ambiguities with concrete event quantifiers

Let us now turn to the second type of expression relating to the part structure of an event, namely, concrete event quantifiers — that is, expressions that involve only quantification over the parts of a concrete event. We will see that all concrete event quantifiers, as long as they do not specifically make reference to the temporal part structure of the event, systematically exhibit multiple readings, which, again, can be traced to the event's having different part structures in different dimensions. In what follows, I will examine a broad range of expressions, which, presumably, exhaust, more or less, the various instantiations of concrete event quantifiers in natural language.

6.6.1. *Same/Different* in the internal reading

Apparent ambiguities due to multiple part structures of a concrete event are displayed by an already familiar construction — namely, *same/different* in the internal reading discussed in Chapter 4.

In Chapter 4, I argued (following Carlson 1987) that *same/different* in the internal reading involves quantification over the parts of an event. In that chapter, we also saw that *same/different* does not involve any specific part structure of the event, but rather may apply to various kinds of event part structures — for example, a participant-related part structure (which is specified by a plural argument), as in (93a), an event-type-related part structure (which is specified by a conjoined event predicate), as in (93b), a temporal part structure, as in (93c), or a spatial part structure, as in (93d):

(93) a. John and Mary saw different films.
    b. John praised and criticized different films.
    c. John played in the house and the garden at different times.
    d. Different people saw John yesterday and today.

In (93a), *different* involves an agent-related part structure; in (93b), an event-type-related part structure; in (93c), a location-related part structure; and in (93d), a time-related part structure.

It is then expected that if in the same sentence, several part structures of the event are specified in several different dimensions, *same/different* exhibits apparent ambiguities. This is borne out by examples such as the following:

(94) a. John and Mary praised and criticized different films.
     b. John praised and criticized different people yesterday and today.
     c. John and Mary saw different people in the garden and in the house.
     d. Different people played in the garden and in the house yesterday and today.
     e. John and Mary praised and criticized different people yesterday and today.

Example (94a) has two readings. On one reading, the films that John praised and criticized were different from the films that Mary praised and criticized. On the other reading, the films that John and Mary praised were different from the films that John and Mary criticized. Similarly, (94b)–(94d) have two readings, and (94e) has three readings.

What is crucial in these examples is that a third or, in the case of (94e), fourth potential reading is excluded. For example, in (94a), a third reading is excluded in which the films that John saw were different from the films that John criticized, from the films that Mary saw, and from the films that Mary criticized. Given the part-quantificational account of *different*, this means that the event described in (94a) cannot have an additional part structure with four parts. Rather, it has only two part structures (containing two parts), each in a different dimension. These dimensions correspond to different kinds of information about the event. The information provided by (94a) specifies a complex event part structure in the following two dimensions: a dimension corresponding to the agents John and Mary and another dimension corresponding to the event types of praising and criticizing. Only one of these dimensions can be the target of the semantic operation associated with *different*.

More formally, the multidimensional part structure of the event e described in (94a) consists of the two simple part structures given in (95a) and (95b), where E is the set of general parts of e, e_1 is an event of John and Mary praising films, e_2 an event of John and Mary criticizing films, e_3 an event of John praising and criticizing films, and e_4 an event of Mary praising and criticizing films:

(95) *The multidimensional part structure of the event described in (94a)*
      a. $(s_1, (E, <), \{e_1, e_2\}, <_{s1})$, whereby
          $FF\text{-INT-WH}(e_1, s_1)$ for $F = \lambda e[(\exists x)(\text{films}(x)\ \&\ \text{praise}(e, \text{John and Mary}, x))]$ and $F'F'\text{-INT-WH}(e_2, s_1)$ for $F' = \lambda e[(\exists x)(\text{films}(x)\ \&\ \text{criticize}(e, \text{John and Mary}, x))]$
      b. $(s_2, (E, <), \{e_3, e_4\}, <_{s2})$, whereby
          $FF\text{-INT-WH}(e_3, s_2)$ for $F = \lambda e[(\exists x)(\text{films}(x)\ \&\ \text{praise and criticize}(e, \text{John}, x))]$ and $F'F'\text{-INT-WH}(e_4, s_2)$ for $F' = \lambda e[(\exists x)(\text{films}(x)\ \&\ \text{praise and criticize}(e, \text{Mary}, x))]$

In order to evaluate *same/different* with respect to an event with a multidimensional part structure, the part-structure-selection function r has to apply so that the semantic operation associated with *same/different* can apply to a single part structure.

The multidimensional part structure of a concrete event is closely related to the event description — more so than in the case of objects. A concrete event may have a part structure in a dimension D only if it is described as having a part structure in D. That is, unlike in the case of objects, a reading relating to a particular part structure cannot come about on the basis of (nonlinguistic) contextual information alone. Consider the examples in (96) and (97):

(96) a. John ate at the same time.
b. John ate the apple and the pear at the same time.
(97) a. John evaluated different people.
b. John praised and criticized different people.
c. John praised and criticized different people yesterday and today.

Example (96a) cannot have (96b) as a reading, even when it is known that all John ate was the apple and the pear. (97a) cannot have (97b) as a reading, even when it is known that John's evaluation of people consisted in praising and criticizing them. Moreover, (97a) cannot have the two readings that (97c) has, even when it is known that John's evaluation of people consisted in praising and criticizing them yesterday and today. Thus, the part structure of a concrete event is totally dependent on the description given by the sentence.[12] This means that concrete events behave like abstract events with respect to their dependence on the event description.

6.6.2. Apparent ambiguities with predicates of concrete events

There are a number of simple adverbs that act as predicates of events and have a lexical meaning that makes reference to the parts of the event. They include *simultaneously, similarly*, and *differently* with an internal, nonindexical reading, as is possible in (98a, b):

(98) a. John simultaneously admired and despised Sue.
b. Mary writes and composes similarly / differently.

On this reading, (98a) means that John's admiring Sue is simultaneous with John's despising Sue, and similarly for (98b).

---

[12] Interestingly, the strict dependence on the description holds only when the events are described by a verb, not when they are referred to by a nominalization, as in (1):

(1) John's evaluations involved different people.

Example (1) may have various readings readings, corresponding to different divisions of John's evaluations. For example, it can mean that John's evaluations involved different people than his negative evaluations or that his evaluations yesterday involved different people than his evaluations today.

Simultaneously can be analyzed as an event predicate which specifies that the parts of an event are at the same time; *similarly* can be analyzed as an event predicate which specifies that the parts of an event are similar (and analogously for *differently*). The lexical meaning of *simultaneously* then is the property given in (99), where t is the function mapping an event to the time at which it takes place:

(99) $[simultaneously]^S = \lambda e[(\forall e')(\forall e'')(e' <_s e \,\&\, e'' <_s e \rightarrow t(e') = t(e''))]$

The parts of the event that *simultaneously*, *similarly*, and *differently* make reference to are specified in the familiar ways — that is, as in the case of the internal reading of *same/different*. Thus, in (98a), the parts of the described event are John's admiring Sue and John's despising Sue; and in (98b), the parts of the described event are Mary's writing and Mary's composing. Of course, the event parts may also correspond to participants or locations, as in (100a, b):

(100) a. John and Mary write similarly.
      b. John writes differently at home and at school.

Like *same/different*, *simultaneously*, *similarly*, and *differently* also display apparent ambiguities:[13]

(101) a. John and Mary simultaneously criticized and praised Bill.
      b. John and Mary simultaneously read the newspaper and talked on the phone.
      c. The three politicians argued simultaneously for and against Bill's proposal.

Here, *simultaneously* may relate either to the members of the relevant group participant or to the parts of the complex event type given by the conjoined event predicates (i.e., conjoined verbs in (101a), VPs in (101b), and PPs in (101c)).[14]

---

[13] Of course, the apparent ambiguities with *simultaneously* are expected already because *simultaneously* is equivalent to *at the same time* with the internal reading of *same*. Note, though, that *simultaneously* differs from *at the same time* in that it cannot take a quantified antecedent:

(1) a. Every child screamed at the same time.
    b. # Every child screamed simultaneously.
    c. All children screamed at the same time / simultaneously.

The fact that *simultaneously* is acceptable with plural quantifiers in (1c) is due to the fact that plural quantifiers may range over subgroups. These subgroups individuate group events to which *simultaneously* can relate in the same way as when it takes a definite plural antecedent.

[14] It is worth noting that the event predicates discussed in this section also impose part-structure-sensitive semantic selectional requirements. For example, *simultaneously* is

6.6.3. 'Floated quantifiers' ranging over events

The multidimensional part structure of events and the various ways of specifying event part structures show up also with simple quantifiers ranging over event parts — namely, *all, each*, and *both* in a function parallel to floated *all* and *both* with nominal antecedents (as in *the people all / each / both made a mistake*). *All, each,* and *both* in the event-related construction in (102) look just like floated quantifiers ranging over events:

(102) a. Mary laughed and screamed, both / each this afternoon.
     b. John criticized and praised Bill, both / each for several reasons.
     c. Mary became pale, trembled, and cried, all / each because of Bill.

In (102), *all, each,* and *both* range over subevents described by conjunct event predicates. The following examples show that they may range also over event parts corresponding to locations, event qualities, and participants:

(103) a. John played in the garden and in the house, both for several
       hours.
     b. John played the sonata slowly and fast, both for several hours.
     c. John wrote to Sue and Mary, both this afternoon.

Like floated *all, each*, and *both* with nominal antecedent, *all, each,* and *both* with event antecedent act as quantifiers ranging over the parts of the event without further specification (*both* imposes only the additional restriction that the event must consist of exactly two parts). Thus, they should display apparent ambiguities. This is in fact the case, as seen in the examples in (104):

(104) a. Mary laughed and shouted at Bill and at John, both / each for the
       same reason.
     b. Mary became pale, trembled, and cried because of Bill, of Mark,

---

subject to the Accessibility Requirement, as seen in (1), and the Integrated Parts Requirement, as seen in (2):

(1) # John built the house simultaneously.
    (i.e., John accomplished every part of building the house at the same
    time.)
(2) a. # John got the information simultaneously.
    a'. John got the pieces of information simultaneously.
    b. # John destroyed the furniture (OK the chairs) simultaneously.
    b'. John destroyed the chairs / furniture and the jewelry simultaneously.

Examples (2a) and (2b) do not provide any means of characterizing the part structure of the described event as consisting of integrated parts. They involve only mass participants and no event group predicates. Thus, the Integrated Parts Requirement is not satisfied.

and of John, all / each in front of a friend.

Example (104a) has two readings: either Mary laughed for the same reason as she shouted (at Bill and at John), or Mary laughed and shouted at Bill for the same reason as she laughed and shouted at John. Example (104b) displays a parallel apparent ambiguity.

Floated event quantifiers behave the same way as *same/different* and simple event predicates in another respect, too. Like *same/different* and event predicates like *simultaneously*, *all* as a floated event quantifier exhibits the 'description-dependence' of the event part structure. Only if the part structure has been specified descriptively can *all* range over the parts of that part structure. This can be seen from the following contrast:[15]

> (105) a. # The message was announced all at the same time.
>   b. The message was announced in several places all at the same time.

So far we have considered concrete event quantifiers only insofar as they make reference to the parts of an event in a neutral way and therefore may apply to any of the part structures the concrete event may have in the relevant situation. We will next see that there are also concrete event quantifiers that make reference to a particular part structure of the event — namely, the temporal part structure.

6.6.4. Binary distributive event quantifiers

6.6.4.1. German *jeweils* as a neutral binary distributive event quantifier

There are two instances of concrete event quantifiers that belong to the class of *binary distributive quantifiers* (using the term I introduced in Moltmann 1991a). Quantifiers of this type occur as both quantifiers ranging over the parts of an event and quantifiers ranging over the parts of an NP-referent. The latter have often been discussed in the syntactic and semantic literature and are exemplified by the *each*-construction in (106):

> (106) The three men bought two books each.

---

[15] Again (see footnote 12), *all* as a quantifier ranging over the parts of a verbal event argument differs from *all* as a quantifier ranging over the parts of an NP-referent. The latter does not exhibit the description-dependence of the part structure. Thus, *all* in (1) may range over the spatial parts of the event, without the event being explicitly located in space:

> (1) The noise came all from different places.

The *each*-construction in (106), *binominal each* as Safir/Stowell (1988) call it, has been discussed by Postal (1975), Burzio (1986), Choe (1987), and Safir/Stowell (1988). Crucially, *each* in (106) is a binary quantifier relating to two terms, one being *the three men*, the *D-NP* in Safir and Stowell's terms, and one being *two books*, the *R-NP* in Safir and Stowell's terms. The parts of the referent of the D-NP provide the quantification domain for the universal quantifier expressed by *each*. The R-NP is the NP immediately preceding *each.*

There are also binary distributive quantifiers that relate to events (as arguments of verbs). For them, I will use the more general notions *D-term* and *R-term*. Event-related binary distributive quantifiers take various forms. Of particular interest in the present context is a distinction between two types of binary distributive event quantifiers: quantifiers that make reference to the parts of an event in a neutral way (*neutral binary distributive event quantifiers*) and quantifiers which make reference to the temporal parts of the event (*temporal binary distributive event quantifiers*).

Neutral binary distributive event quantifiers are exemplified by the German quantifiers *jeweils* 'each' and *je* 'each' (which are basically synonymous and share the relevant properties). *Jeweils* (or *je*) acts as a binary distributive quantifier in a variety of ways, only one of which will be relevant for the present concerns. *Jeweils* may take three types of group antecedent: [1] a deictic group antecedent, as in (107a) (which might be a group of families); [2] a group referent of an NP, as in (107b); and [3] an event, as in (108a) and arguably (108b) and (108c):

(107) a. Jeweils zwei Söhne wurden getötet.
'Of each of them two sons were killed.'
b. drei Kinder aus jeweils zwei Schulen
'three children from two schools each'
(108) a. Maria kritisierte und lobte jeweils zwei Bücher.
Mary criticized and praised each two books
'Mary criticized two books and praised two books.'
b. Hans spielte im Garten und im Haus für jeweils zwei Stunden.
'John played in the garden and the house for two hours each.'
c. Die Kinder bekamen jeweils ein Geschenk.
'The children received one gift each.'

In (108a), *jeweils* expresses a universal quantifier ranging over the parts of the described event (a subevent of criticizing and a subevent of praising) and associating two books with each subevent. Thus, the D-term of *jeweils* in (108a) is the complex event predicate *criticized and praised*. In (108b), *jeweils* expresses a universal quantifier ranging over the two subevents of John's playing in the garden and in the house, the D-term being *spielte im Garten und im Haus*. In (108c) (on one reading), *jeweils* expresses a universal quantifier ranging over the three subevents of the three children's receiving gifts, the D-term simply being *bekamen*.

The semantic function of event-related *jeweils* is to associate the parts of the event argument of the D-term with referents of the R-term. Like binominal *each,* as described by Safir/Stowell (1988), this association between the parts provided by the R-term and the referents of the D-term must be a one-to-one mapping; that is, each part must be mapped onto a different referent of the R-term. For instance, (108a) implies that the two books that Mary criticized are different from the two books that she praised; and (108c) implies that each child received a different gift.[16]

Thus, the denotation of (108a) will be as in (109) in the relevant respects:

(109) $\lambda s[(\exists e)(\exists x)([\textit{kritisierte und lobte}]^S(e, \text{Mary}, x) = 1 \ \&$
$(\forall e\,')(\forall e\,'')(e\,' <_s e \ \& \ e\,'' <_s e \ \& \ e\,' \neq e\,'' \rightarrow (\exists x\,')(\exists x\,'')(x\,' <_s x$
$\& \ x\,'' <_s x \ \& \ [\textit{zwei Bücher}]^S(x\,') = 1 \ \& \ [\textit{zwei Bücher}]^S(x\,'') = 1 \ \& \ x\,' \neq$
$x\,'' \ \& \ [\textit{lobte und kritisierte}]^S(e\,', \text{Mary}, x\,') = 1 \ \& \ [\textit{lobte und}$
$\textit{kritisierte}]^S(e\,'', \text{Mary}, x\,'') = 1)))]$

Thus, (108a) describes situations in which there is an event e of Mary's criticizing and praising an entity x such that for any two distinct parts $e\,'$ and $e\,''$ of e, there are two distinct groups $x\,'$ and $x\,''$ of two books that are part of x such that $e\,'$ is a praising and criticizing of $x\,'$ and $e\,''$ is a praising and criticizing of $x\,''$. (Here it is assumed that an event can be a praising and criticizing even if it consists only of a praising or only of a criticizing event.)

The formal compositional analysis of the sentence meaning in (109) (involving a transitive verb with the object being the R-term) can be based on the syntactic relation in (110a) (presupposing adequate identification conditions for R-terms and D-terms) and the associated semantic operation in (110b):

(110) a. *The syntactic relation for event-related* jeweils
          Let f, g, and h be constituents in a syntactic structure S.
          $<f, g, h> \in je\text{-EVENT}(S)$ iff $f = je$, g is a verb and the D-term of
          f in S, and h is the R-term of f in S.
       b. *The semantic operation for event-related* jeweils
          Let R be a three-place situated relation and P a situated property.
          $je\text{-event}(R, P) = \lambda s \lambda e y[(\exists x)(R^S(e, y, x) = 1 \ \& \ (\forall e\,')(\forall e\,'')(e\,' <_s e$
          $\& \ e\,'' <_s e \ \& \ e\,' \neq e\,'' \rightarrow (\exists x\,')(\exists x\,'')(x\,' <_s x \ \& \ x\,'' <_s x \ \& \ P^S(x\,')$
          $= 1 \ \& \ P^S(x\,'') = 1 \ \& \ x\,' \neq x\,'' \ \& \ R^S(e\,', y, x\,') = 1 \ \& \ R^S(e\,'', y, x\,'')$
          $= 1)))]$
       c. $<je\text{-EVENT}, je\text{-event}> \in$ corr

On this analysis, the R-term enters the syntactic relation associated with *jeweils* to the verb, rather than counting as an argument of the verb. This certainly requires further elaboration; but that will lead too far away from the present issue — namely, the role of part structures in the semantics of event quantifiers.

As the examples in (108) illustrate, the event parts that *jeweils* ranges over are specified in the familiar ways, and *jeweils* can relate to any such event part structure. It is therefore expected that *jeweils*, when acting as an event quantifier, may exhibit apparent ambiguities. This is in fact the case, as seen in the following examples:

---

[16] This is discussed in greater detail in Moltmann (1991a).

(111) a. Hans kritisierte und lobte Maria am Morgen und am Nachmittag
       aus jeweils zwei Gründen.
       'John criticized and praised Mary in the morning and in the
       afternoon each for two reasons.'
    b. Hans kritisierte und lobte Maria und Anna aus jeweils zwei
       Gründen.
       'John criticized and praised Mary and Ann, each for two reasons.'
    c. Maria spielte mit zwei Bällen im Garten und im Zimmer mit
       jeweils einem Partner.
       'Mary played with two balls in the garden and in the room, each
       with one partner.'

In (111a), *jeweils* can relate either to the parts of the described event that consist of
an event of criticizing and an event of praising or to the parts of the described event
that took place either in the morning or in the afternoon. Crucially, *jeweils* in
(111a) cannot relate to both of these sets of event parts simultaneously, requiring
that two reasons be associated with each of the four event parts. This, again, shows
that the two sets of event parts belong to different dimensions. Example (111b) also
has exactly two readings, which can be traced to whether *jeweils* ranges over the
participant-related parts of the described event (which relate to Mary and Ann) or
over the event-type-related parts of criticizing and praising. Example (111c) displays
a similar two readings.

   The apparent ambiguities that *jeweils* exhibits show that *jeweils* involves the
parts of an event in an unspecified way. In this respect, *jeweils* contrasts minimally
with another binary distributive quantifier, which I will discuss in the next section.

6.6.4.2. The English *at a time*-construction as a temporal binary distributive event quantifier

The binary distributive event quantifier that I will discuss now differs from *jeweils*
in that it imposes a sortal restriction on the quantification domain — namely, a
restriction to temporal parts. It consists of a weak quantifier followed by *at a time*:

(112) a. John sold the apples one / two / several / many / a few at a time.
    b. Mary ate the meat a little bit at a time.

Example (112a) intuitively means that there is an event e of John's eating the apples
such that, for every temporal part e' of e, there is a different apple x' of the group of
apples so that e' is an eating of x' by John. Similarly, (112b) intuitively means that
there is an event e of Mary's eating the meat such that, for every temporal part e' of
e, there is a different quantity x' of the meat which is 'a little bit' and e' is an eating
of x' by Mary.

   Note that instead of a weak quantifier, the *at a time*-construction also allows for
measure-phrase constructions such as *one piece* and *one chapter*:

(113) a. John ate the cake one piece at a time.

   b. Mary read the book one chapter at a time.

The expression *at a time* relates to the following two terms: a verb as an event-denoting expression (the D-term) and the quantifier immediately preceding *a time* (the R-term). Unlike binominal *each* and *jeweils*, the *at a time*-construction involves quantification over the parts of two entities: the event denoted by the D-term and an event participant which the D-term is related to. In (113a), the latter is the referent of *the cake*; and in (113b), it is the referent of *the book*. Let me call *the cake* in (113a) and *the book* in (113b) the *R'-term* of *at a time*. Then, we have the labelling of (113a) as in (114a), which is contrasted with the binominal *each* construction in (114b), which lacks an R'-term:

(114) a. John   **ate**   **the cake one piece** *at a time.*
              D-term R'-term   R-term
     b. **The children** ate **two apples** *each.*
           D-term   R-term

Like all binary distributive event quantifiers, the *at a time*-construction involves a one-to-one mapping of the parts of the event to entities that the R-term ranges over. Thus, (113b) implies that Mary read a different chapter of the book in each temporal subevent of her reading the book.

A *time* in the *at a time*-construction acts as a quantifier ranging over the parts of the event denoted by the D-term. But, unlike event-related *jeweils*, *a time* does not range over *any* kind of parts an event may have, but only over temporal parts. This restriction manifests itself in the fact that, unlike event-related *jeweils*, the *at a time*-construction does not display apparent ambiguities:

(115) a. John ate bread and cake one piece at a time.
     b. John wrote and sang songs two at a time.

(115a) cannot mean that John ate one piece of bread and one piece of cake; that is, it cannot have a reading in which *a time* ranges over participant-related parts of the event. (115a) can only mean that, at a given temporal subevent of John's eating bread and cake, John ate one piece of bread or cake. Similarly, (115b) cannot mean that John wrote two songs and sang two songs; that is, the range of *a time* may not consist in the two event-type-related parts that are maximal events denoted by conjoined verbs. (115b) can only mean that during a given temporal subevent of John's writing and singing songs, John wrote or sang two songs.

Thus, *a time* may only quantify over the parts of an event that constitute *temporal units*. Such temporal units are specified as parts of the event not by the event description but rather by the inherent semantic content of *a time*. *A time* imposes a metrical requirement on the part structure of the event and requires that the parts of the event be temporally distant from each other. As in the case of frequency adverbials, this metrical requirement can be conceived of as a component of the lexical meaning of *time*. So the lexical meaning of *time* (in this particular construction) can be construed as a two-place situated relation which holds between an event e' and an event e in a situation s just in case e' is a part of e in s and the temporal-distance function m_t is a metric on the parts of e in s:

(116) $[time]^S = \lambda e' e [e' <_s e$ & METRIC$(m_t, \{e'' \mid e'' <_s e\}, s)]$

The denotations of the sentences in (112) and (113) can now be given formally. The construction with binominal *a time*, strictly speaking, involves two operations of part quantification: one involving the parts of the event denoted by the D-term and one involving the parts of the participant denoted by the R'-term. The former operation is associated with *a time*; the latter with the quantifier preceding *a time* — that is, *one, two, several, many*, or *a few* in (112a), *a little bit* in (112b), *one piece* in (113a), and *one chapter* in (113b). Also, in this case, the lexical meaning of the quantifier specifies the relevant parts, namely parts that are 'one', 'two', 'several', 'many', 'a few', 'a little bit', 'one piece', or 'one chapter'. The denotation of (112a) with *one* then is, simplified, as follows:

(117) $\lambda s[(\exists e)([sold]^S(e,$ John, $sum_{<s}'([the\ apples]^S) = 1$ & $(\forall e')(\forall e'')(e'$
$<_s e$ & $e'' <_s e$ & $[time]^S(e', e) = 1$ & $[time]^S(e'', e) = 1$ & $e' \neq e''$
$\rightarrow (\exists z')(\exists z'')(z' <_s sum_{<s}'([the\ apples]^S)$ & $z'' <_s sum_{<s}'([the$
$apples]^S)$ & $z' \neq z''$ & $[one]^S(z') = 1$ & $[one]^S(z'') = 1$ & $[sold]^S(e',$
John, $z') = 1$ & $[sold]^S(e'',$ John, $z'') = 1)))]$

Thus, on this analysis, (112a) is true of of situations in which there is an event e of eating involving John and the apples such that for any two parts of e that belong to the set of temporally disconnected parts of e, the following holds: there are two distinct parts of the apples that are 'one' in number such that the event parts, John, and the parts of the apples are related to each other by the relation of eating.

The denotations of the other examples in (112) and (113) are exactly parallel. The differences in the overall meanings reside only in the particular lexical meanings of the nouns, verbs, and quantifiers in questions.

The denotation of (112a) as given in (117) can be obtained compositionally on the basis of the following syntactic relation and semantic operation (where it is assumed that *at a time* simply has the denotation of *time*):

(118) a. *The syntactic relation for the* at a time-*construction*
Let f, g and h be constituents in a syntactic structure S.
$<f, g, h> \in$ BIN-TIME(S) iff f is a verb and the D-term of g in S, $g = $ *at a time*, and h is the R-term of g in S.

b. *The semantic operation associated with the* at a time-*construction*
Let R be a three-place situated relation, R' a two-place situated relation, and A a situated set.
For reference situations s' and s'' and a situation s,
$bin\text{-}time(<R, R', A>) = \lambda exz[R^S(e, x, z) = 1$
& $(\forall e')(\forall e'')(e' <_s e$ & $e'' <_s e$ & $e' \neq e''$ & $R'^S(e', e) = 1$

$$\& \; R'^{S}(e'', e) = 1 \rightarrow (\exists z')(\exists z'')(A^{S'}(z') = 1 \; \& \; A^{S''}(z'') = 1 \; \& \; z' \neq$$
$$z'' \; \& \; R^{S}(e', x, z') = 1 \; \& \; R^{S}(e'', x, z'') = 1)))]$$

    c. <BIN-TIME, *bin-time*> ∈ *corr*

Here the R'-term itself is neglected; the relation BIN-TIME only involves the argument position that the R'-term occupies. This means that, on the basis of (118), we get the denotation of discontinuous expressions like *sold ... one at a time.* Clearly, for a more general definition, the R'-term plays a role at least in specifying the argument position that is to be affected.

The *at a time*-construction differs from event-related *jeweils* also with respect to semantic selectional requirements — in particular, the Integrated Part Requirement. As the examples in (112b) and (113) show, the *at a time*-construction does not require that the event be specified as having integrated parts (e.g., by means of a conjoined event predicate or a group participant), and so in this respect, the *at a time*-construction patterns with frequency expressions. The reason for this is that the Integrated Parts Requirement is already independently satisfied — namely, because of the metrical component involved in *a time*. The metrical component specifies the temporal part structure of the event as consisting of subevents that are maximally connected in time and thus are integrated wholes.

In contrast to the *at a time*-construction, the Integrated Parts Requirement is imposed by the German *jeweils*-construction. This can be seen in the contrast between (119a) and (119b):

(119) a. (?) Die Schmuckstücke wurden jeweils mehreren Leuten gezeigt.
         'The pieces of jewelry were shown to several people.'
       b. # Der Schmuck wurde jeweils mehreren Leuten gezeigt.
         'The jewelry was shown to several people.'

Example (119b) is impossible because the D-term is a mass NP — in contrast to (119a), which contains a plural NP and hence is acceptable.

We have seen with German *jeweils* that binary distributive event quantifiers involving event parts without further specification may apply to any part structure of a possibly multidimensional event part structure. They contrast in that respect with quantifiers of the type *one at a time*, which make explicit reference to the temporal part structure and therefore do not exhibit different readings based on different part structures. Moreover, the *at a time*-construction, unlike *jeweils*, does not fall under the Integrated Parts Requirement. This is because the lexical meaning of *time* itself imposes a metric on the event parts and thus by itself specifies the event parts as integrated wholes.

In the next section, we will consider a number of other binary distributive quantifiers that range over the parts of an event. These quantifiers share with *jeweils* the property of not imposing a temporal metric; but still they specify a particular sort of participant part for their quantification domain.

6.6.4.3. Other binary distributive event quantifiers: *in groups of four, piece-by-piece, . . .*

Besides the *at a time*-construction, there is another class of adverbials that quantify both over event parts and participant parts. It includes *in groups of four, piece-by-piece*, and a German construction with the suffix *-weise* such as *schichtenweise* 'by layers' and *stückweise* 'piece by piece'. This class of adverbials differs from the *at a time*-construction in that it is not restricted to temporal parts of the event and does not impose a metrical condition on the temporal part structure.

Like the *at a time*-construction, the adverbials in question all have a component that specifies what sort of participant parts are under consideration. Thus, in *groups of three*, the part sortal for the participant is 'group of three'; in *piece-by-piece*, it is 'piece'; and in *chapter-by-chapter*, it is 'chapter':

(120) a. John sold the apples three at a time.
        b. John sold the apples in groups of three.
(121) a. John ate the cake one piece at a time.
        b. John ate the cake piece-by-piece.
(122) a. Mary read the book one chapter at a time.
        b. Mary read the book chapter-by-chapter.

Like the *at a time*-construction, the adverbials under consideration relate the parts of the event to specified parts of a participant. For example, in (120b), *in groups of three* relates the subevents of selling to subgroups of the apples that have three members, and similarly for *piece-by-piece* in (121b) and *chapter-by-chapter* in (122b). Also the condition obtains that two distinct event parts be associated with distinct participant parts (of the relevant sort). So the denotation of (120b) will be as in (123):

(123) $\lambda s[(\exists e)([sold]^S(e, \text{John}, sum_{<_S'}([the\ apples]^{S'})) = 1 \;\&\; (\forall e')(\forall e'')(e'$
    $<_S e \;\&\; e'' <_S e \;\&\; e' \neq e'' \rightarrow (\exists x')(\exists x'')(x' <_S' sum_{<_S'}([the\ apples]^{S'})$
    $\&\; x'' <_S' sum_{<_S'}([the\ apples]^{S'}) \;\&\; x' \neq x'' \;\&\; [group\ of\ three]^{S'}(x')$
    $= 1 \;\&\; [group\ of\ three]^{S'}(x'') = 1 \;\&\; [sold]^S(e', \text{John}, x') = 1$
    $\&\; [sold]^S(e'', \text{John}, x'') = 1)))]$

Notice that (123) is exactly parallel to the way the *at a time*-construction was analyzed in the preceding section. In fact, almost the same syntactic relation and semantic operation can be used:

(124) a. *The syntactic relation for binary distributive quantifiers of the type* in groups of three
        Let *f, g*, and *h* be constituents in a syntactic structure *S*.
        <f, g, h> ∈ BIN-DISTR(*S*) iff *f* is a verb and the D-term of *g* in *S*, *g = jeweils*, and *h* the R-term of *g* in *S*.
       b. *The semantic operation for binary distributive quantifiers*
        Let *R* be a three-place situated relation and *A* a situated set. Then,

for reference situations s' and s'' and a situation s,

$bin\text{-}distr(<R, \emptyset, A>) = \lambda exy[R^S(e, y, x) = 1 \,\& \, (\forall e')(\forall e'')(e' <_s e$
$\&\, e'' <_s e \,\&\, e' \neq e'' \rightarrow (\exists x')(\exists x'')(x' <_s' x \,\&\, x'' <_s' x \,\&\, x' \neq$
$x'' \,\&\, A^S(x') = 1 \,\&\, A^{S''}(x'') = 1 \,\&\, R^S(e', y, x') = 1 \,\&\, R^S(e'',$
$y, x'') = 1)))]$

   c. <BIN-DISTR, *bin-distr*> $\in$ *corr*

Here *jeweils* is treated as a syncategorematic expression denoting the empty set (cf. Chapter 2).

The adverbials under consideration differ from the *at a time*-construction in one respect, however: they do not impose a temporal metric on the event and do not necessarily range over temporal parts of the event. Consider the contrast between the *at a time*-construction in (125a) and adverbials of the sort under discussion in (125b) and (125c):

(125) a. Mary wrote the book one chapter at a time.
       b. Mary wrote the book in chapters.
       c. Mary wrote the book chapter-by-chapter.

In (125a), Mary must have worked on each chapter of the book during a different time. But in (125b), Mary may have worked on several chapters of the book at the same time. Even though the *by*-construction in (125c) implies that the chapters were written during different time intervals, it does not require that these intervals are disconnected from each other. The *by*-construction makes reference to temporal parts of the event without imposing a metric on the temporal part structure of the event.

Both the sortal restriction to temporal parts and the metric condition imposed by the *at a time*-construction are captured by the lexical meaning of *time* in (116). In the case of the other adverbials, the neutrality regarding the sort of parts and the lack of a metrical condition follow from the lack of any specification of parts. Only the *by*-construction requires reference to temporal parts.[17]

---

[17] One might also analyze *individually* as a binary distributive quantifier. From a semantic point of view, the treatments of *individually* as a perspective shifter and as a binary distributive quantifier actually amount to the same. Consider (1):

(1) The people left individually.

As a perspective shifter, the meaning of *individually* in (1) amounts to the condition that the people are not an integrated whole with respect to the activity of leaving, but consist of parts that are integrated wholes with respect to that activity. As a binary distributive quantifier, *individually* in (1) requires that for each subevent of the event of the people's leaving, there is an individual person who is the agent of that subevent of leaving. Notice that *individually*, unlike *one at a time*, does not imply temporally disconnected events, as seen in the contrast between (2a) and (2b):

(2) a. John wrapped the presents individually.
     b. John wrapped the presents one at time.

The semantic analysis of the binary distributive event quantifiers given in this section has a general implication regarding distributivity. Like the *at a time*-construction, binary distributive event quantifiers make reference to particular parts of the relevant participant as specified by measure expressions such as *one, one chapter*, or *a little bit* in *one at a time, one chapter at a time*, and *a little bit at a time* or *piece* in *piece-by-piece* or *group of four* in *groups of four*. Thus, the quantifiers do not simply involve parts that are contextually determined. But then their analysis bears on the treatment of distributivity. Recall that in Chapter 2, distributive interpretation was conceived of as an association of the relevant parts of a participant with parts of the event. This treatment of distributivity, however, seems to conflict with the semantic analysis of the adverbials in question. Consider (126):

(126) The children danced pairwise and sang songs in groups of four.

What is the part structure of the referent of *the children* in (126)? Does it consist of pairs of children, of subgroups of four children, or of individual children? Given the analysis of adverbials like *pairwise* and *in groups of four* above, the part structure of the group of children must consist both of groups of two children and groups of four children, since both adverbials involve universal quantification over the parts of the children (with a sortal restriction to certain kinds of parts).

There is a way of testing whether the part structure indeed includes both kinds of parts. This is the us of unrestricted part quantifiers — for instance, the floated quantifier *all*, as in (127):

(127) The children sang songs in groups of four and all received a gift.

In (2a), John must have wrapped the presents one after the other. By contrast, in (2b), John may have wrapped some presents simultaneously. (2b) implies only that each present has undergone a process of wrapping that does not involve any of the other. These individual processes, of course, may have taken place at the same time; that is, they may constitute event parts that are not temporal parts (but rather parts that are determined by the event type of a complete 'present wrapping').

From the first meaning of *individually* in (1), it follows that the people were not involved in one collective act of leaving, but rather in individual subevents of coming. Hence the first meaning implies the second. The second meaning implies that each person acts as an integrated whole with respect to the activity of coming; since the people cannot at the same time act as a collective agent, the second meaning implies the first. There are some arguments in favor of the treatment as a perspective shifter and others in favor of the treatment as a binary distributive quantifier. The first treatment would give a unified account of *individual* as an adjectival modifier and *individually* as an adverbial. An advantage of the second treatment is that it would explain the restriction of *individually* to the dimension of a described action for establishing integrity among the group members.

Note that the same two options arise for the treatment of *wholly*.

Example (127) seems acceptable in the reading on which each single child received a gift. But this means that the part structure of groups may consist of layers of overlapping parts. The part structure of the group of children in (127) thus consists of all individual children as well as some groups of four children.

The four types of expressions — *same/different*; simple event predicates such as *simultaneously*; binary distributive quantifiers such as *jeweils*, and 'floated event quantifiers' — seem to more or less exhaust the types of expressions making reference to the parts of an event. Unless they make reference to a specific event part structure, they all exhibit apparent ambiguities. This can be traced to the event's having multiple part structures in several dimensions. The prediction then is that this should hold for any event part quantifier, which seems correct.

6.7. Conclusions

We have seen how multidimensional part structures of events show up with two types of event part quantifiers: [1] quantifiers involving quantification over both parts of an abstract event and parts of a concrete event (expressions of completion) and [2] quantifiers involving only the parts of a concrete event (concrete event part quantifiers).

Expressions of completion are not always able to apply to any part structure the event may have but often are subject to restrictions as to what kind of part structure may be selected. These restrictions involve at least two parameters: [1] the integrity of the part structure and [2] the kind of involvement in the event of the entity determining the part structure — for example, depending on whether or not the entity undergoes a change in the event.

We have seen the first parameter at work with English *completely* and German *ganz*, and the second parameter with *completely* and *partly*, which are subject to the requirement that the participant responsible for the participant-related reading has to undergo a change during the event.

Both sorts of restrictions seem to be absent in the case of concrete event part quantifiers. For example, unlike *partly* and *completely*, concrete event part quantifiers may always relate to the location of the event, as in (128a, b):

(128) a. The message was simultaneously announced in America and
          Europe.
       b. The message was announced in America and Europe, both at the
          same time.

Unlike expressions of completion, concrete event part quantifiers do not seem to impose restrictions on the dimension of the part structure they can apply to. Thus, in (129a–c), the event expressions involve a location-related reading, a reading unavailable for both English *completely* and German *ganz*:

(129) a. John slept on the bed and on the floor in the same position /
          differently.
       b. The glasses are standing individually on the shelves.

    c. John played in the garden and in the house both for two hours.

Event quantifiers of the second type can apply to any part structure the concrete event may have. Such a part structure is available only on the basis of how the event is described. That is, a part structure is available only if the event is described by an appropriate complex event predicate.

    The question why expressions of completions and concrete event quantifiers differ in their restrictions on the event part structure they may apply to is an interesting one, but unfortunately also one I have to leave open for further research.

7

The Mass-Count Distinction for Verbs and Adverbial Quantification over Events

7.1. Verbs and the mass-count distinction

This chapter deals with the question of whether a mass-count distinction obtains for verbs with respect to their event argument place. In relation to that, it also gives a formal semantic analysis of certain types of adverbial quantifiers ranging over events such as *a lot* and *frequently*.

Let me first clarify what exactly the issue is. As was mentioned in Chapter 1, there is a syntactic and a semantic mass-count distinction. Verbs (at least in English) obviously lack a syntactic mass-count distinction. But still one may ask whether it makes sense to apply a semantic mass-count distinction to verbs. In order to answer this question, let us consider the ways in which a semantic mass-count distinction may be relevant. First of all, a semantic mass-count distinction constitutes the content of the syntactic mass-count distinction. But there are other ways in which a semantic mass-count distinction may play a role in natural language. Whether a category is classified as semantically mass or count may be relevant in two respects: [1] the category may have to be classified syntactically as mass or count for some purposes — for example, for the purpose of agreement; [2] the category may classify semantically like categories that are 'mass' or like categories that are 'count' in contexts that are sensitive to the distinction.

What this chapter will show is that verbs uniformly classify as a mass category in important ways. This holds for both respects in which a semantic mass-count distinction may be drawn for a category lacking a corresponding syntactic distinction. First, verbs (with respect to their event argument position) pattern in many ways like mass nouns semantically. Second, if verbs (with respect to the event argument position) have to be classified as mass or count for syntactic purposes, they will be classified as mass.

This result is quite surprising, since verbs (or verbal projections) have traditionally been classified, by analogy to the three nominal categories, into the categories singular count (accomplishments and achievements), plural (repetitive verbs or verbs with plural participants), and mass (process verbs and statives) (cf.

Mourelatos 1981, Bach 1986, Langacker 1987a, Pelletier/Schubert 1989, Jackendoff 1991). The criteria generally used for drawing such a distinction are the extensional mereological ones. Accomplishment and achievement verbs or VPs such as *die, build a house*, or *eat the apples* are neither divisive nor cumulative, and hence they are classified as singular count. VPs such as *rotate, sing songs*, or *build houses* are cumulative, but not divisive; and hence they are classified as plural. Stative or activity verbs such as *lie, know*, and *run* are divisive (more or less) and cumulative, and hence they are classified as mass. So the traditional classification of verbs is as follows:

(1) singular count:
     die, build a house, eat the apple
     plural:
     rotate, sing songs, build houses
     mass:
     lie, know, run

The results of this chapter show that this analogy between nouns and verbs is rather misleading.

I will give three sorts of evidence supporting the claim that verbs behave like mass expressions in either syntactic or semantic respects: [1] adverbial quantification over events, [2] pronominal reference to events, and [3] coordination of deverbal nominalizations. The chapter will be somewhat inconclusive, as I will only consider, but not adopt, a possible explanation for the mass behavior of verbs.

When discussing adverbial quantification, I will also show that the formal analysis developed so far for quantified noun phrases can directly be carried over to the semantic analysis of adverbial event quantifiers. Thus, no special devices have to be introduced for adverbial quantification that have not already been motivated for the nominal system.

7.2. Adverbial event quantifiers as mass quantifiers

There are three classes of adverbial event quantifiers: simple mass quantifiers, frequency adverbs, and measure-phrase constructions:

1. Simple mass quantifiers:
   a lot, little, much
2. Frequency adverbs:
   frequently, rarely, constantly, habitually, usually
3. Measure-phrase constructions of the form numeral-count quantifier-*times*:
   three times, several times, once and *twice* (which are semantically, though not morpho-syntactically, of this form)[1]

---

[1] There are still other adverbial quantifiers that relate to events. Three kinds of event quantifiers were discussed in Chapter 6, Sections 6.4.4.–6.4.6. Also measure adverbials like *for half an hour, until noon*, and *worldwide* relate to events. However, measure

We will see that these three quantifier types represent precisely the quantifier types characteristic of mass categories. Before showing this, however, the question has to be answered why the adverbials above should be classified as event *quantifiers* rather than as event *predicates*. This requires first some general remarks about the quantifier status of adverbials.

Whether an adverbial is an event quantifier or an event predicate can be decided by applying similar diagnostics as for referential and quantified NPs — namely, scope interactions and variable binding. Let us apply these tests to the adverbials listed above.

First, an adverbial quantifier should be able to take wide scope over an indefinite NP. This is the case with frequency expressions and measure-phrase constructions, as seen in (2a) and (2b), which can be about different movies and different French women respectively:

(2) a. John frequently saw a movie.
     b. Three times, John married a French woman.

Simple mass quantifiers, though, allow only indefinite plural or mass NPs, but not indefinite singular count NPs, to take narrow scope, as in (3a), as opposed to (3b):

(3) a. John wrote letters / poetry a lot.
     b. # John wrote a letter / a poem a lot.

I will come to this peculiarity of simple mass quantifiers later.

Adverbial quantifiers should also be able to bind pronouns or definite NPs like *the beginning*, as in (4), where *the beginning* is bound by *every book*:

(4) Every book is boring at the beginning.

Both frequency adverbs and measure-phrase constructions allow for variable binding, as shown in (5a) and (5b). Simple mass quantifiers, though, perhaps for syntactic reasons, do not seem to be able to bind a variable, as seen in (5c):

(5) a. Frequently, *the rain* lasted several hours.
     b. Several times, *the problems in John's firm* turned out to be intractable.
     c. # John managed to solve *the problems in his firm* a lot.

In (5a), the semantic values of *the rain* may depend on the occasions that *frequently* ranges over. In this reading, for each of these occasions, *the rain* refers to the process of rain on that occasion. In (5b), the semantic values of *the problems* may depend on the occasions *several times* ranges over. Such an interpretation is hard to get for

---

adverbials are not quantifiers ranging over events; rather, they are quantifiers ranging over the parts of the measuring entity (a time interval or spatial region), and as such, they take wide scope over the event quantifier (cf. Hinrichs 1985 and Moltmann 1989, 1991b, who follow the analysis of Dowty 1979).

(5c) (that is, an interpretation in which the evaluation of *the problems* depends on the events that *a lot* ranges over).

The three classes of adverbial quantifiers represent exactly the types of quantifiers that may apply to mass nouns. In fact, they have not only the syntactic form of mass quantifiers but also their semantic behavior.

Simple mass quantifiers in English (as in many other languages) are formally identical to the nominal mass quantifiers. Moreover, they exhibit a semantic property typical of mass quantifiers in that they impose the Homogeneity Requirement on the event predicate (cf. Chapter 4, 5). Quantifiers that are formally mass seem to be the only simple quantifiers that can act as adverbials. Natural languages generally do not use bare count quantifiers such as *several* or *two* as simple adverbial event quantifiers.

Frequency adverbs can also be considered mass quantifiers, both syntactically and semantically. As we saw in Chapter 5, frequency expressions generally apply to mass nouns and are syntactically neutral between plural and mass. Unlike simple mass quantifiers, frequency adjectives as well as adverbials do not impose the Homogeneity Requirement. The reason for this is that they involve a metrical component which specifies a complex event as having a discrete part structure. As we have seen with frequency adjectives, this metrical component is completely independent of the mass-count distinction, and it is responsible for why frequency expressions in general may apply not only to count expressions but to mass expressions as well, counting the parts of a discrete part structure.

Measure-phrase constructions also have the form of quantifiers characteristic of mass categories. They are combinations of the form 'count quantifier-measure phrase', a construction typical of mass expressions. The measure phrase, in this case, is *time(s)* (apparently the only measure phrase that can apply to verbs in English). Adverbial measure-phrase constructions are exactly parallel to constructions with measure phrases that apply to mass nouns such as *two grams of salt* or *several liters of wine*. The only way for a count quantifier or numeral to apply to events as arguments of verbs (as with any mass category) appears to be in conjunction with a measure phrase which 'individuates' temporal units of subevents. Constructions such as *John came two* or *John came several* are generally absent in languages such as English, in which verbs do not exhibit a syntactic singular-plural distinction.

In the next sections, I will discuss the three types of adverbial event quantifiers in more detail and give formal semantic analyses of sentences in which they occur.

7.2.1. Adverbial simple mass quantifiers

I will discuss adverbial simple mass quantifiers with data from German since English adverbial *a lot* has secondary meanings and does not behave consistently, and English adverbial *much* is restricted to negative or 'high-degree' environments.

German has two adverbial mass quantifiers, *viel* 'much' and *wenig* 'little'. They are formally identical to the corresponding nominal mass quantifiers and also behave semantically like them: first with respect to the Homogeneity Requirement and second with respect to the requirement that the event be structured into distinguishable parts, a requirement that was traced to the lexical meaning of vague mass quantifiers as part-structure predicates in Chapter 4.

Adverbial mass quantifiers such as *viel* and *wenig* require the event predicate they modify (the verb, the VP, or the VP together with the subject) to be homogeneous. In particular, the event argument position of the event predicate must be cumulative. Divisivity, as usual, is not required in a strict sense.

Let me note in this respect that measure adverbials such as *for two hours* and *until noon* also impose the Homogeneity Requirement. And in fact, the Homogeneity Requirement with event predicates has been discussed only in the context of measure adverbials (cf. Hinrichs 1985; Krifka 1989; and Moltmann 1989, 1991b, 1992a).

For adverbial simple mass quantifiers, cumulativity of the event argument position is met in three cases:

1. The verb is an activity verb, as in (6):

   (6) a. Hans ist viel gerannt.
            'John has run a lot.'
        b. Anna hat viel / wenig geschlafen.
            'Ann has slept a lot / little.'
        c. Hans hat den Wagen viel geschoben.
            'John has the pushed the car a lot.'

2. The verb is an achievement or accomplishment verb, and certain arguments are either bare mass NPs or bare plurals (*the Homogeneity and Indefiniteness Requirement*). The arguments that have to meet this requirement are those that can undergo an event of the relevant kind only once — that is, destroyed or produced objects. Thus, (7a) is acceptable (with bare plural and mass nouns), but (7b) is not:

   (7) a. Maria hat viel / wenig Briefe / Poesie geschrieben.
            'Mary has written letters / poetry a lot / little.'
        b. # Maria hat viel einen Brief / zwei Briefe geschrieben.
            'Mary has written a letter / two letters a lot.'

The event predicates in (7a) are cumulative, but those in (7b) are not. For the sum of two events of Mary writing letters is again an event of Mary writing letters; and the sum of two events of Mary writing poetry is an event of Mary writing poetry. But the sum of two events of Mary writing a letter (or two letters) is not an event of Mary writing a letter (or two letters). Rather, it is an event of Mary writing two (or four) letters.[2]

---

[2] Notice that the NPs *letters* and *poetry* in (7a), which have to meet the Homogeneity and Indefiniteness Requirement, must be in the syntactic scope of the event quantifier. NPs not subject to this condition may take wide scope over the event quantifier. Consider (1) and (2):

3. The verb receives a repetitive interpretation, as is possible in (8):

    (8) a. Hans ist viel / wenig gefallen.
            'John has fallen a lot / little.'
        b. Maria ging viel / wenig in die Stadt.
            'Mary went to town a lot / little.'

Example (8a) in the repetitive reading means that there were many / few events of John's falling, and (8b) in the repetitive reading means that Mary took many or few walks to town. Recall that a repetitive interpretation

---

    (1) a. Maria hat die Sonaten viel gespielt.
            'Mary has played the sonatas a lot.'
        b. Maria hat sehr eindrucksvolle Sonaten sehr viel gespielt.
            'Mary has played very impressive sonatas very much.'
    (2) a. # Hans hat die Briefe / einen Brief viel geschrieben.
            'John has the letters / a letter written a lot.'
        b. Hans hat viel sehr lange Briefe geschrieben.
            'John has written very long letters a lot.'
        c. ?? Hans hat sehr lange Briefe viel geschrieben.
            'John has written very long letters a lot.'

The bare plural *sehr eindrucksvolle Sonaten* in (1b) is outside the scope of the event quantifier because the verb allows for a repetitive interpretation, as in (1a). But the produced object *sehr lange Briefe* in (2b) may not be outside the scope of the adverbial quantifier, since, as indicated by (2a), the argument must meet the Homogeneity and Indefiniteness Requirement. The data make sense only if bare plurals and mass nouns may have quantifier status and interact with other quantifiers in scope and, thus, are not generally referential terms referring to kinds (as argued by Carlson 1977).

Parallel observations can be made for NPs with the determiners *many* and *much*. The extension of *many* N' or *much* N' is homogeneous or at least cumulative. The sum of a group of 'many' or a quantity of 'much' is itself 'many' or 'much'. Like bare plurals and mass NPs, *many* N' and *much* N' in a relevant argument position may define a predicate as homogeneous. Consider the sentences in (3) and suppose that Mary did not visit any museum more than once:

    (3) a. (?) Maria besuchte während der Reise viel viele Museen.
            'Mary visited during the journey many museums a lot.'
        b. # Maria besuchte während der Reise viel diese Museen / zehn Museen /
            ein Museum.
            'Mary visited during the journey the museums / ten museums / a museum
            a lot.'

The contrast between (3a) and (3b) shows that *viele Museen* is responsible for the homogeneity of the predicate in a situation in which a museum is uniquely related to an event. *Viele Museen*, thus, semantically acts as an existential quantifier ranging over a cumulative domain of groups of many museums and taking narrow scope with respect to the event quantifier.

consists simply in the verb's referring to a group of events, rather than to an individual event (cf. Chapter 2).

There is another type of predicate that allows for vague adverbial event quantifiers and arguably involves a repetitive interpretation. Predicates of this type are predicates of performance like *use* or *play*. Their object arguments determine the shape of an event, but existence of those objects, unlike consumed, destroyed, or produced objects, is not affected by the event:

(9) a. Hans hat dieses Wort viel / wenig verwendet.
         'John has used this word a lot / little.'
     b. Hans hat die Sonate viel / wenig gespielt.
         'John has played the sonata a lot / little.'

The sum of two events of using the word or playing the sonata counts again as an event of using the word or playing the sonata.

Formally, adverbial mass quantifiers can be analyzed in exactly the same way as focused nominal quantifiers. On such an analysis, *viel* and *wenig* are predicated of the group of events described by the relevant event predicate. Thus, (10a) has the semantic analysis in (11a), and (10b) the one in (11b):

(10) a. Maria schlief wenig.
          'Mary slept little.'
      b. Maria schrieb viel Briefe.
          'Mary wrote letters a lot.'

(11) a. $\lambda s[[wenig]^S(sum_{<_s}(\{e \mid (\forall e')(e' <_s e \rightarrow [schlief]^S(e', \text{Mary}) = 1)\}))$
          $= 1]$

      b. $\lambda s[[viel]^S(sum_{<_s}(\{e \mid (\forall e')(e' <_s e \rightarrow (\exists x)([Briefe]^S(x) = 1$
          $\& [schrieb]^S(e', \text{Mary}, x) = 1))\})) = 1]$

The sentence meaning (11a) holds of a situation s if *wenig* holds of the maximal event e whose parts in s are events of Mary's sleeping — which basically means that the parts of e must count as 'little' relative to what is expected in s.

The Homogeneity Requirement should now be derived in the same way as with nominal mass quantifiers. However, this is possible only if verbs somehow do not characterize events as integrated wholes and thus count as mass expressions semantically with respect to the event-argument position. If the subevents are not integrated wholes, then an event consisting of such subevents has a homogeneous part structure. Consider the denotations of (12a) and (12b) as given in (13a) and (13b), respectively:

(12) a. # Maria schrieb viel einen Brief.
          'Mary wrote a letter much.'
      b. # Maria schrieb viel die Briefe.
          'Mary wrote the letters much.'

(13) a. $\lambda s[[viel]^S(sum_{<_s}(\{e \mid (\forall e')(e' <_s e \rightarrow (\exists x)([letter]^{S'}(x) = 1 \&$

$[schrieb]^S(e', z, x) = 1)\})) = 1]$

b. $\lambda s[[viel]^S(sum_{<_S}(\{e \mid (\forall e')(e' <_S e \to [schrieb]^S(e',$ Mary, the letters$) = 1)\})) = 1]$

The analysis in (13a) explains the unacceptability of (12a) as follows. Every subevent of the event e that *viel* applies to must be an event of Mary writing a letter. But if verbs do not properly specify events as integrated wholes, no such subevent is an integrated whole, because *viel* does not specify the parts of the event e as being integrated wholes. But then sum formation with subevents is unrestricted, and the sum of any subevents e' and e'' (which are both events of Mary writing a letter) will be part of e. But such a sum should also be an event of Mary writing a letter, which cannot be the case, since it is an event of Mary writing *two* letters (given, of course, that no letter is written twice).

The analysis in (13b) explains the unacceptability of (12b) simply by the fact that it involves quantification over the parts of the event e that *viel* applies to. Since the part relation is not reflexive, and since quantification should not be vacuous, e will have at least two subevents. Each of these subevents should be an event of Mary writing the letters, which is impossible if the letters are not written twice.[3]

The lexical meanings of *viel* and *wenig* that are presupposed in the formulas (11) and (13) are the same that *viel* and *wenig* have as nominal quantifiers (cf. Chapter 4) — that is:

(14) a. $[viel]^S = \lambda x[eval(\{y \mid y <_S x\}) > @_S]$

b. $[wenig]^S = \lambda x[eval(\{y \mid y <_S x\}) < @_S]$

Thus, *viel* expresses the property that holds of an entity x in a situation s iff the quantitative evaluation of the relevant parts of x in s exceeds the expectation value in s (i.e., the value of @ applied to s).

According to (14), *viel* and *wenig* count the parts of the entity they apply to, rather than measuring the extent of an entity (with respect to its natural dimension of measurement); in fact, examples such as (24a) and (24b) in Chapter 4, repeated here as (15a) and (15b), gave independent evidence for this:

---

[3] There is another respect in which the analysis of adverbial mass quantifiers given in (11) proves adequate — namely, scope interactions with other quantifiers. For instance, *everybody* in (1) takes wide scope over the event quantifier *a lot*.

(1) Everybody wrote letters a lot.

This is accounted for in the analysis of adverbial mass quantifiers in (11a, b) in the text. On the basis of this analysis, (1) has the following denotation:

(2) $\lambda s[(\forall x)([person](x) = 1 \to [a\ lot]^S(sum_{<_S}(\{e \mid (\exists y)([letters]^S(y) = 1 \&$

$[wrote]^S(e, x, y) = 1)\})) = 1)]$

The sentence meaning in (2) holds of situations in which every person has participated in a different group of events of writing letters.

(15) a. John is of great height / weight.
      b. # John is of a lot of height / weight.

Example (15b) is bad because a height or a weight does not have distinguishable
parts that could be counted by *a lot*.

The same phenomenon can be observed with adverbial mass quantifiers. In fact,
adverbial mass quantifiers display the phenomenon in a much more prominent way
than nominal mass quantifiers. Adverbial mass quantifiers generally do not measure
the event with respect to its temporal duration (and even less so with respect to its
spatial extent); rather, they count parts of the event that are more or less well-
distinguished from each other in some way. There are several sorts of evidence that
show that *a lot, much,* and *little* count such well-distinguished parts of an event.
First, they contrast with adverbials like *for a long time,* which do measure the
temporal extent of an event. Compare (16a) with (16b):

(16) a. John traveled for a long time.
      b. John traveled a lot.

Intuitively, *for a long time* in (16a) measures the temporal length of one single
event of traveling. In contrast, *a lot* in (16b) counts the number of times John 'took
a trip' — that is, it counts the number of distinguishable events of traveling.
Similar contrasts are found in (17)–(19):

(17) a. John used this expression for a long time.
      b. John used this expression a lot.
(18) a. Mary played this sonata for a long time.
      b. Mary played this sonata a lot.
(19) a. ?? Mary fell down for a long time.
      b. Mary fell down a lot.

In (17a), *for a long time* measures the duration of John's habit of using the
expression. In contrast, in (17b), *a lot* counts the number of times John used the
expression. In (18a), *for a long time* measures the duration of Mary playing the
sonata (whereby Mary may have played the sonata very slowly, for a single time);
in contrast, in (18b), *a lot* counts the number of times Mary played the sonata.
Example (19a) shows that adverbial mass quantifiers are possible with events that
are separated in time (for example, events that are described by achievement verbs in
a repetitive reading). In contrast, temporal measure adverbials are rather awkward
with achievement verbs, forcing an unnatural 'continuous-repetition' reading, as in
(19b). Thus, temporal measure adverbials measure a continuous event, whereas
adverbial mass quantifiers may count temporally separated subevents.

In the examples in (17) and (18), participants that determine the 'shape' of an
event (*the sonata* or *the expression*) specify well-distinguished subevents of the
event, and so allow for a satisfaction of the condition on *a lot* and *little*.[4] Other

---

[4] How is the acceptability of adverbial mass quantifiers in (17b) and (18b) to be
explained? Examples (17b) and (18b) can be considered cases of repetitive interpretation.

kinds of arguments that distinguish parts of an event are objects that are consumed or produced in the event. *A lot* and *little*, when applied to an event consisting of events of eating apples, as in (20), or writing letters, as in (21), generally count subevents in which one apple is consumed or one letter produced:

(20) a. John has eaten apples a lot.
     b. John has not eaten apples a lot.
(21) a. John has written letters a lot.
     b. John has not written letters a lot.

Intuitively, depending on the number of single apples eaten or single letters written, either (20a) is true and (20b) false, or vice versa; and either (21a) is true and (21b) false, or vice versa. In these cases, consumed or produced participants determine the subevents that are counted.

When *a lot* or *little* is applied to an activity (such as running or sleeping), no semantic information is available about event parts that could be counted. In this case, units of activities must be specified by the nonlinguistic context in order for there to be a basis for counting. Relevant examples are (22a) and (22b):

(22) a. John ran a lot.
     b. John ran little.

Example (22a) can be true and (22b) false in two kinds of situations. In the first situation, John ran for a long time on a stretch. Here, the parts of a partitioning of one event of running are most likely what is counted by *a lot* or *little*. In the second situation, John was engaged in the activity of running many times. Here, temporally separated activities of running are most likely what is counted by *a lot* or *little*.

Then, the extensions of the event predicates in (17b) and (18b) are certainly cumulative and, to some extent, divisive (and therefore homogeneous). Thus, the event predicate *Mary plays the sonata* denotes the property in (1), where '$play_{sing}$'' denotes single events of playing.

(1) $\lambda x[(\exists X)(X \neq \varnothing \ \& \ (\forall e)(e \in X \rightarrow play_{sing}(e, \text{Mary, the sonata}) = 1)$
    $\& \ x = sum_{<s}(X))]$

That this analysis makes sense can be seen as follows: in contrast to objects that can be consumed or produced, the existence of expressions does not depend on events of using them, and the existence of sonatas does not depend on events of playing them. Suppose there are two events e and e' which are both playings of the sonata. Then how does one refer to the sum of e and e'? Here, the plural is not used to relate the sonata to the sum of e and e'. A situation in which Mary played the sonata twice is simply described by *Mary played the sonata* and not by *Mary played the sonatas*. The plural is obligatory only for relating the sum of two events to consumed or produced objects. But this means that not only single events, but also event groups, may stand in the relation 'play' or 'use' to a single sonata or a single expression.

With some predicates, adverbial mass quantifiers seem to always be excluded. In particular, mass quantifiers seem impossible with stative predicates such as *know* in (23):

(23) # John knew a lot that he would once be famous.

But even stative or dispositional predicates may, under certain conditions, take mass quantifiers — for example, in (24):

(24) Mary was polite a lot.

Example (24) is acceptable if it refers to specific situations in which Mary behaved politely. Then, *a lot* counts concrete manifestations of Mary's being polite. Clearly, manifestations of a disposition of politeness are in general well-distinguished from each other.

Example (24) shows that the applicability of mass quantifiers does not strictly depend on the type of the verb. Rather, additional pragmatic factors may play a role. If instantiations of a state are appropriately individuated in the context, a mass quantifier may apply even to a stative predicate.

To sum up, according to the analysis in (11) and (13) based on (14), adverbial *viel* and *wenig* count the parts of an event that is the maximal entity whose parts are subevents falling under the event predicate in question. In order for simple mass quantifiers like *a lot* to count the parts of such an event, the event parts must be well-distinguished from each other. We have seen various ways in which events may be specified as having well-distinguished parts. In particular, there are four kinds of events with well-distinguished parts:

1. Events with group participants that are consumed or produced in the event (such as eatings of apples or writings of letters)
2. Events with group participants that are abstract objects determining the shape of subevents (such as uses of an expression or playings of a sonata)
3. Activities that are naturally divided into temporally separated subactivities
4. Dispositions or states that have distinguishable manifestations

In all four cases, simple mass quantifiers do not measure the temporal extent of the event but count the relevant subevents. In this respect, they contrast with temporal measure adverbials such as *for a long time*, which do measure the temporal duration of an event.

7.2.2. Frequency adverbs

As was mentioned earlier, the adverbial event quantifiers of the second type — that is, frequency adverbs, may formally count as mass expressions. However, they do not require that the event predicate be homogeneous. For example, (25) with a predicate lacking cumulativity is acceptable:

(25) Mary frequently wrote a letter.

The absence of the Homogeneity Requirement with frequency adverbials corresponds to its absence with German metrical determiners, as discussed in Chapter 5. As in the latter case, this follows from the lexical meaning of frequency adverbials — in particular, the metrical component. The metrical component specifies an entity with a discrete part structure in the relevant situation (cf. Chapter 5).

Frequency adverbials can be analyzed in the same way as the event quantifiers of the first class. The difference between the two kinds of quantifiers can be located entirely in their lexical meaning, in particular the special lexical meaning of frequency adverbials. Then, the denotation of (25) is as in (26):

(26) $\lambda s[[frequently]^S(sum_{<S}(\{e \mid (\forall e')(e' <_S e \rightarrow (\exists x)([letter]^{S'}(x) = 1 \&$
$[write]^S(e', Mary, x) = 1))\})) = 1]$

Example (26) holds of a situation s iff the maximal event whose parts (in s) are writings (in s) of a letter by Mary has many and only temporally separated parts (in s).

The absence of the Homogeneity Requirement can now be derived in exactly the same way as in the case of German metrical determiners.[5]

To summarize, the difference between adverbial simple mass quantifiers and frequency adverbs with respect to the Homogeneity Requirement supports the following generalization:

(27) Groups of events that are arguments of verbs have a homogeneous
    part structure if there is no further lexical specification to the contrary.

Thus, event groups act as homogeneous quantities if only verbs and predicates like *much* and *little* hold of them in the relevant situation. However, other lexical information such as the metrical condition imposed by frequency adverbials may specify such events with a discrete part structure. The third class of quantifiers provides further evidence for this generalization.

7.2.3. Adverbial measure-phrase constructions

Measure-phrase constructions such as *twice* or *three times* are typical mass quantifiers, both from a formal and a semantic point of view. The measure phrase *times* does not appear accidentally in adverbial measure-phrase constructions, but rather has a particular semantic function. In fact, it has the same semantic function here as *time* has in binary distributive quantifiers like *one at a time* (cf. Chapter 6). *Times* imposes a metrical requirement on the events in the range of the numeral

---

[5] The present discussion has neglected frequency adverbials of habituality such as *usually, habitually,* and *constantly.* Their semantics is more complicated, involving notions of modality.

quantifier to the effect that the event parts be separated in time. Consider the examples in (28):

(28) a. John made a mistake three times.
       b. The three men carried the piano three times.

Example (28a) implies that none of the mistakes were made at the same time; (28b) implies that the three men are involved in three events of carrying the piano, none of which happened at the same time.

The lexical meaning of *times* in adverbial measure-phrase constructions can be conceived as a property of event groups as in (29), where m_t is the function measuring temporal distance:[6]

(29) *The lexical meaning of* times
       $[times]^S = \lambda e[\text{METRIC}(m_t, \{e' \mid e' <_s e\}, s)]$

Thus, *times* specifies events as consisting of temporally separated subevents in essentially the same way as frequency adverbials. It is then expected that the Homogeneity Requirement should not hold. This is in fact the case; for example, the event predicate in (28a) is not homogeneous.

An event group that is specified by *times* has the part structure of a group consisting of integrated wholes. Because of this part structure, count quantifiers and numerals may apply to such an event group. *Three times* thus consists of two lexical specifications: a metrical specification by *times*, which characterizes the part structure of the event group, and a numerical specification by *three*, which counts the so individuated parts.

We have seen that adverbial event quantifiers can be divided into three types, all of which act as mass quantifiers in morpho-syntactic and semantic respects. Let me now turn to two other sorts of evidence that show that verbs behave as a mass category with respect to the event argument position: pronominal reference to events and agreement with nominalizations.

7.3. Pronominal reference to events

Anaphoric pronouns generally must agree with their antecedents in the categories singular count, plural, or mass. Singular pronouns in English formally belong to both the category of mass nouns and the category of singular count nouns. However, groups that are denoted by plurals generally require plural pronouns as anaphors:

---

[6] A minor problem with (29) is how to account for the quantifier *once*, which seems to have the singular *time* as a semantic component. *Once* relates to a reference set of occasions, so that the metric does not apply to a single occasion, but rather to the reference set of occasions. This set seems to have semantic status as the reference set involved in the semantics of *most* discussed in Chapter 4.

(30) The dogs slept. They / # It slept for hours.

Since verbs do not have a singular count-plural-mass distinction, the syntactic category of pronouns that refer anaphorically to an event argument of a verb can be taken as indirect evidence for the status of verbs with respect to the singular count-plural-mass distinction.

The evidence from anaphoric pronouns in fact suggests that verbs are generally classified as mass expressions with respect to the event-argument position. Geis (1975) and Neale (1988) have observed that pronouns that anaphorically refer to a verbal event argument must be in the singular, regardless of whether the event is a single event or a group of events. In their examples, a group event consists of events described by the conjuncts of a clausal or verbal conjunction, as in the following:

(31) a. John stumbled, and Bill stumbled. They did it / # them in the park, and they did it / # them at noon. (Geis 1975)
      b. Mary danced, fell, broke her neck and died. It / # They happened yesterday.
      c. It was raining and it was very warm; but it / # they did not last for a long time.
      d. John talked and Mary danced. It / # They took place in this room.

The same can be observed with an event group that owes its group structure to a group participant, such as the event argument of *were killed* in (32):

(32) The horses were killed.

On the analysis of distributive interpretation given in Chapter 2, for (32) to be true, the relation denoted by *were killed* must hold between a group event e of being killed and the group of horses x such that for each member x' of x there is a subevent of e that is a killing of x'. The following examples illustrate that anaphoric reference to such a group event requires singular, rather than plural, pronouns:

(33) a. The horses were killed. It / # They was (were) very painful for them.
      b. John and Mary solved the math problems. It / # They took a long time.
      c. John, Sue, and Bill talked about future projects separately. It / # They took place here.

The data in (31), (32), and (33) show that verbs (with respect to their event-argument position) are classified as mass expressions, rather than as singular count or plural; and this is independent of the kind of event that is described. Only full NPs like *these events* can refer back to an event argument of a verb:

(34) Mary danced, fell, and broke her neck. These events happened

yesterday.

The reason this is possible is that a full NP carries lexical content of its own, allowing the events to be attributed additional properties which verbs cannot attribute to them.

Even more direct evidence that verbs are classified as a mass category comes from pronominal quantifiers in German. German pronominal quantifiers exhibit a formally sharply differentiated mass-count distinction. In German, quantifiers do not require a head noun but can always occur pronominally; and pronominal quantifiers ranging over verbal event arguments take the form of mass quantifiers, rather than plural quantifiers:

(35) Maria las Zeitung, schrieb Briefe, führte Telephongespräche und
      ärgerte Hans. Alles / Vieles / Viel / Einiges / # Alle / # Viele /
      # Einige tat sie mit Begeisterung.
      'Mary read the newspaper, wrote letters, made phone calls, and
      bothered John. She did all (mass) / many (mass) / much / several
      (mass) / all (plur.) / many (plur.) / several (plur.) with enthusiasm.'

Note that quantifiers ranging over verbal event arguments may also belong to the class of quantifiers that are semantically count, but formally mass, such as *vieles*, discussed in Chapter 4. Their status as mass quantifiers is evidenced by the fact that they act as being of the category singular, rather than plural.

Under certain circumstances, however, plural pronouns in English may refer back to a group of verbal event arguments, in exactly those cases in which the predicate involves a comparison between the members of the event group. The examples in (36) are acceptable at least for a number of speakers:

(36) a. Mary lost her job, and John broke his leg. They happened at the
          same time.
      b. Mary was depressed, and John was elated. They generally never
          happen together.

Obviously, in this case, the Integrated Parts Requirement is at stake. Apparently, a plural pronoun can satisfy the Integrated Parts Requirement even if it refers to an entity that, when first introduced, was not characterized as a group. For instance, *they* in (36a) refers to a collection of propositions that, according to the first sentence, classifies as a quantity. But this means that plural pronouns must implicitly characterize a referent as a group. In other words, plural pronouns require that the parts of the referent be specified as integrated wholes by the nonlinguistic context. Thus, plural pronouns have a lexical meaning parallel to German vague count quantifiers. Accordingly, *they* holds of an entity x in a situation s only if every part x' of x in s is an integrated whole in s. However, unlike German vague mass quantifiers, plural pronouns always are syntactically plural, requiring plural agreement.

The possibility for a syntactically plural pronoun to relate anaphorically to a mass expression in English may be traced to the fact that agreement in English may be semantically determined — that is, agreement need not take into account the syntactic category of the phrase it agrees with, but rather may take into account the kind of entity the phrase refers to, as in (37) (see Morgan 1972, 1984 and Reid 1984 for discussions of the semantic conditioning of agreement in English):

(37) The group of students do not agree.

Support for the thesis that semantically conditioned agreement is correlated with the possibility of plural reference to verbal event arguments comes from German. German does not have semantically conditioned agreement and completely excludes reference to verbal event arguments by pronouns that are syntactically plural. This is seen in (38a) and (38b):

(38) a. Das Kommittee stimmte / * stimmten nicht überein.
      'The committee did not agree (sg.) / (pl.).'
   b. # Maria verlor ihren Job, und Hans brach sich das Bein. Sie
      passierten genau zur selben Zeit.
      'Mary lost her job, and John broke his leg. They happened at
      exactly the same time.'

Thus, it appears that in a language with semantically conditioned agreement, a plural pronoun may refer to an event argument of a verb under the condition that the event be specified as a group event in the relevant situation— that is, as an entity whose parts are integrated wholes in that situation. The event argument in the second sentence in (38b) in fact must be specified as a group, because the predicate *happened at the same time* imposes the Integrated Parts Requirement, requiring that the subject referent be a group.

7.4. N'-Conjunction with deverbal nominalizations

N'-conjunction is sensitive to the mass-count distinction in the following way: N'-conjunction of singular count nouns requires that the conjuncts refer to the same individual if the verb takes singular agreement (as a case of 'appositional conjunction'):

(39) a. The secretary and lover of John was at the party.
   b. The most immoral person and greatest artist of this century is
      Picasso.
   c. # The wife and son of John was at the party.
   d. # The dog and cat is in the garden.

In contrast, N'-conjunction of plural or mass nouns allows the conjuncts to refer to different groups or quantities. The conjoined NP then refers to the group composed of those groups or quantities, as in (40):

(40) a. The woman and children were rescued.

   b. The bread and wine is on the table.

Examples (39) and (40) motivate a generalization about N'-conjunction and the mass-count distinction whose formulation, though, first requires a clarification of the semantics of N'-conjunction. N'-conjunction can be interpreted either by *property conjunction* or by *group formation*. Property conjunction is defined in (41):

(41) *Property Conjunction (PC)*
     Let $A_1, \ldots,$ and A_n be situated sets.
     $PC(A_1, \ldots, A_n) = \lambda s \lambda x [A_1{}^S(x) = 1 \ \& \ \ldots \ \& \ A_n{}^S(x) = 1]$

The relevant semantic operation of group formation is defined in (42):

(42) *Group Formation (GF)*
     Let $A_1, \ldots,$ and A_n be situated sets.
     $GF(A_1, \ldots, A_n) = \lambda s \lambda x [(\exists x_1) \ldots (\exists x_n)(A_1{}^S(x_1) = 1 \ \& \ \ldots \ \& \ A^S(x_n)$
     $= 1 \ \& \ x = sum_{<s}(\{x_1, \ldots, x_n\}))]$

The generalization then is that, if N'-conjunction is interpreted by group formation, the category of the conjoined N' may differ from the category of the N'-conjuncts. This is the case when the conjuncts are singular count N's that do not refer to the same entities. If singular count nouns with nonintersecting extensions are conjoined, the result must be interpreted by group formation. The resulting NP is then categorized syntactically as a plural NP, requiring plural agreement of the verb. In contrast, the conjunction of singular count or mass NPs does not result in a different category. The result of conjoining mass N's is always a plural N', requiring plural agreement of the verb. Thus, the following condition on N'-conjunction obtains:

(43) *Condition on N'-conjunction*
     If $f_1, \ldots, f_n$ are N's, then f_1 and $\ldots$ and f_n must be of the same
     mereological category (i.e., 'singular count', 'plural', or 'mass')
     as $f_1, \ldots, f_n$.

   Given (43), N'-coordination can now be considered a diagnostic for whether nouns (when occurring as conjuncts in an N'-conjunction) are mass nouns or count nouns (either singular count nouns or plurals): if N's which denote different entities are conjoined and if verb agreement is singular, then the N's must be mass.
   This criterion can now be applied to event-denoting nouns. Underived event-denoting nouns like *storm* and *fire* behave the same way as other singular count nouns: when underived event-denoting nouns refer to different events, the conjunction of these nouns cannot count as a singular N':

(44) a. # The storm and fire was terrible.
     b. # The earthquake and hurricane takes place every year.
     c. # The picnic and game was pleasant to everybody.

Notice that *storm, fire, earthquake, hurricane, picnic,* and *game* are all singular count nouns.

Deverbal nominalizations behave differently. In fact, they pattern together with mass nouns, as seen in (45) with the possibility of singular verb agreement:

(45) a. The arrest of Mary and execution of John was done in a hurry.
     b. The singing of songs and drinking of wine was very relaxing.
     c. The treatment of Mary and accusation of John was embarrassing.

Notice that *arrest* and *execution* in (45a) are syntactically singular count nouns. Notice also that *the arrest of Mary and execution of John* in (45a) cannot refer to a fact or a group of facts. For, as (46) shows, *was done in a hurry* cannot be predicated of facts (as described by *that*-clauses):

(46) # That Mary was arrested and that John was executed was done in a hurry.

The difference between facts and events based on distinct classes of acceptable predicates has been discussed extensively by Vendler (1967) (see also Zucchi 1989).

Otherwise, of course, the acceptability of (45a) would be explained straightforwardly, since facts never trigger plural agreement of the verb under conjunction. (See the appendix to this chapter.)

There is another explanation one might suggest for singular agreement in (45a): *arrest of Mary* and *execution of John* somehow refer to the same event. But this is just too implausible: the arrest of Mary is just not the execution of John.[7]

Thus, the data with N'-conjunction of deverbal nominalizations can best be explained if verbs are classified as mass expressions. Deverbal nominalizations then carry this classification over to some extent, even though their overt syntactic category may be that of singular count nouns. Notice that the condition on N'-coordination was formulated as a condition referring to the semantic, not the syntactic, mass-count distinction. Since the acceptability of conjunctions of deverbal nominalizations with singular verb agreement cannot be due to the fact that the conjuncts refer to events, the verbs from which *arrest* and *execution* are derived must count as mass expressions (with respect to the event argument position). Events denoted by *arrest* and *execution* are therefore specified as quantities, not as

---

[7] In these examples, plural verb agreement is possible as well:

(1) a. The arrest of Mary and execution of John were done in a hurry.
     b. The singing of songs and drinking of wine were very relaxing.
     c. The treatment of John and accusation of Mary were embarrassing.

This is also the case with conjoined mass NPs in English:

(2) The bread and butter are / is on the table.

Most plausibly, plural agreement in both (1) and (2) is licensed because English allows for semantically conditioned agreement, as was mentioned in the previous section.

individuals, by the lexical meanings of the verbs *arrest* and *execute* (which are, of course, also the lexical meanings of the nouns *arrest* and *execution*). So group formation applied to events, classified as quantities, yields quantities as well, satisfying the condition on group formation with N'-conjunction.

7.5. A possible explanation of the mass-status of verbs

In this last section, I turn to the crucial question, Why do verbs classify as mass expressions with respect to the event argument position? One possible answer is that categories that lack a syntactic mass-count distinction are, as the default case, classified as a mass category whenever such a classification is necessary. But this cannot suffice as an answer. We have seen that verbs behave not only syntactically as a mass category but also in semantic respects. This is rather mysterious, because verbs seem to often specify events as integrated wholes (achievements and accomplishments).

A speculation as to the special behavior of events relies on the multidimensionality of the part structure of events. We have seen that events may have several part structures. In particular, events may be integrated wholes or may consist of subevents that are integrated wholes with respect to one part structure, but not another — for example, with respect to a participant-related, but not a time-related, part structure. Consider (47):

(47) Mary destroyed the chairs.

The event of destruction in (47) may be a temporally continuous event and thus an event without integrated parts in the temporal dimension. But at the same time, it is a group event by the fact that subevents stand in a one-to-one-relation to independent integrated wholes, the chairs. With respect to the first part structure, the event counts as a quantity; but with respect to the second, it counts as a group.

The status of events as quantities then may be the result of a particular informational conflict among several part structures of the event. If an event should be classified with respect to the semantic mass-count distinction, then such a classification might generally be based on one of the part structures of the event in which the event is not an integrated whole and does not have subevents that are integrated wholes.

But this line of explanation is deficient. We have seen that an event has a multidimensional part structure only when it is described as such. No additional part structure should be available when the only information about the event is given by a telic predicate. In this case, the event should not classify as a quantity. But verbs systematically behave as mass expressions, regardless of whether the event is specified with multiple part structures or not.

Thus, an alternative explanation must be found for the mass status of verbs. It is quite plausible, in particular in view of the data in the appendix, that the difference has to do with some general, perhaps modal, semantic distinction between verbs and nouns. (For a proposal in this direction see Gupta 1980, who maintains that only nouns provide a principle of individuation allowing the identification of entities across different possible worlds.)

Appendix:
Clauses and the Mass-Count Distinction

7A.1. Clauses and the diagnostics of mass categories

In this appendix, another category will be examined that lacks a syntactic mass-count distinction — namely, clauses. As it turns out, clauses also classify as a mass category in relevant respects. This will be shown by a number of tests, some of which are the same as the ones that were used for verbs before. This appendix, though, has purely observational character, since no explanation for the mass status of clauses will be given. (Clearly, no explanation is available in terms of the multidimensionality of the part structure of propositions.)

7A.2. Pronominal reference to propositions

The test of pronominal anaphoric reference shows that clauses generally count as mass expressions. It was already noted in Chapter 6 that German prosentential vague quantifiers (i.e., quantifiers ranging over propositions) are mass, rather than count, quantifiers. In German, the mass quantifiers *viel* and *vieles* (the quantifier that is semantically, but not syntactically, plural) and not the plural count quantifier *viele*, act as bare quantifiers ranging over propositions. The same holds for English. For instance, *little,* rather than *few,* is used as such a quantifier:[8]

(A1)   John knew little / # few.

Also definite prosentential pronouns are mass, rather than singular count, since they generally are in the singular, rather than in the plural, when referring to a group of propositions:

(A2)   Mary knows that John is crazy and that Bill is a genius. She
       discovered it / # them recently.

As in the case of pronouns referring to events, however, plural pronouns may sometimes act as prosentential pronouns — at least for some speakers. As with

---

[8] Notice that in English *everything* also acts as a prosentential quantifier. But *everything* can be classified as a mass quantifier, with *thing* being a numeral classifier — in analogy to *liters* in *two liters of wine.*

event-referring pronouns, the condition is that the propositions be explicitly regarded as a group with distinct members, rather than as an undifferentiated collection. Again, the context must provide some reason for regarding a collection of propositions as such a group. A group of propositions actually *has* to be regarded as a group with distinct members if the predicates involve a binary relation between group members, imposing the Integrated Parts Requirement. An example is the predicate *contradict each other*, which involves a comparison between distinct parts of a group argument:

(A3) Mary found out that x is four and that x is a prime number, but (?) they / # it contradict(s) each other.

(A4) a. That x is four and that x is not a prime number is true. Mary discovered it / # them recently.

      b. John is intelligent and Mary is brilliant. Bill knew it / # them.

Example (A3) is acceptable for many speakers with the plural pronoun *they*. It contrasts with (A4a) and (A4b), which do not contain a predicate that imposes the Integrated Parts Requirement and thus do not provide a context in which there is reason to regard the collection of propositions as a group with distinct members.

The fact that the Integrated Parts Requirement is satisfied with plural pronouns can be traced to the fact that, as in the case of event-referring pronouns, plural pronouns referring to propositions impose implicit integrity conditions on the parts of the collection of propositions.

7A.3. Clauses and agreement

A further test for the classification of clauses with respect to mass and count is verb agreement with conjoined clauses. A conjunction of clauses, like a conjunction of mass NPs, generally requires singular agreement, and in that respect classifies as a mass expression:

(A5) That Mary travels a lot and that John does not go to work is / # are well-known.

Plural agreement is permitted only under certain conditions. One context in which it is permitted is when the propositions denoted by the clausal conjuncts are explicitly considered as being unrelated (as in the case of anaphoric plural reference to clauses). Such a reading may in fact be suggested by certain predicates — for instance, the predicate *are surprising* in (A6), where each of the two propositions may have triggered an individual event of surprise:

(A6) That Mary travels a lot and that John does not go to work is / are surprising.

The semantic conditioning of agreement with conjoined clauses in English corresponds to the conditions on agreement with mass NPs, which are sometimes also semantic, rather than syntactic, in nature (see also fn. 7).

As expected, plural agreement is possible (and in English even required) with conjoined clauses if the content of the predicate makes explicit reference to single propositions as group members. Predicates of this kind involve a binary relation between group members and thus require arguments with integrated parts (i.e., they impose the Integrated Parts Requirement). The examples in (A7) illustrate the point:

(A7) a. That x is four and that x is a prime number contradict / # contradicts each other.
      b. That x is four and that x is a prime number form / # forms a contradiction.

The possibility of conjoined clauses taking plural verb agreement, again, can be correlated with the general property of English of allowing for semantically conditioned agreement. For in languages that prohibit such agreement — for example, German — conjoined clauses seem to be unable to take plural verb agreement. This is illustrated in the German translation of (A7a) in (A8):

(A8) Daß x vier ist und daß x eine Primzahl ist stellt / # stellen einen Widerspruch dar.
      'That x is four and that x is a prime number forms / form a contradiction.'

7A.4. Plurals and concealed propositions

NPs such as *the election of Mary* may, in certain contexts, refer to propositions, rather than to events. And they *must* do so with predicates like *hope*, which can take only propositions, not events, as object arguments (cf. Vendler 1967):

(A9) John hoped for the election of Mary.

Thus, in (A9), *the election of Mary* does not refer to the event of electing Mary, but rather to the proposition that Mary will be elected. Event-describing NPs that receive an interpretation as a proposition, rather than as an event, are so-called *concealed propositions* (cf. Grimshaw 1979, see also Pesetsky 1982).

Now the crucial point is that, if an NP with the head *election* refers to an event, it must be in the plural if that event is a group of distinct subevents, as in (A10); but the same NP may be, and in fact has to be, in the singular when acting as a concealed proposition referring to a group of distinct propositions, as in (A11):

(A10) The elections of Bill and Mary were observed by several international organizations.
(A11) John and Mary hoped for the election / # the elections of Bill and

Sue.
(I.e., John hoped for the election of Bill and Mary hoped for the election of Sue.)

This shows that NPs that are concealed propositions pattern with mass NPs, rather than count NPs, regardless of the category of the head noun (which, in the case of (A11), is singular count).

7A.5. Requirements on the countability of situations

Another phenomenon that can be related to the classification of clauses as a mass category is Kratzer's (1989a) observation that *if*-clauses and *when*-clauses differ with respect to certain requirements on their semantic content. In her generalization, *when*-clauses must contain either an indefinite NP or a stage-level predicate. Stage-level predicates are predicates that describe nonpermanent states of an individual, processes, or events (in the narrow sense). Examples are *be happy* or *laugh*. They contrast with individual-level predicates, which describe permanent states (or states perceived as such) of an individual. The restriction imposed by *when*-clauses is illustrated in (A12):

(A12) a. # When Bill knows French, Mary wants to know it, too.
       b. When Bill knows a foreign language, Mary wants to know it, too.
       c. When Bill laughs, Mary wants to laugh, too.

If-clauses are not subject to this restriction:

(A13) If Bill knows French, Mary wants to know it, too.

Kratzer suggests that this is related to the fact that *when*-clauses can act as the restriction of an adverb of quantification, but *if*-clauses cannot:

(A14) a. When Bill knows a foreign language, Mary often wants to know it, too.
       b. # If Bill knows a foreign language, Mary often wants to know it, too.

When-clauses share this property with other 'specifiers of situations'. The *when*-clause in (A14a) characterizes a certain set of situations — namely, the set of situations in which Bill knows a foreign language. *Often* in (A14a) ranges over these situations. In a similar way, indefinite NPs may specify a set of situations in generic sentences.[9] An example is (A15), in which the occurrences of *a dog* and *a cat*

---

[9] For a discussion of the role of indefinite NPs in generic sentences see Schubert/Pelletier (1989).

characterize the set of situations over which the quantifier *often* ranges (in the most plausible reading):

(A15)   A dog often frightens a cat.

In this reading, (A15) means that for most (appropriate) situations containing a dog and a cat, the dog frightens the cat in such situations.

Generally, then, *often* in the examples in (A14) and (A15) counts situations as specified by the situation specifier, that is, a *when*- or *if*-clause in (A14a, b) and a set of indefinite NPs in (A15).

I assume that *often* denotes a relation between a group *s* of events or situations and another group *s´* of events or situations so that *s* is a subgroup of *s´*, the parts of *s* are distant from each other with respect to the temporal metric in *s*, and the cardinality of the parts of *s* is greater than what is expected in *s*.

Given these assumptions, the situations specified by the situation specifier must meet the requirement of being distant from each other with respect to the relevant metric. For clauses, this metric need not necessarily be temporal, but may be any sort of metric — as provided by the context. In order for a group of situations to minimally satisfy the metrical requirement, it suffices that the situations be well-distinguished from each other and, thus, be countable.

How is this countability requirement met? Let us look again at Kratzer's restriction on *when*-clauses. This restriction can be interpreted as a countability requirement on situations. Consider (A12a) and (A12c). Situations characterized only by Bill's knowing French are not differentiated at all. In contrast, situations characterized by Bill's laughing may be sufficiently differentiated by distinct events of laughing by Bill. What is crucial in these two cases is that an individual-level predicate such as *know French* generally denotes states that do not have a natural temporal limitation, but rather are perceived as permanent, whereas an event predicate such as *laugh* naturally denotes temporally limited events, which are well-distinguished units. Furthermore, the situations characterized by Bill's knowing a foreign language may be differentiated by involving different languages and thus be welldistinguished from each other in that respect. (Notice that this may be considered an instance of the condition Integrating Parts on the Basis of Relations of Chapter 3.)

The distinction between *if*- and *when*-clauses shows that situations as specified by clauses are not countable *per se*. That is, they do not generally act as groups like the referents of plurals. Rather, they must meet specific conditions in order to be conceived of as countable and thus act as groups with integrated parts. These conditions are met, for instance, if the clause contains an indefinite NP whose referents distinguish situations. They are also met if the clause describes events, rather than permanent states.

This indicates that situations as described by clauses classify in the unmarked case as homogeneous quantities. But, with the help of particular specifications, they may classify as well-distinguished members of groups. Then they meet the metrical requirement of frequency adverbs and are considered countable.

This constitutes another argument for the mass status of clauses. Referents of mass nouns are, in the unmarked case, homogeneous; but nonetheless, under appropriate conditions, they can be modified by frequency expressions — namely, if the metrical requirement is met by the way the quantity is individuated in the context.[10]

---

[10] This account of the restriction on *if-* and *when*-clauses has other implications apart from the issue of the mass-count distinction. Kratzer (1989a) has introduced the data regarding the distinction between *if-* and *when*-clauses in order to argue that only stage-level predicates, but not individual-level predicates, have an argument position for events. The operator associated with a *when*-clause has to 'unselectively bind' some argument position. This requirement can be satisfied by either an indefinite NP or an eventive verb. Given the present account of the difference between *if-* and *when*-clauses in terms of individuation conditions on situations, the relevant data cease to present an argument either for unselective binding or for the lack of an event argument position of individual-level predicates.

8

Concluding Remark about Part Structures and Natural Language

This book has examined and analyzed a broad range of natural language phenomena that involve part structures. These phenomena all involved situated part structures, part structures entities have in a particular situation. Moreover, the relevant part structures included conditions of integrity, which may be either essential or accidental for an entity.

The claim was not, though, that situated part structures are the only part structures that natural language may be about. There are expressions and constructions in natural language that clearly involve other, or perhaps more specific, notions of part structure. One example is the *have/lack*-construction in (1) and (2):

(1) a. The house has a door.
    b. The house lacks a door.
(2) a. The dinner has a first course.
    b. The dinner lacks a first course.

The *have/lack*-construction involves a specific notion of part — namely, the notion of *functional part*. This can be seen from the unacceptability of the following *a*-examples, where the parts are not functional. The *b*-examples show that the noun *part* can still apply in those cases:

(3) a. # The house has a stone.
    b. The stone is part of the house.
(4) a. # The dinner has potato.
    b. The potato is part of the dinner.

Another kind of expressions involving part structures other than situated part structures are nouns such as *edge*, *surface*, *bottom*, and *front*, which denote very specific kinds of parts of particular kinds of objects.

Thus, specific lexical items may involve notions of part other than the notion of situated part. But still the notion of situated part appears to play the most important role in natural language, as the range of phenomena investigated in this book should testify.

Bibliography

Bach, E. (1986). 'The algebra of events.' *Linguistics and Philosophy* 9, 5–16.

Bartsch, R. (1987). 'Context-dependent interpretations of lexical items.' In J. Groenendijk et al. (eds.), *Foundations of Pragmatics and Lexical Semantics*. Foris, Dordrecht, 1–26.

———— (1986/7). 'The construction of properties under perspectives.' *Journal of Semantics* 5.4, 293–320.

Barwise, J. / Cooper, R. (1981). 'Generalized quantifiers and natural language.' *Linguistics and Philosophy* 4, 159–219.

Barwise, J. / Perry, J. (1983). *Situations and Attitudes*. MIT Press, Cambridge.

Bennett, J. (1988): *Events and Their Names*. Hackett Publishing, Indianapolis.

Bennett, M. (1972). 'Accommodating plurals in Montague's Fragment of English.' In R. Rodman (ed.), *Papers in Montague Grammar*. UCLA Occasional Papers in Linguistics 2, 25–65.

———— (1974). 'Some extensions of a Montague fragment.' Ph. D. dissertation, University of California, Los Angeles.

Blau, U. (1981). 'Collective objects.' *Theoretical Linguistics* 8, 101–130.

Bunt, H. (1985). *Mass Terms and Model-Theoretic Semantics*. Cambridge University Press, Cambridge.

Burge, T. (1972). 'Truth and mass terms.' *Journal of Philosophy* 59, 263–282.

Burzio, L. (1986). *Italian Syntax*. Reidel, Dordrecht.

Carlson, G. (1977). 'Reference to kinds in English.' Ph. D. dissertation, University of Massachusetts, Amherst. Published 1980, Garland Publishers.

———— (1987). '*Same* and *different*. Some consequences for syntax and semantics.' *Linguistics and Philosophy* 10, 531–565.

Carlson, L. (1981). 'Aspect and quantification.' In P. Tedeschi / A. Zaenen (eds.), *Syntax and Semantics* 14. Academic Press, New York, 31–64.

Cartwright, H. (1970). 'Quantities.' *Philosophical Review* 79, 25–42.

Cheng, C. Y (1973). 'Response of Moravcik.' In J. Hintikka et al. (eds.), *Approaches to Natural Language*. Reidel, Dordrecht, 286-288.

Choe, J.-W. (1987). 'Anti-quantifiers and a theory of distributivity.' Ph. D. dissertation, University of Massachusetts, Amherst.

Cooper R. (1993). 'Generalized quantifiers and resource situations.' In P. Aczel et al. (eds.), *Situation Theory and Its Applications:* CSLI Lecture Notes. CSLI, Stanford, 191–212.

Cruse, T. A. (1979). 'On the transitivity of part-whole relations.' *Journal of Linguistics* 15, 29–38.

Davidson, D. (1967). 'The logical form of action sentences.' In N. Rescher (ed.),

The Logic of Decision and Action. Pittsburgh University Press, Pttsburgh, 81–95.

de Swart, H. (1991). 'Adverbs of quantification. A generalized quantifier approach.' Ph. D. dissertation, University of Groningen.

Devlin, K. / D. Rosenberg (1993). 'Situation Theory and cooperative action.' In P. Aczel et al. (eds.), *Situation Theory and Its Applications*. CSLI Lecture Notes. CSLI, Stanford, 213–264.

——— (1994). 'Sums and quantifiers.' *Linguistics and Philosophy* 17, 509–550.

Dowty, D. (1979). *Word Meaning and Montague Grammar*. Reidel, Dordrecht.

——— (1986): 'A note on collective predicates, distributive predicates, and *all*.' In F. Marshall (ed.): *Proceedings of the Third Eastern States Conference on Linguistics (ESCOL)*. Ohio State University, Columbus, 97-115.

Fine, K. (1982). 'Acts, events and things.' In W. Leinfellner / E. Kramer / J. Schank (eds.), *Sprache und Ontologie*. Proceedings of the Eighth Wittgenstein Symposium, Hoelder-Pichler-Tempsky, Vienna, 97–105.

Geach, P. (1962). *Reference and Generality*. Cornell University Press, Ithaca New York.

Geis, M. (1975). 'Two theories about action sentences.' *Working Papers in Linguistics*. Ohio State University, Columbus, 12–24.

Gillon, B. (1987). 'The readings of plural noun phrases in English.' *Linguistics and Philosophy* 10, 199–220.

——— (1992). 'Towards a common semantics for English count nouns and mass nouns'. *Linguistics and Philosophy* 15, 597–639.

Griffin, N. (1977). *Relative Identity*. Oxford University Press, Oxford.

Grimshaw, J. (1979). 'Complement selection and the lexicon.' *Linguistic Inquiry* 10, 270–326.

——— (1990). *Argument Structure*. MIT Press, Cambridge.

Guéron, J. (1980). 'On the syntax and semantics of PP Extraposition.' *Linguistic Inquiry* 11, 637–678.

Gupta, A. (1980). *The Logic of Common Nouns. An Investigation in Quantified Modal Logic*. Yale University Press, New Haven, Connecticut.

Hale, K. (1989). 'Warlpiri categories.' Presented at the Linguistics Department, MIT, December.

Heim, I. (1985). 'Notes on comparatives and related matters.' Unpublished manuscript. University of Texas, Austin.

Heim, I. / Lasnik, H. / May, R. (1991). 'Reciprocity and plurality.' *Linguistic Inquiry* 22, 97–101.

Higginbotham, J. (1981). 'Reciprocal interpretation.' *Journal of Linguistic Research* 1, 43–70.

——— (1985). 'On semantics.' *Linguistic Inquiry* 16, 547–593.

——— (1987). 'Indefiniteness and predication.' In E. J. Reuland / A. ter Meulen (eds.), *The Representation of (In)definiteness*, MIT Press, Cambridge, 43–70.

Higginbotham, J. / B. Schein (1989). 'Plurals.' In J. Carter et al. (eds.), *Proceedings of the Northeastern Linguistic Society (NELS)* 19. Graduate Linguistics Student Association, University of Massachusetts, Amherst, 161–175.

Hinrichs, E. (1985). 'A compositional semantics for *aktionsarten* and NP reference in English.' Ph. D. dissertation, Ohio State University.

Hoeksema, J. (1983). 'Plurality and conjunction.' In A. G. B. ter Meulen (ed.), *Studies in Model-Theoretic Semantics*. Foris, Dordrecht, 63–83.

——— (1988). 'The semantics of non-Boolean *and*.' *Journal of Semantics* 6, 19–40.

Humberstone, L. (1981). 'From worlds to possibilities.' *Journal of Philosophical Logic* 10, 313–344.

Jackendoff, R. (1990). 'Parts and boundaries.' *Cognition* 41, 9–45.

Kaplan, D. (1977). 'Demonstratives.' In J. Almog et al. (eds.), *Themes from Kaplan.* Oxford University Press, Oxford.

Kratzer, A. (1989a). 'Stage-level and individual-level predicates.' *Papers on Quantification,* University of Massachusetts, Amherst.

———— (1989b). 'An investigation into the lumps of thoughts.' *Linguistics and Philosophy* 12, 607–653.

Krifka, M. (1989). 'Nominal reference, temporal constitution and quantification in event semantics.' In R. Bartsch et al. (eds.), *Semantics and Contextual Expression.* Foris, Dordrecht, 75–115.

———— (1990). 'Four thousand ships passed through the lock: object-induced measure functions on events.' *Linguistics and Philosophy* 13, 487–520.

Landman, F. (1985). *Towards a Theory of Information.* Foris, Dordrecht.

———— (1989). 'Groups I.' *Linguistics and Philosophy* 12, 559–605; and 'Groups II.' *Linguistics and Philosophy* 12, 723–744.

Langacker, R. (1987a). 'Nouns and verbs.' *Language* 63, 53–94.

———— (1987b). *Foundations of Cognitive Grammar.* Stanford University Press, Stanford.

Langendoen, D. T. (1978). 'The logic of reciprocity.' *Linguistic Inquiry* 9, 177–197.

Lasersohn, P. (1989). 'On the readings of plural noun phrases.' *Linguistic Inquiry* 20. 130–134.

———— (1990). 'Group action and spatio-temporal proximity.' *Linguistics and Philosophy* 13, 179–206.

Lieb, H. (1983). *Integrational Linguistics.* Benjamins, New York.

Lewis, D. (1986). *On the Plurality of Worlds.* Basil Blackwell, Oxford.

Link, G. (1983). 'The logical analysis of plurals and mass terms. A lattice-theoretical approach.' In R. Bäuerle et al. (eds), *Meaning, Use and Interpretation of Language.* de Gruyter, Berlin, 302–323.

———— (1987). 'Generalized quantifiers and plurals.' In P. Gärdenfors (ed.), *Generalized Quantifiers.* Reidel, Dordrecht, 151–180.

Löbner, S. (1987). 'Natural language and Generalized Quantifier Theory.' In P. Gärdenfors (ed.), *Generalized Quantifiers.* Reidel, Dordrecht, 181-202.

Lønning, J. - T. (1987). 'Mass terms and quantification.' *Linguistics and Philosophy* 10, 1–52.

———— (1989). 'Some aspects of the logic of plural noun phrases.' Department of Mathematics, *Cosmos Report* 11, University of Oslo.

May, R. (1977). 'Logical Form.' Ph. D. dissertation, Massachusetts Institute of Technology, Cambridge.

McConnell-Ginet, S. (1982). 'Adverbs and logical form.' *Language* 58, 144–184.

———— (1981). 'An intensional logic for mass terms.' *Philosophical Studies* 40, 105–125.

Milsark, G. (1977). 'Towards an explanation of certain peculiarities of the existential construction in English.' *Linguistic Analysis* 3, 1–30.

Moltmann, F. (1989). 'Measure adverbials as part quantifiers.' In E. J. Fee et al. (eds.), *Proceedings of the West Coast Conference in Formal Linguistics (WCCFL)* 8. Stanford Linguistics Student Association, Stanford University, 247–261.

———— (1990a). 'Semantic selection and the determination of part structures in the use of natural language.' In M. Stokhof et al. (eds.), *Proceedings of the*

Seventh Amsterdam Colloquium in Semantics. ITLI, University of Amsterdam, Amsterdam.

——— (1990b). 'The multidimensional part structure of events.' In A. Halpern (eds.), *Proceedings of the West Coast Conference in Linguistics (WCCFL)* 9. Stanford Linguistics Student Association, Stanford University, Stanford, 361–378.

——— (1990c). 'Multiple semantic functions and bipartite interpretation in the semantics of NPs.' In D. Meyer et al. (eds.), *Proceedings of the Meeting of the Formal Linguistics Society of Midamerica (FLSM)* 1. University of Madison, Madison (Wisconsin), 205-221.

——— (1991a). 'On the syntax and semantics of binary distributive quantifiers.' In T. Sherer (ed.), *Proceedings of the North Eastern Linguistic Society (NELS)* 19, 279–292.

——— (1991b). 'Measure adverbials'. *Linguistics and Philosophy* 14, 629–660.

——— (1992a). *Individuation und Lokalität. Studien zur Ereignis- und Nominalphrasensemantik.* Fink Verlag, Munich.

——— (1992b). 'Reciprocals and *same/different.* Towards a semantic analysis.' *Linguistics and Philosophy* 15, 411–462.

——— (1994). '*Together* and *alone.*' Ms. UCLA, Los Angeles.

Morgan, J. L. (1972). 'Verb agreement as a rule of English.' *Proceedings of the Chicago Linguistic Society (CLS)* 8, 278–286.

——— (1984). 'Some problems of the determination of English number agreement.' *Proceedings of the First Eastern States Conference on Linguistics (ESCOL).* Ohio State University, Columbus, 96–78.

Mourelatos, A. P. D. (1981). 'Events, processes, and states.' In P. J. Tedeschi / A. Zaenen (eds.), *Tense and Aspect (Syntax and Semantics, 14).* Academic Press, New York, 191–212.

Neale, S. (1988). 'Events and "logical form".' *Linguistics and Philosophy* 11 303–323.

Ojeda, A. (1991). 'Definite descriptions and definite generics.' *Linguistics and Philosophy* 14, 367–397.

——— (1993). *Linguistic Individuals.* CSLI Lecture Notes 13, CSLI, Stanford.

Parsons, T. (1979). 'An analysis of mass and amount terms.' In F. J. Pelletier (ed.), *Mass Terms: Some Philosophical Problems.* Dordrecht, Reidel, 137–166.

——— (1985). 'Underlying events in the analysis of English.' In E. Lepore (ed.), *Actions and Events.* Basil Blackwell, New York, 235–267.

——— (1990). *Events in the Semantics of English. A Study in Subatomic Semantics.* MIT Press, Cambridge.

Pelletier, J. F. / L. Schubert (1989). 'Mass expressions.' In D. Gabbay / F. Guenthner (eds.), *Handbook of Philosophical Logic.* Reidel, Dordrecht, 327–407.

Pesetsky, D. (1982). 'Paths and categories.' Ph. D. dissertation, MIT, Cambridge.

Postal, P. (1975). *On Raising.* MIT Press, Cambridge.

Quine, W. V. O. (1960). *Word and Object.* MIT Press, Cambridge.

Reid, W. (1984). 'Verb agreement as case of semantic redundancy.' *Proceedings of the First Eastern States Conference on Linguistics (ESCOL).* Ohio State University, Columbus.

Rescher, N. (1955). 'Axioms for the part relation.' *Philosophical Studies* 6, 8–11.

Roberts, C. (1987). 'Modal subordination, anaphora, and distributivity.' Ph. D. dissertation, University of Massachusetts, Amherst.

—— (1991). 'Distributivity and reciprocal distributivity.' In S. Moore / A. Z. Wyner (eds.), *Proceedings from Semantics and Linguistic Theory (SALT)* I. Cornell University, Ithaca, New York, 209–230.

Roeper, P. (1983). 'Semantics for mass terms with quantifiers.' *Nous* 17, 251–265.

Safir, K. / Stowell, T. (1988). 'Binominal *each*.' In J. Blevins et al. (eds.), *Proceedings of the Northeastern Linguistic Society (NELS)* 18. Graduate Linguistics Student Organization, Department of Linguistics, University of Massachusetts, Amherst, 424–450.

Sánchez, L. (1995). 'Aspectual adjectives and the event structure of DP.' *Probus* 7, 167-180.

Scha, R. (1981). 'Distributive, collective and cumulative quantification.' In J. Groenendijk et al. (eds.), *Formal Methods in the Study of Language*. Vol. 2, Mathematical Centre Tracts, Amsterdam, 483–512.

Schein, B. (1986). 'Event logic and the interpretation of plurals.' Ph. D. dissertation, Massachusetts Institute of Technology, Cambridge.

—— (1994). *Plurals and Events*. MIT Press, Cambridge.

Schubert, L. / Pelletier, F. J. (1989). 'Generically speaking, or using Discourse Representation Theory to interpret generics.' In G. Chierchia et al. (eds.), *Properties, Types and Meaning*. Reidel, Dordrecht, 193–268.

Schwarzschild, R. (1992a). 'Types of plural individuals.' *Linguistics and Philosophy* 15, 641–675.

—— (1992b). '*Together* as a non-distributivity marker.' In P. Dekker / J. van der Does (eds.), *Proceedings of the Ninth Amsterdam Colloquium*. ITLI, University of Amsterdam.

—— (1994). 'Plurals, presuppositions and the sources of distributivity.' *Natural Language Semantics* 2, 201–248.

Sharvy, R. (1980). 'A more general theory of descriptions.' *Philosophical Review* 89, 607–624.

Siegel, M. E. A. (1979). 'Measure adjectives in Montague Grammar.' In S. Davis / M. Mithun (eds.), *Linguistics, Philosophy, and Montague Grammar*. University of Texas Press, Austin.

Simons, P. (1987). *Parts. A Study in Ontology*. Clarendon, Oxford.

Stalnaker, R. (1979). 'Assertion.' In P. Cole (ed.), *Syntax and Semantics* 9, Academic Press, New York, 315–332.

Strawson, P. (1960). *Individuals. An Essay in Descriptive Metaphysics*. Methuen, London.

Stump, G. (1981). 'The interpretation of frequency adjectives.' *Linguistics and Philosophy* 4, 221–257.

Szabolsci, A. (1985). 'Comparative superlative.' In *MIT Working Papers in Linguistics*. Massachusetts Institute of Technology, Cambridge.

Tenny, C. (1987). 'Grammaticalizing aspect and affectedness.' Ph D dissertation, Massachusetts Institute of Technology, Cambridge.

ter Meulen, A. (1980). 'Substances, quantities and individuals.' Ph. D. dissertation, Stanford University, Stanford.

Thomason, R. (1972). 'A semantic theory of sortal incorrectness.' *Journal of Philosophical Logic* 1, 209–258.

van Benthem, J. (1987). 'Semantic automata.' In J. Groenendijk et al. (eds.), *Studies in Discourse Representation Theory and the Theory of Generalized Quantifiers*. Foris, Dordrecht, 1–25.

van der Does, J. (1992). 'Applied quantifier logics: collectives and naked infinitives.' Ph. D. dissertation, University of Amsterdam.

Vendler, Z. (1967). 'Verbs and times.' In Z. Vendler, *Linguistics in Philosophy*.
    Cornell University Press, Ithaca, New York, 97–121.
———— (1972). *Res Cogitans*. Cornell University Press, Ithaca, New York.
Verkuyl, H. / van der Does, J. (1991). 'The semantics of plural noun phrases.' In J.
    van der Does / J. van Eijck (eds.), *Generalized Quantifier Theory and Appli-
    cations*. Dutch Network for Language, Logic and Information, Amsterdam,
    403–442.
Westerståhl, D. (1985). 'Logical constants in quantifier languages.' *Linguistics and
    Philosophy* 5, 387–413.
Wiggins, D. (1981). *Sameness and Substance*. Clarendon, Oxford.
Zemach, E. M. (1970). 'Four ontologies.' *Journal of Philosophy* 67, 231–246.
Zucchi, A. (1989). 'The language of propositions and events: issues in the syntax
    and semantics of nominalizations.' Ph. D. dissertation, University of Massa-
    chusetts, Amherst.

Index